WAGING SOVEREIGNTY

WAGING SOVEREIGNTY

Native Americans and the Transformation of Work in the Twentieth Century

COLLEEN O'NEILL

THE UNIVERSITY OF NORTH CAROLINA PRESS
Chapel Hill

© 2026 Colleen O'Neill

All rights reserved

Designed by Jamison Cockerham
Set in Scala by codeMantra

Manufactured in the United States of America

Cover art: *Top:* Blackfeet WPA sewing-project workers, 1936. From the Annual Report of Extension Workers, January 1, 1936, to December 31, 1936. *Bottom:* Construction workers at Boulder Dam in Nevada, 1935. NAID 298638. Both in RG 75, National Archives and Records Administration, Washington, DC.

LIBRARY OF CONGRESS CATALOGING-IN-PUBLICATION DATA
Names: O'Neill, Colleen M., 1961– author.
Title: Waging sovereignty : Native Americans and the transformation of work in the twentieth century / Colleen O'Neill.
Description: Chapel Hill : The University of North Carolina Press, [2026] | Includes bibliographical references and index.
Identifiers: LCCN 2025041377 | ISBN 9781469693279 (cloth ; alk. paper) | ISBN 9781469693286 (pbk. ; alk. paper) | ISBN 9781469687209 (epub) | ISBN 9781469693293 (pdf)
Subjects: LCSH: Indians of North America—Employment—Social aspects—20th century. | Indians of North America—Employment—Political aspects—20th century. | Indians of North America—Government relations—Social aspects—20th century. | Indians of North America—Ethnic identity—Social aspects. | Indians of North America—Cultural assimilation—Social aspects.
Classification: LCC E98.E6 O54 2026
LC record available at https://lccn.loc.gov/2025041377

Portions of chapter 2 first appeared in Colleen O'Neill, "Charity or Industry? Gendering of Work Relief in Indian Country in the New Deal Era," in *Indigenous Women and Work: From Labor to Activism*, edited by Carol Williams (University of Illinois Press, 2012). Used with permission.

Portions of chapter 4 first appeared in "Jobs and Sovereignty: Tribal Employment Rights and Energy Development in the 20th Century," in *Indians and Energy: Opportunity or Exploitation?*, edited by Sherry L. Smith and Brian Frehner (School of Advanced Research Press, 2010). Used with permission.

Portions of chapter 5 first appeared in "Civil Rights or Sovereignty Rights? Understanding the Historical Conflict between Native Americans and Organized Labor." Occasional Paper Series 43. Las Vegas: Center for Gaming Research, UNLV University Libraries, 2018. Used with permission.

For product safety concerns under the European Union's General Product Safety Regulation (EU GPSR), please contact gpsr@mare-nostrum.co.uk or write to the University of North Carolina Press and Mare Nostrum Group B.V., Mauritskade 21D, 1091 GC Amsterdam, The Netherlands.

For John Nelson

CONTENTS

List of Illustrations ix

Acknowledgments xi

Abbreviations and Acronyms xvii

Introduction Beyond the Civil Rights Paradigm: Thinking about Class, Native American Workers, and Colonial Legacies   1

1. The Civilizing Machine: Indian Boarding Schools as Labor Contractors   19

2. Building, Digging, and Sewing: Working for Wages on Federal Relief Projects in the 1930s   41

3. The Limits of "Positive Programming": American Indians, Gender, and the Postwar Urban Relocation Program   63

4. Jobs and Sovereignty: The Development of the Tribal Employment Rights Movement   91

5. Labor Rights or Sovereignty Rights? The Challenge of Gaming   109

Conclusion Sovereignty Rights and Work: Anti-Colonial History in the Making   141

Notes   149

Bibliography   185

Index   211

ILLUSTRATIONS

- 4 "Loafers and Laborers," *Puck*, 1880
- 11 Ojibwe wild rice harvest, 1971
- 24 Estelle Reel, the national superintendent of Indian schools, 1898–1910
- 28 Girls in ironing class at Carlisle, 1901
- 35 Boys digging for potatoes at Carlisle, 1901
- 42 Diné worker at a WPA mattress-making project, 1940
- 46 Northern Cheyenne CCC-ID workers, 1941
- 53 Blackfeet WPA sewing-project workers, 1936
- 65 Francisco Castillo, Wingate Ordnance Depot worker, 1944
- 66 Grace Thorpe at General MacArthur's headquarters, 1945
- 75 Rena Jones, Diné worker in Los Angeles, 1952
- 79 Navajo Nation Tribal Council Relocation Committee, 1960
- 80 Byron Chee, Diné worker at North American Aviation, 1960
- 95 Navajo Generating Station, October 28, 2019
- 96 Kenneth White, first compliance officer, Office of Navajo Labor Relations
- 102 Conrad Edwards and Dan Press, December 2007
- 124 Foxwoods Resort Casino, August 2008
- 132 Winstar World Casino, September 2012

ACKNOWLEDGMENTS

This book is long overdue. I was inspired to begin this project in 2006 when I discovered that Congressman J. D. Hayworth (R-AZ), who represented my hometown in Arizona, had sponsored the Tribal Labor Relations Restoration Act (for more on that, read chapter 5) the previous year. Hayworth, mired in the corruption associated with the Abramoff scandal and clearly not an advocate for Native Americans or organized labor, was not reelected. But other members of Congress have introduced versions of the legislation ever since. Given my somewhat unique field of study, blending US labor with Indigenous history, I felt compelled to lend my expertise to unpack the complicated issues that such legislation over simplified. So, I suppose my first acknowledgment should be to Hayworth. Without his underhanded dealing, I might not have been inspired to tell this complicated story and lend historical context to the changing nature of work and sovereignty in Native American nations.

Since then, scores of scholars, editors, activists, relatives, and institutions of higher learning have offered the support I needed to finish this book and weather national economic crises, a global pandemic, and a series of personal and family tragedies. First and foremost, I want to thank those who trusted me with their stories and who helped me understand the thorny legal and historical issues at the center of this work. The list includes Diné labor activist Kenneth White and his family and the founders of the Council for Tribal Employment Rights (CTER), Conrad Edwards, Larry Ketcher, Rodney "Fish" Gervais, and John Navarro, as well as Daniel Press, CTER's dedicated general counsel. They kindly allowed me to attend their national conferences and invited me to address their convention in December 2012. Sharing my historical research on CTER and the development of the Tribal Employment Rights Ordinance with a ballroom filled with CTER founders and younger tribal officials was the highlight of my career. I also thank Deron

Marquez for answering my questions about the politics of Indian gaming in California. He served as the chair of the Yuhaaviatam of San Manuel Nation in Southern California at a crucial time when organized labor and tribal governments were facing off over who had the right to regulate trade unions on reservation lands. I appreciate his time, patience, and candid responses to my questions. Thanks to David Kamper, professor of American Indian Studies at San Diego State University for arranging that meeting. Thanks also to Ron Cobb, president of Teamsters Local 886, and to an anonymous teamster organizer, for discussing their efforts to organize casino workers in Oklahoma. I also thank Keri Hohne, an organizer of the United Food and Commercial Workers union (UFCW) in Connecticut, and an anonymous UFCW activist for sharing their knowledge and experience working at the Foxwoods Resort Casino.

Like most historians, I am eternally grateful to archivists and librarians for helping me locate primary sources. Special thanks to National Archives and Records Administration staff, including Eugene Morse at College Park, Maryland; William Creech at Washington, DC; Randy Thompson at Riverside, California; Gwen E. Granados, Eileen Bollinger, and Cody White at Denver, Colorado; Deborah Osterberg at San Bruno, California; and Ken House at Seattle, Washington. I also appreciate Nathan Sowry, reference archivist at the National Museum of the American Indian; and Holy Wilson and Delphine Best from the US Equal Employment Opportunity Commission library. Great thanks, to Lisa Marie Yazza and Shanidiin Jeff, for their eleventh-hour help in securing a photo from the Navajo Nation Museum.

Historical societies and university special collections were also indispensable for my research. Thanks to Pat Ragains at the University of Nevada, Reno; Bob Diaz, in Special Collections at the University of Arizona; Julia Huddleston, in Special Collections at the University of Utah; Wendi Goen and Sativa Peterson, at Arizona State Library, Archives, and Records Management. Many thanks to Micaela Connolly and Mark Fritch from the Mansfield Library at the University of Montana; to Priscilla Finley at the University of Nevada, Las Vegas Library (UNLV); and to other unsung archivists at UNLV who expertly curated the Katherine A. Spilde Papers on Native American Gaming. I am also blessed with terrific help from the archivists and librarians at Utah State University (USU), where I have been teaching since 2004. Special thanks to Dean of Libraries Jennifer Duncan and to Clint Pumphrey, the manuscript curator at USU's Merrill-Cazier Library, Special Collections and Archives.

I have always viewed research and writing as a kind of collective effort. Indeed, I have enjoyed the intellectual companionship found in dynamic scholarly gatherings, formal and informal. I am grateful for the opportunity to develop my work in nurturing research environments created by Sherry L. Smith and Brian Frehner as part of a Clements Center for Southwest Studies symposium. I am honored to have been included in that conversation and in the resulting anthology, *Indians and Energy*. Thanks also to Carol Williams, who organized a fabulous research weekend at Trent University in Peterborough, Ontario, a kind of smart girls' slumber party that yielded the fantastic collection, *Indigenous Women and Work from Labor to Activism*. I am also grateful for the pivotal time I spent as a fellow at University of Utah's Tanner Humanities Center. Thanks to Bob Goldberg, John Boyack, Beth James, and Susan Anderson for their hospitality, intellectual support, and good humor during the 2016–17 academic year. My work also benefited a great deal from the time I spent at the Center for Gaming Research and Special Collections at UNLV. Thanks to David Schwartz and Su Kim Chung for making my brief stay in Las Vegas so productive. And I owe a great debt to Marc Landry, at the University of New Orleans, who graciously offered a space for me to spend my most recent sabbatical to finally finish this book.

More informal intellectual communities greatly helped to advance my work, including a research group organized by the incredible Tammy Proctor for the USU's history department. It proved to be a useful sounding board as I was developing parts of the book early on. Thanks to my colleagues who offered helpful criticism, including Tammy Proctor, David Rich Lewis, James Sanders, and Lawrence Culver. And a shout-out to Chris Conte, for his willingness to provide me more than his share of collegial counseling sessions. As the manuscript started to take shape, I created a nurturing digital community that included some of the best minds out there. Thanks to Kevin Whalen, Farina King, Erika Bsumek, Coll Thrush, Boyd Cothran, Doug Miller, Cathleen Cahill, Tisa Wenger, Chantal Norrgard, Andy Fisher, and Victoria Haskins for your brilliance and friendship.

The richest part of this kind of work is in the relationships you develop out of a common commitment to research and teaching. I first met Brian Hosmer at a Western History Association (WHA) conference when I was a graduate student. Since then, we have been friends, fellow travelers, and collaborators. I met Sasha Harmon in a similar way. I was already a great fan of her work and was flattered when she turned to me at the WHA and said, "We should talk." From that exchange grew a collaboration on a piece we wrote together with Paul Rosier for the *Journal of American History*. Again, the WHA provided a great place to develop ideas and create networks of amazing colleagues and friends. Paul Rosier has been a constant in my orbit over the years, from helping me buy cowboy boots in Oklahoma City, to collaborating on an article, to writing letters of recommendation. I have learned a great deal from him, particularly as I was developing my analysis of settler colonialism in the Cold War Era. Jessica Cattelino's early commentary on my work at a conference served as a constructive intervention, inspiring me to complicate my research questions. And thanks to my mentor, Alice Kessler-Harris, for her continuous support, and for helping me keep one foot in labor history while remaining connected to the wonderful Labor and Working-Class History Association. I am deeply grateful to the editorial staff at the University of North Carolina Press, particularly to Mark Simpson-Vos, for his patience, intellectual rigor, and unwavering support for this project.

Institutional funding from the College of Humanities and Social Sciences, the Women and Gender Research Institute, and the Mountain West Center for Regional Studies at Utah State University supported my travel to conferences and archives. A subvention grant from the College of Arts and Sciences and an Arts & Humanities Research and Creative Endeavors Outcomes Grant defrayed the cost of indexing. I also appreciate the extra assistance I received from Dean Joseph Ward and History Department Chair Ravi Gupta, who funded my research assistants, Jonah Bibo and Megan Fairbanks. I appreciate Bibo's and Fairbanks's work in checking notes and locating hard-to-find sources. Former students of mine, Joe Lamb, Kathy Teufel, and Mary Thompson, provided great help transcribing my oral interviews, particularly since they did that work before Google translate and other AI tools were invented. The Eadington Visiting Fellowship at the Center for Gaming Research at UNLV and the Obert C. and Grace A. Tanner Humanities Center Visiting Research Fellowship at the University of Utah Tanner Humanities Center offered me wonderful environments in which to conduct my research and write. Other funding sources, including the Charles Redd Faculty Travel Grant from Brigham Young University's Charles Redd Center for Western Studies, and a Summer Stipend from the National Endowment of Humanities, helped me complete a significant portion of the manuscript. The Charles Redd Center along with the Wenner-Gren Foundation for Anthropological Research provided support for a conference where many of the ideas for this book took root. That gathering, which I had organized with Alexandra Harmon and Paul Rosier, called "Indians, Labor, and Capitalist Culture: A Colloquium of Historians, Ethnohistorians, and Anthropologists," and held at the Newberry Library, eventually produced a jointly authored piece in the *Journal of American History*. Thanks to Brian Hosmer and Laurie Arnold for hosting us.

David Reichard deserves a paragraph of his own. I have known David since fall 1989, when as first year graduate students, he and I bonded over a discussion of Kathy Peiss's work, *Cheap Amusements*. A master teacher and dedicated scholar, David has been a lifelong friend. He read every word of this book more than once, raised my spirits on many occasions, helped me clarify and organize my thoughts, prodded me to sharpen my prose, and led me through the mysterious world of legal research. For all that, and for the opportunity to meet other amazing scholars, Thomas Patterson, Kathy Walker, and Peter Gran, I am deeply grateful for the short detour to Temple University on the road to my PhD work at Rutgers.

I could not have started this journey without the incredible, wise women who have guided me over the years: my mother, Freda Gay O'Neill, who taught me about resilience; Salle Sherrod, who showed me how to be a compassionate friend and rigorous teacher; Jill Jones, whose guidance helped me survive the ups and downs of academe; Joan M. Jensen, my scholarly fairy godmother; and my lifelong friend Marguerite McIntyre, whose intellect, humor, and creative energy continue to inspire me.

I am profoundly grateful for my husband, partner in crime, and research assistant extraordinaire John Nelson. I still wonder how I got so lucky to find him. His love, humor, caretaking, and proofreading skills have sustained me and provided me the peace I needed to stay centered. Through him, I have become part of a family, stepmother to three wonderful human beings, a mother in-law to a lovely young man, and now a grandmother to the most adorable baby boy I could have imagined. John, my love, this book is for you.

ABBREVIATIONS AND ACRONYMS

BIA	Bureau of Indian Affairs
CCC	Civilian Conservation Corps
CCC-ID	Civilian Conservation Corps–Indian Division
CERT	Council of Energy Resource Tribes
CETA	Comprehensive Employment and Training Act
CTER	Council for Tribal Employment Rights
CWA	Communication Workers of America
DNA	Diné be'iiná Náhiiłna be Agha'diit'ahii
EEOC	Equal Employment Opportunity Commission
HERE	Hotel Employees and Restaurant Employees Union
HUD	Department of Housing and Urban Development
IECW	Indian Emergency Conservation Work
IGRA	Indian Gaming Regulatory Act
MPTN	Mashantucket Pequot Tribal Nation
NCAI	National Council of American Indians
NIYC	National Indian Youth Council
NLRA	National Labor Relations Act (1935)
NLRB	National Labor Relations Board
OIA	Office of Indian Affairs
ONLR	Office of Navajo Labor Relations
TERO	Tribal Employment Rights Ordinance
UAW	United Auto Workers
UFCW	United Food and Commercial Workers
WPA	Works Projects Administration

WAGING SOVEREIGNTY

INTRODUCTION

Beyond the Civil Rights Paradigm

THINKING ABOUT CLASS, NATIVE AMERICAN WORKERS, AND COLONIAL LEGACIES

> *Education and industrial training for Indian Youth,* for all Indian youth, *will, in a very short period, end Indian wars and, in a not very long period, end appropriations to feed and clothe them. I don't believe anything else will.*
>
> RICHARD HENRY PRATT, FROM BATTLEFIELD AND CLASSROOM

> *When the Grandfather told me to live like white people, I told him to send me six teams of mules, because that is the way white people make a living, and I wanted my children, the Lakotas, to have these things to help them make a living. I also told him to send me two spans of horses with wagons. . . . I was advised to follow the ways of the white man, and that is why I asked for those things. I want you to tell the Grandfather to send me some agricultural implements, so that I will not be obliged to work barehanded. . . . It is your doing that I am here; you sent me here and advised me to live as you do, and it's not right for me to live in poverty.*
>
> SITTING BULL, AUGUST 22, 1883

Richard Henry Pratt's words, quoted above, illustrate US federal policymakers' faith in the power of education to detribalize Native Americans and to erase their claims to the land and resources promised to them in treaties and in previous legislation.[1] Boarding schools like the institution Pratt founded, the United States Indian Industrial School in Carlisle, Pennsylvania, were supposed to accomplish that task by readying Native American children for a place in the rapidly industrializing American economy. Pratt and other reformers believed that Native students could assimilate, and they were confident that, with enough exposure to hardworking white Christians, the children would adopt the values, behavior, and work ethic they were taught. As workers, Native students could then assimilate into white society, and subsequently, Native claims to lands, sovereignty, and cultures would become irrelevant. A new appreciation of American civilization, or so policymakers thought, would prompt Native people to leave their communities, traditions, and cultural identity behind. As a result, the conflict and violence of the recent past between Native Americans and the US government would fade from memory. Historian Frederick Hoxie describes Pratt and his contemporary reformers as embracing "total assimilation": the notion that Native Americans could abandon their cultures, lands, and identities and completely absorb the supposed ideals and practices of American society. However, by the turn of the twentieth century, such optimism, at least from the policymakers perspective, started to wane. They were beginning to think that assimilation was not possible and that Native people were suited only for low-level manual labor.[2]

Sitting Bull, also quoted above, challenged the sincerity of "Grandfather's" (the US federal government) assimilation plan.[3] With his characteristic sarcasm, the Hunkpapa Lakota leader spoke out against federal efforts to divide his people's land into individual allotments. Four years later, in 1887, Congress passed the Dawes Act, legislation that would make allotment a centerpiece of US Indian policy. Unlike Pratt's scheme, which was supposed to introduce Native people to the civilizing influence of wage work, these reformers hoped that the Dawes Act would assimilate them to the ways of white farmers. For Sitting Bull, neither plan seemed plausible. He doubted that working for wages or farming individual plots would solve his people's problems. Living like the white man required capital, not assimilation schemes, to make a living. And Sitting Bull knew that material support from the federal government would not be forthcoming. In fact, carving up Native land without providing significant capital to develop it (or the power to decide how to use their wealth) would instead make most Native people poor.[4] Furthermore, assimilating into the world of wage work would do little to remove the racial discrimination they faced in the workplace, nor would it restore their collective wealth in land. Unlike European peasants, who lost their access to common lands because of structural economic change over the course of several centuries, Native Americans moved from self-sufficiency to wage work at the hands of federal policymakers over the course of fifty-seven years.[5]

Contrasting Pratt's and Sitting Bull's words hints at the central contradiction in US Indian policy that was supposed to offer Native people a way to make a living but instead reinforced a racialized labor system that undermined Native economies. Despite the increased bureaucratic surveillance of their homes, bodies, and cultures, and the dispossession of their natural resources, Native people continued to struggle to adapt and to maintain economies that included both seasonal wage work and their culturally defined ways of making a living. They resisted federal policy initiatives and created new economic and governing institutions that asserted their sovereignty over their lands, cultures, and governance structures. This book charts Indigenous people's efforts over the twentieth century to expand the notion of sovereignty to include the terms and conditions of work itself.

Indigenous economies have been subject to European and American assault since the early days of colonial contact. Particularly for the Spanish, whose wealth depended on the exploitation of Indigenous labor throughout the Americas, taking control of the ways Native people made a living was pivotal to the success of their colonial expansion efforts. Settler-colonial powers, such as the British and Americans, whose thirst for Native land outpaced their interest in Native labor, attempted to remake American Indians into people who would embrace private property and patriarchal gendered norms, social values central to the colonial land system. Even though the United States continued to acknowledge tribal sovereignty into the late nineteenth century, the federal government chipped away at those rights and eroded tribal land claims by incorporating Native people into the republic, but on the margins—as individuals, but without the rights that accompanied citizenship, until the mid-twentieth century.[6]

The acquisition of Native land required the transformation of Indigenous people into individual workers. The 1880 *Puck* cartoon "Loafers and Laborers" brutally illustrates the role of work, or at least waged work, in settler-colonial expansion. The image shows Uncle Sam leading a group of immigrant and American-born workers. "At the end of his patience and his territory," Uncle Sam says, "Now durn your pesky copper skins, you've got to Work [sic] or Jump [sic]."[7] This satirical engraving seems to offer Native people a choice:

"Loafers and Laborers," *Puck*, September 29, 1880, 53.
Courtesy Library of Congress Prints and Photographs
Division, Washington, DC (LC-USZ62-101954).

They can either join the ranks of the American working class or be crushed by the train of civilization barreling toward them. The connection between work and colonialism could not be clearer.

Recent tribal histories reveal a much more complicated story, describing how American Indians shaped regional labor markets and maintained the cultural integrity of their communities. And these works offer important regional and tribally specific case studies that counter the idea that wage work was corrosive to Native culture.[8] Historian Chantal Norrgard, in *Seasons of Change*, describes the ways that the Ojibwe incorporated wage work into their seasonal round. The Ojibwe asserted control over their labor and their subsistence practices as a treaty right. In *We Were All Like Migrant Workers Here*, historian William Bauer argues that people from the Round Valley Reservation in California used wage work to enhance and enlarge their reservations. From the start, the voluminous Indian boarding school literature in the United States and in Canada highlighted the kinds of work students performed as part of their assimilationist training, including their work as part of the outing program and the labor they provided to keep the schools running. Historians Kevin Whalen and Victoria Haskins demonstrate that those programs did more than train students to fit into the waged economy. They served as quasi–labor contractors that supplied the settler communities surrounding the schools with agricultural and domestic workers and subjected the Native students to the racial dynamics of those workscapes.[9]

Despite the growing interest in American Indian workers, their stories still seem peripheral to US labor and economic history. Indeed, on the surface, American Indians may seem irrelevant to the history of the labor movement. Given their absence from labor history, it might appear that American Indians were contented in their jobs; or that struggles against colonialism trumped any class-based concerns. Historical evidence suggests, however, that Native laborers were certainly not satisfied with their second-class status in the workplace. Indeed, we know that they confronted energy companies in the Southwest, entrenched labor unions on the Vancouver docks, and commercial farmers in California. Native workers joined unions wherever they lived, and they created their own organizations to contest discrimination in hiring and to maintain control over their work and their communities' natural resources.

BEYOND CIVIL RIGHTS

But, locating a place for Native workers in "labor's story," requires more than adding a racialized population to the civil rights narrative—a narrative prevalent in studies of workers of color, one that explores how workers transformed their unions from organizations concerned primarily with workplace issues into social movements to struggle for broader social change. While Native people confronted racism and sought equality within US civil society, their status as colonized peoples set them apart from other workers of color. Their social movements diverged as well. American Indians have struggled for the right to control (or reclaim) their land, their resources, and their cultures. Rather than target employers or unions, Native activists largely focused their energy on the federal government because of its control over their economies and political structures. To accommodate these differences, our understanding of class, and the historical processes that shaped Native workers' roles in the capitalist economy may require significant retooling to consider how colonialism shaped them as workers, and why sovereignty, not simply the demand for "civil rights," informed their collective experience in the waged economy.[10]

Like other labor histories, Native Americans' story is about contesting racism and discrimination; but Native American workers also faced a colonial legacy of exploitation and a federal bureaucratic system meant to control both their land and their labor. They followed a path different from their non-Native counterparts. Even though they did not play a leading role in the labor movement, Native workers challenged the terms of economic change and eventually demanded greater controls over their workplaces. But that struggle meant something more than advancing class-based demands or other forms of social justice. Instead, improving Native wages and working conditions meant challenging larger federal control over their lands, politics, and cultures. Exploring the changing meaning of wage work from the late nineteenth century to the present explains how Native workers eventually shaped the meaning of sovereignty itself. Indigenous and non-Native workers might share similar histories; but to find Native people in "labor's story," colonialism must be addressed as a significant part of the plot.

In many ways Native workers' experience resembles what Black and Latinx peoples confronted in their workplaces and communities since at least the mid-nineteenth century. Mexican American workers share a parallel story of land dispossession; but their long-term relationship to the US federal government differed considerably, and as a result, Mexican Americans and Native Americans developed goals and strategies for social change that traveled divergent paths.[11] African American and Mexican American workers fought for the right of inclusion and transformed their unions into social movements to make true America's promise of civil rights. Native people confronted racism and sought equality within US civil society too, but their experience under settler colonialism set them apart from other workers of color. Their social movements reflected those differences. Asserting their sovereignty, a practice fought in the courts, on battlefields, and in the minds of Native people for generations, offered a better strategy for reclaiming their land, culture, natural resources, and the power to govern their people rather than simply struggling for civil rights, as individuals, according to federal and state law. Workers' rights—workplace safety, decent wages, respect, and equality on the job—became key issues that defined sovereignty movements in the late twentieth century.[12]

Colonialism, a key factor in the development of capitalism in settler states like the United States, Canada, and Australia, exploited Native people by separating them from their lands; by attempting to destroy their cultures; and by controlling their labor through state-sponsored work programs, education, and access to jobs until at least the mid-1960s. So, to achieve labor rights, Native American workers demanded civil rights; but they also struggled with the settler state, which in most cases had undercut their ability to make a living by the seasonal round, depleted their lands, and tried to erase their cultures. Adapting to the demands of a colonial bureaucracy, incorporating wage work into culturally defined subsistence practices, or developing collective strategies to assert control over their economies cleared a larger historical path for decolonization that is, as Aman Sium, Chandni Desai, and Eric Ritskes describe, a "messy, dynamic, and a contradictory process." It is a multifaceted struggle that involves a rejection of the colonizer's authority to rule and to expropriate Indigenous lives, lands, and cultures. But, as scholars have asserted, decolonization is not simply reactive. It is creative and proactive, a historic moment in which Indigenous people embrace their own traditions (both old and new) and develop sovereign forms of modernity.[13] Scholars and activists have expanded our understanding of decolonization beyond "metaphors" and ideas (moving beyond Fanon's concepts of decolonizing the mind) to reclaiming land, language, and Indigenous notions of citizenship.[14]

In addition to reclaiming land, political authority, and knowledge, contesting colonial power includes gaining control over the terms and conditions of work—whether that means embracing Indigenous ways of living and working on the land, or working as a drag line operator in a coal mine. It might involve rejecting federal official's expectations about how one behaves as a worker or, as other historians have argued, it could potentially mean refusing to recognize the spatial limitations imposed by the colonizer: fishing where one is not supposed to fish, living one's life by the seasonal round, privileging cultural obligations and attending to family needs over the demands of the workplace, or choosing to work in seasonal jobs, such as in agriculture or lumber, because it allows the flexibility to maintain kin relationships.[15] Wage work, a defining component of capitalism, was supposed to disrupt all those practices.

This book argues that anti-colonial struggle, a building block of decolonization, involved conflict over labor—since wage work and how Native peoples made a living—as a focal point for the federal government's assimilationist efforts.[16] Native people have engaged in a wide spectrum of anti-colonial struggle, including adapting to and subverting settler-colonial models of gendered behavior, incorporating wage work into a seasonal round, or building new tribal institutions meant to reclaim power over jobs, working conditions, and control over their economies and resources. Alone, each of these actions might not be seen as an act of decolonization. However, taken together over time, they contribute to a gradual dismantling of settler colonialism's structures through a longer, complex historical process.[17] The chapters that follow describe how Native Americans, emerging from a history of colonial exploitation, persevered and rebuilt their communities and developed distinctive institutions to defend their cultural, political, and economic sovereignty.[18]

WAGE WORK AND SETTLER COLONIALISM

To sort out the role of wage work in settler colonialism, it is important to consider why late nineteenth century reformers, such as Richard Pratt, thought it would put an end to settlers' conflict with Native Americans and the federal government's obligations to them. Native communities made a living on the land in ways that contradicted Euro-American sensibilities. To be civilized, from the settlers' perspective, meant farming the land and living in one place, and of course, practicing Christianity. In their eyes, Native people were savages because of the way they used the land and how they organized their labor. Native women worked. Native men did not. They moved their communities to take advantage of what the land, its waterways, and the seasons provided. Indeed, American policymakers pointed to Native mobility as proof of their savagery. And those who lived a more sedentary life also used the land in ways that conflicted with colonial designs. Beginning in the late nineteenth century, preparing Native people for a place in the permanent waged workforce seemed like the best solution. Doing so would solve problems that frustrated policymakers since the beginning of the republic, and it would encourage Native people to settle in one place. As a result, at least in the imagination of reformers, Native people would adapt to an industrial routine that required the kind of personal discipline employers valued. Preparing Native people for wage work would supposedly make them self-sufficient. Remade into workers, then, Native Americans would have no need for their own collectively held land, and they would eventually disappear into the American working-class landscape.[19]

Becoming a wage worker, with nothing but one's labor to sell to make a living, is not some sort of natural human state of being, nor is it an inevitable but noble characteristic of an unequal economic system. Undoubtedly, those of us who work for wages today see it in those terms, despite the libraries full of books and periodicals in which historians and other scholars have examined the history of wage work and its role in the development of capitalism.

Indeed, the creation of a working class, a central feature of Western capitalist society, was a slow, and often uneven, historical transformation in people's relationship to the natural world and to the systems of power that determined who owned or exploited its resources.[20]

PRECOLONIAL NATIVE WORKSCAPES

Given their cultural, economic, and geographic diversity, painting a generalized portrait of Native economies in North America in a single chapter of a book is impossible. Native workscapes in the precolonial era were as diverse as the environments and peoples who created them. A "workscape"—a concept developed by historian Thomas Andrews in his book *Killing for Coal*—describes a dynamic relationship between people and the landscapes they transform through their labor. Unlike a landscape that might be perceived in a single frame, according to Andrews, a "'workscape' implies something more complex: not just an essentially static scene or setting neatly contained within borders but a constellation of unruly and ever-unfolding relationships." Cultures develop as people create and recreate these workscapes and help them "make sense of and act on their surroundings."[21]

Before Europeans arrived, many Native communities crafted workscapes from the land and animals. Many peoples planted gardens in the spring; gathered fruits, nuts, and root vegetables as they matured in the summer; and harvested their crops in the fall. Depending on where they lived, people fished and hunted throughout the year, gathered with relatives and other villages in the summer, and moved to different locations to seek shelter in the winter. For example, as historian Chantal Norrgard describes, Ojibwe communities living in the Lake Superior Basin moved from family sugaring camps in the spring to larger villages, where in the summer they netted fish, harvested wild plants and berries, and cut birch bark for their canoes. That seasonal movement, or seasonal round, as Norrgard states, shaped a "variety of subsistence activities governed by the shift in seasons and movement to locations where resources were available."[22]

Depending on where they lived, the shifting grounds of colonial settlement, removal, and continuous violence and war, many Native peoples managed to avoid working for wages and to subsist instead on the land and by trading goods in kinship and colonial markets well into the mid-nineteenth century. Of course, those who had suffered genocidal conditions in California, or in other places that underwent rapid industrialization, may have had little choice but to work for miners, rancheros, or commercial farmers, either with or without getting paid.²³

Migrating for work was not new. Many Native Americans had been traveling back and forth between their reservations and nearby cities since at least the late nineteenth century, when, like other rural people, they were finding it harder to make a living by cultivating their own lands. In 1886, Kahnawà:ke men from the south shore of the St. Lawrence River in southern Quebec first started working as riveters in crews constructing railroad bridges for the Canadian Pacific Railroad. By the 1920s. they were gaining respect in "high steel" throughout the northeastern United States, building bridges in New York, skyscrapers in Manhattan, and even traveling to San Francisco to work on the Golden Gate Bridge (1933–1937). With their families, they established homes and developed strong community ties in Brooklyn, New York; they joined unions, intermarried with non-Native people, and established their own churches. American Indians in the Southwest and in California worked alongside Latino, Filipino, and Asian workers harvesting carrots, lettuce, sugar beets, potatoes, and citrus.²⁴

Like their settler counterparts, Native Americans remained aloof from wage work if they could depend on their own lands to make a living. But they could not preserve their independence from expanding commercial markets. Native Americans traded furs and produce and even crafted commodities for non-Native consumers. For example, in what is now Dubuque, Iowa, Fox women mined lead and traded it. In the 1840s, Miwok miners initially participated in the California Gold Rush.²⁵ Those who worked for wages, either as scouts for traders and military officials or as fishers or agricultural laborers, folded that income into their seasonal round and still maintained their self-sufficiency.

Some Native communities transformed their subsistence practices, such as gathering wild berries and rice and other forms of agriculture and fishing, into commercial ventures. The Red Cliff and Bad River Ojibwes developed orchards and successful berry farms in response to the expanding market for produce in northern Wisconsin. But after twenty years, that industry faded. Allotment reduced the size of Ojibwe landholdings, and many of those who were trying to survive as farmers struggled to pay their property taxes.²⁶ The story of Akimel O'odham farmers in southern Arizona mirrors that of the Ojibwe. Their efforts to develop a lucrative cotton industry was thwarted by paternalistic Office of Indian Affairs (OIA) management and the rise of large-scale commercial agriculture that restricted the Native farmers' access to water. Historians have documented other examples involving oil

Ojibwe wild rice harvest, Bois Forte/Nett Lake, Minnesota, 1971.
David Grant Noble Photographs. Courtesy National Museum of the
American Indian Archive Center, Smithsonian Institution, Washington, DC.

and coal mining, including the violence experienced by the Osage and other mineral-rich tribes in the West when they tried to develop their oil reserves.[27]

By the early twentieth century, many Native communities were incorporating wage work into their seasonal round. For example, when Ojibwe communities faced increased pressure from federal officials and settlers, they found work in the lumber industry, canneries, and commercial fisheries; but they also steadfastly defended their treaty rights to maintain their access to their lands and their labor. Similarly, northwestern Native peoples made a living picking hops in Yakima, or berries in western Washington, before moving on to dig clams in the Puget Sound and sell handicrafts to tourists in urban areas. "Moving between seasonal occupations," as historian Paige Raibmon observed, offered those communities an "economic safety net" and some autonomy from Canadian and US officials.[28] Farther south, Native peoples on the Round Valley Reservation were recovering from California's devastating indentured labor system, augmenting subsistence hunting and gardening with domestic work, sheep shearing, and picking hops. Historian William Bauer argues that Round Valley residents used "mobility, fluid reservation boundaries, and cash wages to take control of their work activities and define community."[29] In South Florida, Seminoles supplemented their subsistence hunting by cultivating small gardens and raising hogs, and by working in commercial agriculture picking tomatoes, beans, oranges, eggplant, and peppers for a few weeks out of the year. They also worked in the seasonal tourist industry, making patchwork garments, carving canoes, and entertaining tourists by wrestling alligators.[30]

Nevertheless, in the twentieth century, Native peoples found it increasingly difficult to maintain their seasonal round, even with the incorporation of wage labor. The Navajos (or Diné), for example, faced intrusive federal policies that limited their sheep herds, dictated governance, and ushered in non-Navajo exploitation of their land's minerals such as coal, oil, and uranium. Other policies urged Diné workers to permanently relocate to urban areas.[31] Indigenous communities in the Great Lakes region also incorporated wage work into their seasonal round but found it increasingly difficult to maintain those strategies when states like Minnesota and Wisconsin began enforcing new hunting, fishing, and land use regulations. As historian Brenda J. Child describes, those laws criminalized many of the ways that the Ojibwe used the land and imposed a settler land-use philosophy, one that favored industrial exploitation of timber and agriculture, and that redefined hunting and fishing as a sport rather than as subsistence. As Child observes, "Working the Ojibwe economy was discouraged—unless it was adjusted in ways so that it could be managed by the nation-state."[32]

The growing literature on American Indian workers demonstrates that wage work may have brought about cultural changes, but Native communities managed to resist the complete assimilation of American social values and practices. In many instances, wage work provided Native families the resources they needed to maintain their cultural connections to the land and to each other. While a picture of creative adaptation is emerging in the historical scholarship, considerations of gender remain largely unexplored.[33]

Gendered economic change is not a twentieth-century phenomenon, of course.[34] At different times and in different places, American Indian women's power over the production and distribution of food and their control over livestock often translated into broader cultural and economic influence in their communities. But, when those communities began to produce goods for a larger capitalist market beyond a kinship-centered trading system, women historically lost economic ground to their male counterparts. As anthropologist Jessica Cattelino demonstrates, a federal program that distributed cattle to men exclusively, created a "male gendering of Seminole tradition" and undermined women's economic power.[35] Conversely, as Marsha

Weisiger and other scholars have shown, efforts to reduce livestock herds on the Navajo Reservation (as part of a federally imposed conservation measure) impacted women disproportionally.[36] This book builds on that scholarly tradition and examines how gender shaped Native experience in federal work programs, including in Indian schools and relief jobs as well as in relocation. In those instances, Native women experienced a great deal of pressure to conform to settler-colonial ideas of proper gendered behavior. However, like other working-class women of color, they entered the waged workforce because they were unable to afford the luxury of a white, middle-class settler lifestyle. Their story of anti-colonial struggle most likely falls into the realm of "everyday acts of resistance."[37]

In the 1970s, as the narrative shifts away from Indian policy to Native-centered economic development initiatives, the gendered thread fades. Perhaps a shift in sources suggests that settler-colonial, gendered rhetoric, so transparent in the archives, is not reproduced as clearly when Native people begin to build stronger institutions, wield greater economic political power, and strengthen their sovereignty claims. The answer lies in continued research.

Chapter 1 of this book begins with a discussion of the pivotal role that Indian boarding schools played in federal efforts to transform Native people into wage workers. After 1877, allotment was intended to undermine Indigenous land-based economies along with Native peoples' tribal identities. Boarding schools were supposed to complete that project, turning independent rural peoples into wage workers and market agriculturalists. The schools were supposed to teach Native youths about work and who they were supposed to become in an industrial society stratified by race, class, and gender; these were lessons many Native people had already learned without the help of boarding school matrons.[38]

Chapter 2 explores the federal policies that seemed to reverse earlier initiatives to move Native people off their lands. The Works Progress Administration (WPA) or Civilian Conservation Corps–Indian Division (CCC-ID) projects offered Native people one of few opportunities to earn wages in their own communities, something that many Native people living on reservations would not experience again until the late twentieth century. Indigenous people welcomed the paid work, even if the jobs were only temporary. But relief work did not help to establish sustainable economies on reservation land. New Dealers claimed to have abandoned the assimilationist objectives of earlier policymakers, but such work tended to reinforce assimilationist ideals, inscribing gendered ideas about work and the value of labor on men and women unevenly.[39]

New Deal reforms faded during World War II. Chapter 3 looks at the years that followed, when the federal government waged a new assault on tribal sovereignty and imposed new legislation, a domestic version of a much broader development philosophy meant to "modernize" the developing world in the postwar era. In 1952, Congress unveiled a voluntary program to accelerate American Indians' relocation from their reservation homes to cities, including Chicago, Cleveland, Dallas, Denver, Los Angeles, Oakland, San Francisco, San Jose, Tulsa, and Oklahoma City. Jobs and job training anchored the program. According to BIA officials, off-reservation wage work provided the means to accomplish assimilationist policy goal: to transform Native people into wage workers. Hoping to complete that process and destroy reservations altogether, a year later Congress passed Public Law 280 (Termination), which withdrew federal services, extended states' jurisdiction over Native land, and revoked federal tribal recognition from many American Indian communities.[40]

Policymakers hoped that urbanization would make tribal homelands irrelevant and that individual states could simply absorb the Native population. But they failed to understand that controlling work did not necessarily mean undermining Indigenous collective identity. Native workers and their families struggled with the terms of relocation. Nevertheless, on or off reservations, Native people continued to assert their sovereignty rights. Stories gleaned from the archives reveal a complicated narrative and provide a glimpse into the often-contradictory impact of postwar economic policy in an era of global decolonization.

Native workers learned a great deal from Relocation, including lessons that contradicted the policy's overall objectives. Chapter 4 examines the emergence of a labor sovereignty movement in response to the growth of extractive industries on reservation land in the 1970s. Looking at the history of sovereignty from the perspective of Indigenous workers complicates the story both in how we assess the impact of energy industries on reservation land and in the ways that workers themselves redefined the terms of this development. When Native workers organized to protect tribal employment rights, they expanded the anti-colonial struggle by broadening the meaning of sovereignty to include control over not only natural resource rights but also the jobs that such development created.

The expansion of the Indian gaming industry flipped the script, at least for tribes with the most lucrative casinos. Before the 1980s, when most of the private employers on reservations were non-Native, the connection between sovereignty and workers' rights seemed clear. Tribal leaders and activists demanded access to those jobs and greater authority to regulate their economies, off-reservation corporations, and labor unions dominated by non-Native members. With the development of gaming, tribal governments became the employers, and the workers in the most lucrative casinos were largely non-Native. As a result, the role of labor in the struggle for sovereignty shifted from the right to hold jobs to the right to govern the workplace. Chapter 5 considers these changes in an analysis of the legal battles over gaming in twenty-first century Southern California, Connecticut, and Central Oklahoma. Struggles between tribes, unions, and state and federal governments created a paradigmatic impasse between sovereignty and civil rights, ideals that frame the social movements important to Native Americans and workers, more broadly.

METHODOLOGY

Thanks to a blossoming of rich scholarship over the last generation, we know a great deal about the relationship between settler colonialism and the expansion of capitalism in North America.[41] Historians and Indigenous studies scholars have clearly charted how the US and Canadian economies expanded at the expense of Native lives, lands, and wealth, beginning in the seventeenth century (at least).[42] Focusing on the twentieth century, *Waging Sovereignty* adds to that story the history of Indigenous workers and their tribal governments. Since many Native people entered the world of wage work by participating in BIA work programs over the course of the twentieth century, examining that pivotal moment of economic transformation in their lives provides an opportunity to understand the connection between colonialism and capitalism from the perspective of Native workers.

This book attempts to balance a policy approach with attention to how Native people navigated around federal programs, first by becoming wage workers and eventually by organizing to gain some control over their working lives in and away from reservation communities.[43] In each chapter, examples from recent tribal scholarship complicate and enrich the policy history with stories that emphasize the agency of Native communities and individuals. To tell that story I rely heavily on Record Group 75: The Records of the Bureau of Indian Affairs of the National Archives and Records Administration (NARA)—located in Washington, DC, as well as in other NARA regional branches—and on government documents, and manuscript collections in various state and university libraries and historical societies. Mindful of the problem of relying on the "colonial archive," I pay close attention to Native voices, pulling their stories out of the archival documents where possible, and including oral histories as the narrative moves closer to the present.[44] I use pseudonyms to protect the privacy of those whose lives were documented by federal bureaucrats. I identify Native American public figures who willingly engaged in public discourse as well as those people whom I interviewed and who agreed to let me use their names. I use the names of BIA agents since they were federal employees and cognizant of the filing system that preserved the historical documents they created.

Native voices can be heard in different ways throughout the book, in their criticism of work relief programs, in the letters they wrote calling for access to jobs, in their letters to BIA relocation officers, in newspaper interviews and oral history archives, and in their responses to a massive survey the BIA conducted to assess the program's success. Native intentions or "hidden transcripts," can be found in federal reports and correspondence by interpreting BIA officials' frustrated rhetoric as they tried to carry out federal labor initiatives.[45] I have supplemented the BIA archive with my own interviews of Native and non-Native leaders and activists.[46]

This book revisits the policy narrative to examine how Native peoples became wage workers, a historical transformation that played a key role in the expansion of settler colonialism in the United States. Work, as imagined by the settler state, remained a central thread in US Indian policy, even as federal officials abandoned the draconian measures meant to suppress Native American cultural practices. Policymakers imagined that turning Native Americans into workers would complete the process of detribalization that started in the early nineteenth century with removal treaties and war, and that culminated in the late nineteenth century with the General Allotment Act (Dawes Act [1887]). The link between work programs and Indian land policy remained strong until the end of the termination and relocation era, in the 1960s.

Indeed, for most of the twentieth century, Native Americans were recovering from the destruction of their precolonial economies and the loss of their land, natural resources, and wealth; and they were becoming increasingly dependent on wages to make a living. Even so, and without much capital, they continued to assert their sovereignty rights by resisting or adapting to assimilationist federal work programs and by demanding access to jobs working in industries operated by non-Native employers on reservation land. In the 1970s, those jobs were located largely in the energy sector and in other extractive industries over which tribes exercised little control. Inspired by the Red Power moment and by their experience during Relocation, activists pushed tribes to develop regulatory bodies to protect the rights of Native workers and to assert the power of tribal governments over non-Native corporations on reservation land. By the late twentieth century, Native people had transformed the meaning of wage work from an assimilationist tool, wielded by federal officials to chip away at tribal identities and culturally specific subsistence strategies, to a sovereignty right, one that Native Americans hoped would allow them to live and work in their communities, either on- or off-reservations, on their own terms.

1

The Civilizing Machine

INDIAN BOARDING SCHOOLS AS LABOR CONTRACTORS

In the late nineteenth century, US federal policymakers set out to finish what the Indian wars had failed to achieve. In Richard Henry Pratt's infamous words, a more enlightened and humane answer to the "Indian problem" was (in his mind) to "kill the Indian in him and save the man," an effort that would require a complete transformation of Native American cultures and economies and an intensive campaign meant to undermine tribal sovereignty.[1] The General Allotment Act of 1887 was supposed to accomplish part of this scheme by dividing the collectively held lands, thereby weakening tribal identities. Boarding schools, the flip side of allotment, were meant to transform Indigenous children into individuals and to teach them the moral value of work—at least according to the Protestant work ethic—and encourage them to conform to settler-colonial gender roles.[2] Channeling Native children into a racialized workforce would complete the transformative process and serve settler-colonial expansion and labor needs.[3] Boarding schools, or "civilizing machines," as Zitkala-Ša called them in her memoir, were supposed to churn out workers, as historian K. Tsianina Lomawaima describes, to do the "hard labor necessary to serve the . . . elite, and [they] anticipated the integration of native people into European American economic and political systems."[4] Wage work would undermine tribal sovereignty, make Indigenous people legible to an expanding state bureaucracy, and extend settler-colonial authority over Native communities and their land. At least that was the plan. Despite such draconian measures, Native people resisted where they could and adapted to the demands of the rapidly changing economy. Through many acts of survivance over the last century, they have retained their sovereign connections to the land and to each other.[5]

Federally sponsored boarding schools (as well as those operated by religious institutions) taught Native children about agriculture and the "domestic arts," everything they needed to know so that they would settle in one place, become subsistence farmers, and abandon the seasonal round.[6] That and good morals, according to Indian school advocates, was all Native Americans needed to prosper in the New Republic as individuals, not as communities.[7] Put simply, Indian boarding schools were meant to implement the objectives of federal Indian policy, lesson by lesson, student by student. Learning those lessons, policymakers hoped, would hasten the alienation of Native peoples from their lands. Yet, as Indian boarding school historians have demonstrated, the curriculum often failed to meet its stated goals. Early boarding school advocates hoped these schools would prepare Native people to successfully tend to their allotted lands. Instead, the curriculum ushered many Native people into the lowest rung of racially segregated wage work.[8]

Non-Native, working-class students, too, were subjected to a school curriculum aimed at molding them to fit into the highly racialized and gendered US economy of the Progressive Era. Educational reformers believed that school curricula needed to be directly tied to the needs of industry. As education historian Harvey Kantor has argued, reformers set out to steer children into the labor market rather than allowing them to wander into jobs without direction. Public schools, according to reformers, should "act as a transmitter between human supply and industrial demand."[9] Historians have argued that those reforms either created greater democratic opportunities for the working class or served as a tool used by elites to control and manage them.[10] Non-Native working-class children's experience might have spanned that continuum, depending on their nationality, geographical, racial, and gendered context. They might have been adequately prepared to work in a factory or even prosper in skilled trades.

Adding a settler-colonial dimension to those educational policies created different results for Native students. Suffering violent displacement, constant bureaucratic surveillance, and federal policies aimed at undermining their collective landholdings and wealth, Native people were supposed to learn to work in the lowest-ranked occupations and embrace the lifeways of the people who occupied their lands. Such training was supposed to pry them away from their communities and undermine their land claims.

LESSONS OF CAPITALISM: THE OUTING SYSTEM

Richard Henry Pratt, the founder of the first federally sponsored Indian boarding school, the Carlisle Indian Industrial School in 1879, developed a tool that was supposed to accomplish those goals: the outing system. His plan, which focused on work in addition to a basic common school curriculum, was, in his mind, the best strategy to achieve assimilationist goals.[11] At first, the outing system placed boarding school students in the homes of rural white families who, in Pratt's estimation, were morally upstanding. In exchange for room and board, and a small stipend, the boys tended livestock, picked crops, and performed other agricultural labor, and the girls served as domestic help, minding white families' children and doing their laundry and other household chores. The students were supposed to learn industrious habits and absorb the "democratizing influence of yeoman agriculture."[12]

In Pratt's vision, Native students needed to remain servile or at least prove their usefulness in order to be incorporated into white society. He acknowledged that Native people could excel in academics and professional occupations. Yet, his boarding school curriculum, and the outing program in particular, mostly trained Native youths for low-waged manual labor. Assimilation could be accomplished, in Pratt's words, "If as individuals the people of one race can be made to add material help to the other, they become proportionally acceptable."[13]

As historian Kevin Whalen has pointed out, the program contradicted its own stated goals. Instead of "uplift," the outing system taught Native youth that they would not enjoy the promises of democracy as independent small farmers. Indeed, that model was already becoming anachronistic. As Sitting Bull observed, Native farmers needed capital, not to mention access to railroads, to succeed in that market. They were not alone. In fact, most non-Native rural people could not compete with large, commercial farmers. Starting in the late nineteenth century, they too were moving to urban areas to search for wage work.[14]

At a 1928 hearing in front of the subcommittee of the commissioner of Indian affairs, Morgan J. Doyle described how the outing system was supposed to operate. As a special agent for the General Land Office of the Department of the Interior, Doyle reported that six girls from the Yuma Reservation had been placed in white homes scattered across California.

One committee member asked, "As household help?" Doyle replied, "Well, yes. You could use them as just rough help, I guess you might call it . . . you couldn't use them as cooks." He then quickly pointed out that the Native girls could be useful as maids, but that was not the point of the outing system. Native children were supposed to be placed in the homes of sympathetic white folks, and those white folks, "in the course of a month or two, will try to teach the girls some of the ways of the white man, they will try to teach the girls sanitation, try and teach them modern cooking of meals, the use of modern cooking utensils and stoves, and they might teach a girl how to set a table and how to serve food, and how to make different sorts of foods, and how to mix them up and cook them."[15]

In his mind, and in the minds of other boarding school critics, the outing system was turning young women into domestic workers but not into good homemakers. Even worse, some staff members were taking advantage of their students. He testified that one superintendent's wife was placing Native children out to work in her sister's Santa Monica home. Doyle's testimony was part of a larger fact-finding project that would eventually become the important study, *The Problem of Indian Administration*, compiled by Lewis Meriam, thus better known as the *Meriam Report*.

Like Doyle, contributors to the *Meriam Report* pointed to the exploitation of Native children as workers as one of the central failures of Indian policy, which, in addition to school crowding, poor sanitation, bad food, inadequate health care, and subpar curriculum, attracted the attention of reformers. For example, authors of the report noted that Native children, as young as eleven, were sent to work in the beet fields of Colorado and Kansas. According to a circular distributed by the Phoenix Office of Indian Affairs, "Beet thinning was light work, though tedious . . . and all done in stooping over or on the hands and knees." Admittedly, beet farmers preferred to hire small boys since they were "very well adapted to this work. . . . It could be done very nicely by boys from 13 to 14 years of age," the circular boasted. Pratt's model boarding schools, which he had hoped would transform Native people into American citizens through exposure to good Christian farmers, became instead quasi–labor contractors.[16]

The outing system and the boarding school curriculum, in general, were supposed to introduce Native people to the capitalist market not as producers and traders, as they had been in the past, but as workers, wielding considerably less power than they had in other markets, such the fur and horse trades.[17] These boarding school lessons taught them who they were supposed to become in an industrial society stratified by race, class, and gender. As William Jones, the commissioner of Indian affairs from 1897 to 1905, wrote, "The great object is to train the Indian to go back to his allotment and live the life of a white man, or to go out and live among the whites."[18]

LESSONS OF CAPITALISM: TIME AND MONEY

By the end of the nineteenth century, living as a "white man" mostly meant working for wages, since self-sufficient farming was largely out of reach for most Native people.[19] Indeed, family farming, the model that had anchored ideas of American civilization for at least 100 years, was becoming obsolete. Most rural peoples in the United States could not compete with those who were farming on an industrial scale. Even so, Native boys were learning how to fix a wagon wheel and plow a field, and Native girls were learning how to iron clothes or can vegetables, skills normally associated with the quickly fading yeoman farming ideal. They were subjected to a curriculum that prepared them to compete in the market economy neither as commercial farmers nor as skilled workers. The children were supposed to conform to a rigid, seasonless time schedule, to submit to the hierarchical authority of an employer, and to acquire the skills necessary for jobs on the bottom rung of a racialized labor market.[20]

But instead of learning self-reliance and budgeting, the system reinforced dependency. Students did not receive the total wages they earned at the end of a pay period, like other workers. Instead, employers sent the money to the schools where it was rationed out to the students at the discretion of the school administrator. This plan, as described by Superintendent of Indian Education Estelle Reel, was part of a larger "civilizing" project. According to Reel, "The teaching of a proper appreciation of the value of money is one of the ends aimed at in Indian education, and by the boy or girl putting aside each month a part of the earnings of his or her own labor, this much-desired result is secured to a very gratifying degree. To earn money by one's own exertions is to appreciate its value a hundredfold more than to obtain it without effort. From this will follow also a proper appreciation of the value of time."[21]

Encouraging Native students to save their money was not necessarily exploitive. However, the school superintendent imposed this system on the students, without their consent. Max Hanley, a Diné man from Shiprock, New Mexico, remembered that after a year working on the "Indian Farm," between 1919 and 1923, officials at the Sherman Institute, issued him money, "just a little at a time."[22] Hopi student at the Phoenix Indian School and future chief Edmund Nequatewa recalled that when he and his fellow

Estelle Reel, the national superintendent of Indian schools, 1898–1910.
Bain News Service Photograph Collection. Courtesy Library of Congress
Prints and Photographs Division, Washington, DC (LC-DIG-ggbain-03707).

classmates returned after working during the summer, they had "a little money saved up." But they did not have ready access to it. Their wages, or documentation thereof, were placed in the office for safekeeping. "If you would need a little money," Nequatewa recalled, "you had to fill out an application blank in order to get any."[23] This was particularly frustrating for him, since he hated the school and was planning to run away. So, one day he snuck into the administrator's office and retrieved his bankbook. He then took the streetcar to Homes Savings Bank where he presented his bankbook to the teller. Nequatewa recalled,

> He looked at me and said, "You want some money?" And I said: "I want my money." "Okay." He looked the account over and says, "Well, your savings here are $110, and your spending money is $7.50. I have strict orders, and I can't let you have this savings money, but I can let you have the spending money, just not the savings." "All right. Just give me my spending money if that's all that I can draw. I would like to have the other, but if you can't do it, there isn't anything I can do about it." "I just can't do it. If I let you have it, I lose my job here."[24]

At the Sherman Institute in Riverside, California, Kevin Whalen found that withholding student wages was commonplace. During the 1920s, students received only one-third to one-quarter of their pay from their employers. Employers sent the balance to school officials who were supposed to deposit it in student savings accounts. Like Nequatewa's experience, the students at Sherman had to request access to their money, in writing. How and when they used their money was subject to the superintendent's approval. Even then, as Whalen describes, "At the close of the 1914 and 1915 school years, male student laborers still awaited 10 to 20 percent of the money earned in those years, respectively."[25] The Office of Indian Affairs (OIA) commonly withheld funds, including wages, money individual Native Americans earned leasing their lands, or royalties non-Native corporations owed the tribes for oil and mineral extraction. The superintendent could deny account holders access to their funds if they judged them to be incompetent.[26]

Even Blackfoot activist and businesswoman Elouise P. Cobell (Yellow Bird Woman) fell victim to this type of rank paternalism when she, at the age of eighteen, tried to find out what was in her own trust account. Cobell, the future treasurer of the Blackfoot Nation, founder of the Blackfeet National Bank, and MacArthur fellowship recipient was told she was "incapable, of understanding accounting."[27] In 1996, she became the lead plaintiff in a class action lawsuit to make the federal government accountable for the money that seemed to have evaporated from Individual Indian Money accounts. She did, in fact, understand accounting. Known as *Cobell v. Salazar*, the historic lawsuit was finally settled after many years of maneuvering through the internecine federal court system.[28] Legal scholar Armen H. Merjian has described the whole affair as a "dreary story of Interior's degenerate tenure as Trustee-Delegate for the Indian trust—a story shot through with bureaucratic blunders, flubs, goofs and foul-ups, and peppered with scandals, deception, dirty tricks and outright villainy."²⁹ It is unclear if boarding school students suffered the same problem collecting wages from school superintendents as Native Americans have experienced trying to collect their money from BIA agents. We know that schools and agency offices normally held back a percentage of Native Americans' wages. Students often wrote to school officials to request their money. But unfortunately, we don't know whether they received their funds. Nevertheless, given the kind of administrative incompetence revealed in *Cobell v. Salazar*, it is reasonable to question whether Native workers also suffered wage theft. Perhaps additional, intensive research will reveal answers.

In addition to lessons on money, the students learned how to tell capitalist time. Zitkala-Ša characterized her boarding school experience as an "iron routine." The famous Yankton Dakota reformer and musician remembered learning about industrial time from "a loud-clamoring bell" that roused her and her classmates out of bed each morning at 6:30 a.m., followed by a "small hand bell vigorously rung," that ushered the students to roll call. For her, this abrupt and regimented schedule signified a stark break with the natural world; a "civilizing machine," that put an end to "happy dreams of Western rolling land and un-lassoed freedom." According to Zitkala-Ša, the clock left little time for joy. She explained, "There were too many drowsy children and too numerous orders for the day to waste a moment in any apology to nature."³⁰

Native children like Zitkala-Ša lived and worked according to an industrial time clock; this was part of a vocational education curriculum that was gaining currency in public education more broadly at the turn of the twentieth century. White working-class, immigrant, and other children of color did not necessarily experience the same type of land dispossession, cultural assault, or forced relocation as part of their education.³¹ Even so, Progressive Era public school teachers taught those non-Native students how to follow orders and the "values of industrial time," too. As K. Tsianina Lomawaima asserts, those lessons were "designed to produce docile, efficient workers . . . and refashion the home, school, and workplace."³²

Francis E. Leupp, who served as commissioner of Indian affairs from 1905 to 1909 and who was one of Pratt's harshest critics, remained committed to the outing system. Estelle Reel, who served under him as superintendent of Indian education, was convinced that the outing system "places the student under the influence of the daily life of a good home, where his inherited weaknesses and tendencies are overcome by the civilized habits which he forms—habits of order, of personal cleanliness and neatness, and of industry and thrift, which displace the old habits of aimless living, unambition, and shiftlessness."

Leupp insisted that teachers in Indian schools embrace the curriculum with gusto. He thought that Native Americans required a full transformation in how they understood time itself. In addition to teaching Native students about the value of land in market terms, Leupp's Indian policy aimed to make the student "understand that a day or an hour frittered away or not counted in the cost of any undertaking, is so much provision for the future wasted. In other words, it must be impressed upon him that the hand-to-mouth, happy-go-lucky mode of existence, which answered for his fathers, will no longer protect him from suffering, and still less his children."[33]

In addition to living and working by the bell, students divided their time between the classroom and work (if they were not on their outing assignment). They usually spent one-half of their days studying basic academic subjects and learning English, Christianity, and white middle-class cultural mores. For the most part, they were forbidden to speak their Native languages and practice their cultural traditions. As historian David Wallace Adams describes, school officials attempted to replace Native ways with new rituals, such as "bugle calls, lining up for inspection, prayers before meals, saluting the flag, and marching drills." Those practices and new holidays, Christianity, sporting events, and gendered behavior "functioned simultaneously as legitimizing and transformative processes."[34]

The children spent the second half of their days working in the barns and agricultural fields and performing tasks that kept schools running such as constructing and maintaining buildings, taking care of the schools' livestock, and working in the kitchens and laundries, and staffing the dormitories.[35] In some cases, students produced agricultural and other goods either to supply other agency facilities or to sell at local markets. For example, as a cost-cutting measure, Pratt hoped to put boys at Carlisle to work making wagons, harnesses, and tinware. In a letter to Wisconsin Congressman Thad C. Pound, he boasted about the plan: "This getting rid of what we make without, by its sale here, imposing on the local trade will be a great relief, and will not only enable us to teach Indian boys the trades, but will be a saving to the Department."[36] Children at Chilocco in Oklahoma, at the Sherman Institute in Southern California, and at Genoa in Nebraska were particularly important for generating revenue that kept the schools running. For example, at Genoa, students tended herds of dairy cows that raised most of the school's income, none of which was shared with the students as wages. Cleaning barns and tending animals were part of the curriculum. The students endured harsh

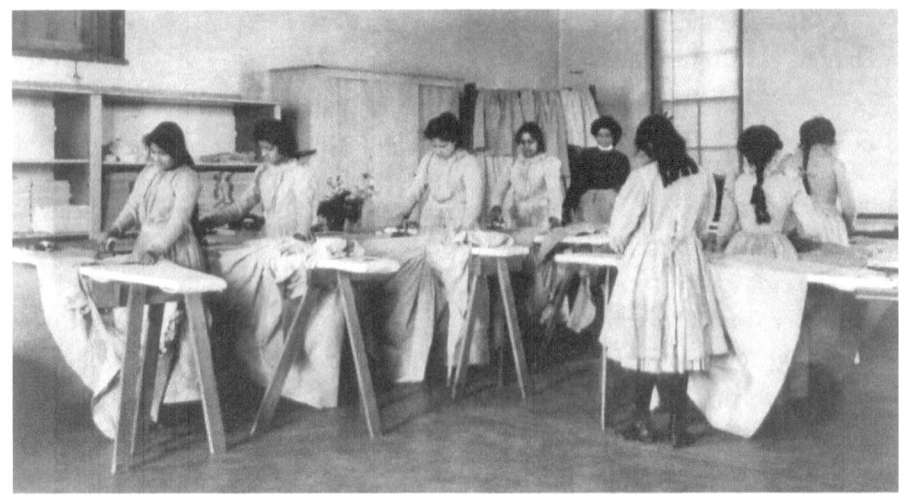

Ironing class, 1901. Photograph by Frances Benjamin Johnston. Carlisle Indian School, Carlisle, PA. Frances Benjamin Johnston Photograph Collection. Courtesy Library of Congress Prints and Photographs Division, Washington, DC (LC-USZ62-26794).

working conditions and as a result many of them contracted bovine tuberculosis.[37] School administrators and boosters heralded this type of work as "vocational." In reality, these lessons were preparing students to work for settlers as agricultural and domestic laborers.

The authors of the *Meriam Report* were particularly concerned about students as young as ten years old "spending four hours a day in more or less heavy industrial work—dairying, kitchen work, laundry, shop." Such work, according to the study, was "bad for children of this age" and could "constitute a violation of child labor laws in most states." Instead, the authors urged schools to limit such work to older students, noting that "a plan of direct pay for actual work is probably better."[38] If Native children were going to be treated like workers, they should get paid.

Like the children at Genoa Indian School, students at many boarding schools cared for livestock, but they did not study the science and economics of animal husbandry. For example, students learned about raising chickens, as part of their chores but not "as a supplement to the usual farmer' resources."[39] They did the work, but they did not learn the business. Indeed, the *Meriam Report* explained, "Most of it is in no sense educational, since the operations are large-scale and bear little relation to either home or industrial life outside." The type of training the students received did not prepare them to be self-sufficient farmers or even good homemakers. While boys tended livestock or thinned beets, girls sewed garments, ironed aprons, and performed a host of domestic duties. However, as the *Meriam Report* pointed out, these jobs yielded little experience that was useful to young women as they started their own families. They were trained to operate institutional equipment that was much different from what they would use in their own homes. Instead of learning "individual laundry and kitchen methods," the school trained them in "machine methods for getting the institutional labor done."[40] Adam Fortunate Eagle, an Ojibwe from the Red Lake Nation, vividly remembered working in the school laundry at Pipestone Boarding School in Southwestern Minnesota:

> The boys on Saturday laundry duty have to learn how to run the great big washing machines, the spin dryer and the hot air dryer. We have to wash and dry hundreds of loads of everybody's clothes and sheets. After that the girls take over the clothes. They press the sheets, pillowcases, and towels on a big hot mangle and then they fold and stack them. The girls iron all our clothes. They take the torn clothes to the sewing room in the girls' dormitory and they patch them back together. The matron is sure to keep us busy so we don't have time to goof off or fool around with the girls.[41]

LESSONS OF CAPITALISM: RACE AND GENDER

In addition to learning about time and what it was worth in wages (or lack thereof), the boarding school experience taught Native students where they fit in a society structured by race and gender. Initially, the boarding school curriculum took shape in the racial environment of post–Reconstruction era reform, and it offers a good example of how the era's Indian policy and racial uplift schemes intended to help African Americans overlap. Richard Pratt, a former Union officer in the Civil War, reenlisted in the military in the years that followed. He eventually commanded the 10th Cavalry, a Black regiment, popularly known as "buffalo soldiers," and he served in various campaigns to subdue Native resistance in the Great Plains and the West. In 1875 Pratt moved from his post at Fort Sill, Oklahoma, to Fort Marion in St. Augustine, Florida, where he supervised the confinement of Native prisoners of war.[42] When the prisoners were released in 1878, he escorted seventeen Cheyenne, Kiowa, and Arapahoe men to the Hampton Normal Institute in Southeastern

Virginia.[43] Founded in 1868, in the wake of the Civil War, Hampton educated newly freed Black people and trained them for jobs in a waged economy.[44]

Pratt's experience at Hampton significantly shaped his vision for Indian education. Unlike some of his contemporaries, who saw Native people and African Americans as sub-human, Pratt thought that their cultural and material circumstances were responsible for their poverty and diminished status. Pratt considered "racial difference" not as inherent or biological but as environmental. Changing environmental conditions and exposing Native students to upstanding white people, according to Pratt, would be the key ingredient that would transform them into ideal citizens, on par with their white counterparts. But educating Native students alongside Black students was not what he had in mind. Doing so, according to Pratt, would "further the segregating and reservating [sic] process."[45]

According to Pratt, Native people needed the opportunity for "observation of our best people."[46] Clearly racist and paternalistic, he contrasted the histories of formerly enslaved people with Native Americans. For Pratt, "the negro," now a citizen, had achieved "the fitness he had for that high place . . . by the training he was given during slavery which made him an individual, English speaking, and capable industrially."[47] Native American students needed to experience something similar. But, according to Pratt, they had arrived at these schools as prisoners, bitter from a legacy of war and neglect on reservations. Pratt believed that Native people and whites would overcome their animosity if they got to know each other. In his mind, when Native Americans learned white ways of doing things, they would embrace "civilization."

Educating Native students alongside previously enslaved people did not offer the civilizing example Pratt had in mind. In his view, Black Americans were not civilized enough to serve as an example to Native people. He worried that his charges would be influenced by the surrounding Black community, including the "woods full of degraded Negroes."[48] He wanted to expose Native students to what he saw as a higher, more virtuous environment. That meant that Native students needed to live and work with white people. So, when he was offered the chance to supervise Native American students at Hampton, he opted instead for starting his own school.

Indian boarding schools were supposed to offer practical experience to Native students and "remove prejudice between the races." To Estelle Reel's mind, when introduced to their white counterparts, animosity between Native and white students would dissolve. Of course, the system's overt racial intent required Native students to conform to the expectations of white culture, and it trained them in the "worth and value of labor and its remuneration."[49]

Indeed, the boarding schools taught Native youths where they stood in the racial matrix of settler society. Their work was essential to the local economies that surrounded the schools and to the operation of the schools themselves. Children attending boarding schools like Genoa, near Lincoln, Nebraska, and the Sherman Institute in Riverside, California, worked hard in the school's fields, barns, and kitchens. Students at Sherman also served as a significant labor force in commercial agricultural operations nearby in the Inland Empire and Imperial Valley. They worked in the summers, as part of their outing placements, alongside adult migrant laborers. By 1925, this practice no longer resembled what Carlisle's founder, Richard Pratt, had originally envisioned. The students were not working in a family environment, and they were not learning the ways of the yeoman farmer. Instead, as Whalen states, students' work experience "funneled young Indians into jobs that would never uplift them from their supposed positions at the bottom of the hierarchy of civilization." When they joined the migrant labor force, they found a racialized working class largely defined, as Whalen states, "as Mexican and Non-Mexican." Farmers and ranchers classified them as the former. And they shared a similar racialized experience. They received lower wages than white workers, they slept outdoors, worked "torturously long days," and slept in "shoddy living quarters" or in racially segregated camps where they had to provide their own bedding.[50]

While farm and ranch supervisors were supposedly teaching Native boys how to be men, boarding schools were hiring out Native girls to be domestic workers. They too received training on how to conform to the gendered and racial expectations of white employers. From their employers' perspectives, for Native people to be civilized, they needed to be of service. That goal did not necessarily include full integration into American society on an equal basis with white Americans, despite the rhetoric of some reformers, like Pratt, who often claimed he was preparing Native people for citizenship.[51]

Boarding school scholars have explained in great detail how the civilization project was clearly meant to undermine Native Americans' tribal identity and collective landholdings and impose a settler-colonial bureaucracy over their everyday lives. The keystone of this plan was the institution of a strict, gendered division of labor. William Torrey Harris, the US commissioner of education from 1889 to 1906 and one of the founders of modern public education in the United States, weighed in on the connection between gender, work, and civilization for Native Americans.[52] According to Harris, "Not only does tribal life prevent intercourse with the present and past history of the human race, but it prevents that division of labor which makes possible any high degree of productivity in the industries. Its agriculture and manufacturers are conducted by the women and superannuate men. The young warrior despises an industrial occupation."⁵³ Federal Indian policy since at least the early nineteenth century was meant to change what settlers perceived as a savage and unproductive organization of work. As Harris recommended to the commissioner of Indian affairs, Indian schools needed to persuade young Native men to settle down and become industrial workers and then, perhaps, Native women might be relieved of their heavy burdens.

In addition to working their outing jobs in the summers and their everyday chores of maintaining the school and its agricultural lands, the boys completed vocational training in various shops, where they made and repaired shoes, harnesses, and wagons. They also learned about carpentry, blacksmithing, "other useful trades." Undoubtedly, marching around the school grounds in uniforms, a practice that was meant to maintain military discipline, offered lessons in settler manliness and, as the superintendent boasted, "thorough obedience to civil authorities."⁵⁴

Unsurprisingly, girls were subjected to the domestic arts. Girls tended to the schools' kitchens, laundries, dormitories, and cared for the chickens. These duties and more were supposed to make them better housewives once they returned to their allotments. Girls also took classes in home economics that taught them about sanitation, sewing, cooking, and childcare. Enola Acord, a matron at the Fort Berthold Indian School, reported that she was teaching her students "the art of housekeeping in a systematic way." Accordingly, "the ideal training for girls is [what] will instill a love for home and make good, neat housekeepers." She urged her fellow teachers to encourage "students to plant shrubs, plants, and flowers . . . [which would] work a great transformation of the surrounds of a home." But, keeping house, according to Acord, accomplished a weightier goal. "The good home makes a good citizen, and the good citizen makes a good government," Acord proclaimed.⁵⁵ Yet, the students rarely had the chance to use the kinds of domestic tools that they might use to take care of their own families. As students, they mostly operated large, industrial sized kitchen and laundry equipment at their school; they still had to adjust to middle-class white ways. The schools often left it up to outing employers to teach students settler cooking and housework methods.

Matrons and teachers at the boarding schools subjected young Native women to a curriculum of subservience. As Margaret Jacobs and Victoria Haskins have documented, that involved policing the young women's behavior on the most intimate level.⁵⁶ At stake was the school's ability to market the girls' labor. School officials assured employers that the girls were ideal employees. Just in case, the superintendent instructed employers to keep them at home in the evenings and to make sure they were always chaperoned. If the young women disobeyed, they could be returned to school.[57] The reputation of the domestic workers and the matrons was at stake. Indeed, the women charged with managing the outing program saw themselves as "maternalist civilizers of Indian women." In their efforts to "uplift" (as they imagined) young Native women, they were reinforcing their own racial and class superiority.[58]

Despite Enola Acord's lofty goals, other teachers and matrons simply prepared students to work in white middle-class homes.[59] Native boarding schoolgirls served roles similar to what other racialized migrants and enslaved women have played since at least the nineteenth to the twenty-first centuries. They worked within a structure of "global motherhood," where they had to privilege the domestic needs of white middle-class women over the care of their own children and households. As a result, their middle-class employers were often freed to pursue other interests and professions. Of course, boarding school students were mostly children. So perhaps, rather than forfeiting their own mothering opportunities, they lost their childhood instead.[60]

And middle-class white employers were eager to hire Native students. The growing middle class in Western cities in the early twentieth century found the availability of cheap domestic workers a selling point for having an Indian boarding school in their midst.[61] Boosters in cities like Phoenix, Arizona, and Riverside, California, were giddy with the promise of young Native labor working in their fields or minding their children for relatively low wages. A newspaper reporter in Grand Junction, Colorado, suggested that these schools provided an ideal solution to the labor shortage. Unlike the authors of the *Meriam Report*, who complained about the school's educational quality in 1928, a reporter for the *Delta (CO) Independent*, in 1902, thought the training was perfect. Self-satisfied, the reporter boasted, "The system of training now bestowed upon the red children at school teaches them to become servile to their superior—the paleface, and the present generation in training have become so accustomed to serving their paleface teachers that they are more than willing to enter the household as servants. Herein may lie the solution of the servant-girl question—for a time, at least."[62]

The authors of the *Meriam Report* singled out the contradiction between the boarding schools' mission to "civilize" Native children by shaping them to live an idealized notion of white, yeoman farm families and the reality of the student's experience. They did not condemn the outing system outright. Yet, the critics thought that the execution of "cooperative part-time learning" had wandered far from Pratt's original vision. "Whatever it may have been in the past," the *Meriam Report* concluded, "at present the outing system is mainly a plan for hiring out boys for odd jobs and girls for domestic service, seldom a plan for providing real vocational training."[63] Boarding schools neither prepared students to compete with non-Native workers in the industrial world nor significantly helped students improve their lives at home. The report noted how the schools' idea of "uplift" was farcical. According to the study's authors, "Any educational policy that looks toward making day laborers of the men and domestic servants of the women is to be deplored, not because these employments are in themselves objectionable but because they represent standards of life too low to be sought as a goal for any race."[64]

SCHOOLS AS LABOR CONTRACTORS

Moving Native people into the low-waged labor force had been the plan all along. From the very start, Indian boarding schools served as quasi–labor contractors for commercial agriculture and other businesses in the areas surrounding the schools. Richard Pratt, who was responsible for supervising Native American prisoners of war from the Southern Plains at Fort Marion in St. Augustine, Florida, initiated the system. Convinced that work and exposure to white society would help to civilize the prisoners, he decided to hire them out to local employers. He set them to work at a local sawmill, polishing "sea beans," and picking oranges.[65] He hired out "five of the sturdiest, each from a different tribe," to a wealthy landowner to clear the ground for a new orchard on Anastasia Island. For six weeks of back-breaking work, which included pulling palmetto roots and moving five acres of soil, each prisoner received thirty-five dollars. With one day off per week, which was spent at the prison, the prisoners' wages amounted to one dollar a day, comparable to the prevailing rate paid to other seasonal farm laborers in the South Atlantic at the time.[66] They slept in tents, isolated on an island and within sight of the prison. After a few weeks, Pratt proudly remembered that after an adjustment to the hard work, "Their physical improvement was very considerable and became an object lesson to the whole party." After that experience, Pratt was happy to accommodate employer requests when they "applied for an Indian" to labor in their fields, shops, or building sites.[67] In the years that followed, Pratt and other Indian policy reformers developed the aptly named

Boys digging for potatoes in field, 1901. Photograph by Frances Benjamin Johnston. Carlisle Indian Industrial School, Carlisle, PA. Frances Benjamin Johnston Photograph Collection. Courtesy Library of Congress Prints and Photographs Division, Washington, DC (LC-USZ62–55420).

"industrial school" system and hired out students—instead of prisoners of war—to serve employers in their surrounding communities.

THE INDIAN EMPLOYMENT BUREAU

Perhaps reflecting the growing pessimism of their assimilationist mission, the OIA instituted its own labor placement program modeled on the outing system. Although originating as a vehicle for placing boarding school graduates into jobs, the OIA's program eventually sidestepped schools entirely, and placed southwestern Native people directly in low level mining, commercial ranching, and railroad jobs, or, as Francis Leupp put it, "wherever else in the outer world a dollar can be fairly earned by days' labor."[68] He considered government philanthropic labor programs that put poor people to work for work's sake, "humbug, even if a benevolent, humbug." Instead, Leupp's program, as he described it in 1910, was "designated to gather up all the able-bodied Indians who, through the pinch of hunger . . . may have been moved to think that they would like to earn some money."[69]

The OIA employment bureau's supervisor was supposed to serve as a go-between, making sure that employers treated Native workers fairly, that they received wages, and that their contracts were legitimate. But Leupp did not want the bureau to manage the Native workers consistently. He expected that once they were familiar with the system, they would "understand that for whatever comes to them thereafter they will have themselves to thank."[70] In that way, according to Leupp, Native workers would gain self-reliance and self-respect.

Leupp appointed Charles E. Dagenett to lead the program. The *Indian Craftsman*, a magazine from Carlisle, described Dagenett as a "quarter blood Peoria" who had studied at Carlisle and Hampton and had served in the outing program. He was married to a "full-blood Miami" woman. Leupp was impressed with Dagenett's experience and eager to extend the outing program's principles beyond the boarding schools to reach "Indians of all ages and conditions and in all classes of industries."[71] Dagenett established his headquarters in Denver and with field assistants, located in Arizona, New Mexico, Utah, Montana, and Colorado, he recruited Native workers for jobs working on the railroads, government reclamation projects and commercial agriculture, particularly in the sugar beet fields of Colorado and Wyoming.[72]

OIA officials had considered developing an Indian employment service for several years before Leupp assumed leadership of the agency. But Henry Pratt staunchly refused to allow the OIA to use boarding school students. It is likely that he felt it was necessary to maintain a strong system of surveillance over the children. Under Leupp and Dagenett, however, the boarding school outing program directly overlapped with the Indian Employment Service. For example, southwestern Indian schools placed Native boys in homes in Rocky Ford, Colorado, where they worked side by side with Native adults in the beet fields. The young boys earned four dollars a month and lived with families. Other recruits were paid twelve to fourteen dollars per month during the contract period.[73] Dagenett boasted that the farmers who used the most advanced irrigation and intensive farming methods employed "as many as 600 workers in this field at one time."[74]

Robert Valentine, the commissioner of Indian affairs from 1909 through 1912, praised Dagenett and claimed that jobs helped to ease conflict between tribes and the federal government. Recalling a rather simplistic version of the story, Valentine described how Dagenett deescalated tensions by putting the Utes to work. He convinced them to take jobs on the Burlington Railroad. And, Valentine noted, "Contrary to expectations, they proved to be very satisfactory laborers, quiet, tractable, and for some time well satisfied with the work. They earned a considerable sum of money and the training they received had a very salutary effect."[75]

As one might expect, the story is much more complicated. These jobs served less as a carrot, and more of a stick. In 1907, a group of White River Utes left their homes in the Uintah Basin and traveled to South Dakota where they hoped to meet with tribes on the northern plains, such as the Crow and the Lakota, to formulate a collective plan to resist further American encroachment on their lands. Rebuffed by the Lakota, they remained steadfast, threatening armed resistance. Federal officials tried to negotiate with the Utes but insisted that they work in exchange for rations and send their children to boarding school. Fearing for their children's safety, the Utes refused the deal. They also believed that the government should provide food and supplies to them as a treaty obligation, not in exchange for work. It was only when federal officials cut their rations in half, and federal troops arrived, ready to put down Ute resistance, that they agreed to take jobs on the Santa Fe Railway and the Burlington Railroad in South Dakota and to send their children to school in Rapid City.[76] They also built fences at the school and performed farm labor. Not long after, the Utes in Rapid City returned to their homes in the Uintah Basin.

MIXED FEELINGS

Recent public revelations about the abuse Native children suffered in boarding schools throughout the United States and Canada make it difficult to craft a generalized portrait of contemporary Indigenous views on the topic. Native memories and critics are somewhat mixed. Notable Native American leaders, particularly members of the National Congress of American Indians (NCAI), pursued a variety of educational options and assumed professional careers in law, medicine, and the arts. Some, like Francis La Flesche and Arthur C. Parker maintained a strong critique of Indian schools, demanded that Native children have access to higher education, and supported a curriculum that centers what we might now call Indigenous knowledge. In the tradition of racial uplift, certain individuals, such as Charles Eastman, embraced the civilization model and defended Indian boarding schools. Others assumed administrative roles in the OIA and worked as boarding school matrons and instructors.[77]

However, the memoirs of former boarding school students suggest that they did not necessarily embrace the meaning that boarding school officials

The Civilizing Machine

attached to their outing work and vocational training.[78] They may have enjoyed learning new things, such as carpentry or using a sewing machine, and their parents might have appreciated the material support the schools provided. Nevertheless, many students challenged school officials' dehumanizing and paternalistic control by quitting their jobs, returning home, or by simply engaging in what anthropologist James C. Scott has called "everyday acts of resistance."[79] Boarding school historians tell stories of students ignoring outing matrons' instructions, feigning incompetence, and continuing to maintain romantic relationships and social lives beyond the reach of their employers.[80] Some students ran away from their schools. And, at times, parents refused to let them attend in the first place. For example, in August 1904, Oscar M. Waddell, the superintendent of the Ouray Boarding School in Randlett, Utah, reported that Ute parents were not cooperative. "About the time school is to open," Waddell complained, "they take their children and go to the mountains hunting, where they stay for weeks and perhaps months, hiding from the police or employees sent to get the children."[81] Yet some students and alumni relied on the schools as a resource when they were looking for work. They knew that if all else failed, they might call on school officials to find them a job as a domestic worker or farmhand.

Living and working for white families, students certainly learned the ways of white culture. They improved their English language skills and observed middle-class consumer behavior. They undoubtedly acquired information helpful for surviving the trauma of dispossession. Using letters from Native students and their parents, Brenda J. Child has revealed how Native families sometimes used the schools to counteract economic hardship. For example, while students at Haskell who were sent to work as domestics in white middle-class homes may have rejected the assimilationist goals of the program, their parents found it "useful because it allowed teenagers to find summer jobs."[82] Indeed, Child explains that Native families sometimes viewed boarding schools as a resource that might help them cope with dire economic and personal tragedies, or as a strategy to avoid the racism Native students experienced at public schools. Even so, parents worried that those boarding schools might endanger the health of their children.[83]

While the experience was outright exploitative, some former students look back on their boarding school days with mixed feelings. Adam Fortunate Eagle, who later became active in the Red Power movement, remembered Pipestone Indian Training School fondly, particularly his friends and teachers. He was proud that at the age of twelve he could "glaze windows, paint the dormitories . . . refinish the floor in the boys' dormitory." Learning how to use "belt sanders, disc sanders and scrapers" on those hardwood floors" paid off. He was also pleased by the quality and efficiency of their work maintaining and repairing school employee housing. "We refinish their floors, paint their ceilings and walls, and they can move back in a week," Fortunate Eagle boasted.[84]

Myrtle Begay, a Diné woman from Canyon De Chelly, also remembered her time at boarding school with mixed emotions. In 1923, when she was eleven years old, she was transferred from a day school near her home to Fort Apache Boarding School. She traveled by wagon, train, and truck, 194 miles south, and arrived at the school late at night, and was "sent to bed, without a meal." Recounting her loneliness, she stated, "I had never been that far from home. Everything was strange. That evening all the girls I came with gathered together. We sat talking about our homes and wept all evening."[85]

After acclimating to the school environment, Begay embraced the experience. She played in the band and enjoyed learning "many subjects." She remembered her teachers at Fort Apache Boarding School as exceedingly strict. "If a girl was naughty," Begay recalled, "she got a spanking with a ruler or a strap." Nevertheless, she warmly recalled that the experience taught her self-discipline, a trait that she greatly valued throughout her life.[86]

But she did not embrace her education as the "uplift" Indian boarding school administrators had envisioned. Instead, she saw her Navajo upbringing and the boarding school curriculum as two useful bodies of knowledge that could help her accomplish the same thing. In Begay's opinion, "Traditional education and Anglo education are similar in many ways. Both teach a student to be independent, to have self-respect, to know the facts of life and so on. Getting involved in home activities gives a young person knowledge of Navajo family life. Then, in school, he must be involved in all the activities to learn, advance and constantly be a better student."[87]

During three of the four summers of her boarding school years, Begay worked in domestic service, as part of Fort Apache's outing program. She recalled: "We called this type of work 'outing.' That was how we learned to work, earn our own money and spend it. The wage we received was five dollars weekly. It was a lot of money to me; so, I was tickled and could not wait for each payday. I enjoyed my work very much."[88]

It is important to note that neither Fortunate Eagle nor Begay fully internalized the assimilationist lessons they learned at boarding school. Despite their hardships and the considerable time they spent in boarding schools, both grew up to be advocates for their communities and cultures. Myrtle Begay embraced her identity as a Diné elder. Adam Fortunate Eagle, known as a "contrary warrior," played a significant role in the Alcatraz takeover in 1969.[89] Both examples, while anecdotal, offer evidence of Native resilience and resistance to the cultural dynamics of settler colonialism. They may have learned about capitalist time and money, but they did not necessarily embrace the worldview that accompanied those lessons.

The next chapter moves the story forward into the 1930s, when the OIA repealed some of the devastating characteristics of allotment and boarding schools and introduce new plans that promised government reform and poverty relief.[90] American Indians welcomed the income. Nevertheless, Native workers who survived the boarding school experience might have been thinking, in the words of rock-and-roll star Pete Townshend, "Meet the new boss, same as the old boss."[91] New policies carried old assimilationist lessons and provided the means for federal officials to impose settler-colonial ideas about gender, labor, and the capitalist workplace onto Native lands, eventually undermining tribal sovereignty.

2

Building, Digging, and Sewing

WORKING FOR WAGES ON FEDERAL RELIEF PROJECTS IN THE 1930s

When the CCC-ID camps were first opened in 1933, the boys had to be taught the meaning of work and discipline before they could be taught any particular job.

M. H. DAVIS, FOREST SUPERVISOR,
HOOPA VALLEY AGENCY, CCC-ID, MARCH 5, 1941

This chapter begins with a picture of a young Diné woman sitting in front of a sewing machine, surrounded by mattress ticking, in what looks like a semi-industrial context. For her, such industrial employment within her reservation community offered great comfort since the Navajo economy, like the rest of the United States, was in deep trouble. Her relatives had suffered as they watched their pastoral way of life slip away, a process largely engineered by federal authorities who reduced the Navajo livestock herds to preserve the tribe's rangelands for long-term economic benefit. But in the short term, without their sheep and goats to sustain them, many Navajos went looking for jobs. Usually, in the depths of the Great Depression, that meant working in a federal work program.[1]

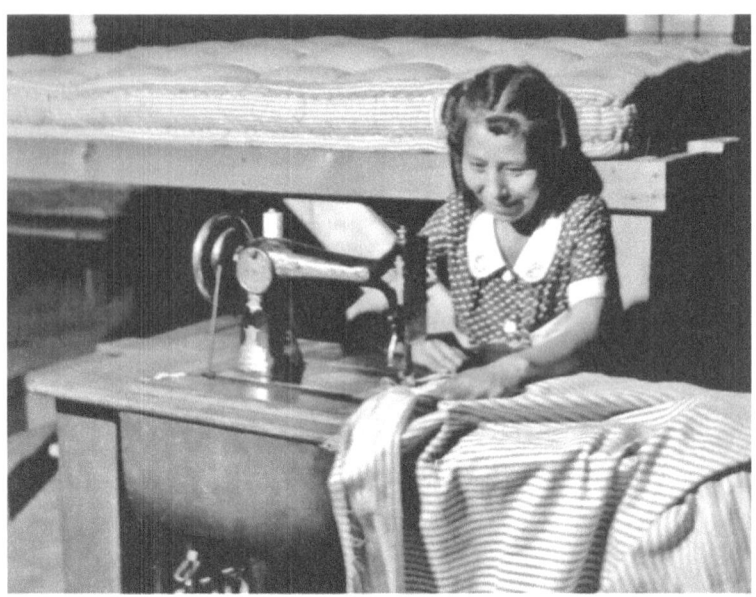

Unidentified Diné woman working at a WPA mattress-making project in Shiprock, NM, 1940. Photograph by Milton Snow. Courtesy Navajo Nation Museum, Window Rock, AZ (16-378).

During the 1930s, thousands of Native Americans found work on federal relief projects specifically designated for Indian reservations and administered by local OIA officials.[2] The WPA employed men on large public works projects, such as building schools and roads, and it put women to work sewing mattresses or repairing used clothing for distribution among the poor. The Civilian Conservation Corps–Indian Division, (CCC-ID) employed Native workers to dig irrigation ditches and wells and to work on other projects meant to improve their lands. Native people embraced the work and welcomed the income, even if the jobs were only temporary.[3]

John Collier, the commissioner of Indian affairs from 1933 to 1945, made sure that Native people had access to that relief work. In fact, he ushered in changes that signified a dramatic departure from earlier policies meant to break down tribal ties and transform Native people into individual landowning Americans. He reversed OIA school and administrative protocol and encouraged Native American cultural expression; he emphasized the development of day schools to replace dreaded boarding schools, and he supported the revival of American Indian languages. He even advocated limited self-government. But his efforts to protect Native American lands and traditions ushered in different kinds of pressures to transform their land use practices, work, political traditions, and gendered behavior.[4]

Like many federal policies intended to "help" Native Americans, such as Indian boarding schools, federal relief programs created new problems. Relief work programs, particularly jobs with the Civilian Conservation Corps–Indian Division were supposed to make the tribes' land more viable for American Indian subsistence.[5] But these projects did not adequately replace the self-sustaining economies that the federal government had destroyed in previous generations, nor did the projects offer adequate income, capital, and the political autonomy Native communities needed to develop on their own. The programs encouraged Native men to work for wages rather than caring for their own land and animals. Indigenous communities now contended with relief-oriented economies and found themselves working on projects that were designed to provide them with subsistence wages and subjected them to the same kind of assimilationist lessons that they might have learned in boarding schools.[6]

THE INDIAN REORGANIZATION ACT

The Wheeler-Howard Act, also known at the Indian Reorganization Act, served as the keystone of John Collier's "Indian New Deal." In addition to repealing allotment, reforming Indian boarding schools, and creating a revolving credit system, the legislation was supposed to offer reservation communities the opportunity to govern themselves, albeit in a limited manner. Under the provisions of the act, if American Indians voted in favor of the law, they could then organize local constitutional governments. Most tribes agreed to do so. However, notable exceptions included the Navajos and several tribes in the Pacific Northwest.[7] To form those tribal governments, the tribes had to conform to settler-colonial political structures and constitutions; but they would not enjoy the same type of authority and autonomy as states. Tribal governments remained subject to OIA oversight, and all decisions they made required the OIA's and Bureau of the Interior's approval.[8] The law was an improvement from the previous military-styled supervision, but it nonetheless reproduced settler-colonial dynamics and constituted a direct effort to undermine tribal sovereignty, at least in the mid-twentieth century.

Therein lies one of the central contradictions in New Deal–era Indian policy. Efforts to supposedly affirm Native culture and identity, in the end, undermined tribal sovereignty. Collier, a passionate reformer, hoped to rebuild subsistence societies but instead designed policies that favored wage work and commercial agriculture. In fact, relief work sometimes contradicted the OIA's stated long-range goals and encouraged Native people to settle around agency headquarters, abandoning their ranches and farms. For example, according to historian Donald Parman, in the 1930s, residents of the Lower Brule Reservation moved close to OIA agency headquarters in search of work. By the end of the decade, they depended on the CCC-ID and other relief programs for 50 percent of their income and earned only an additional 18 percent of their income from agriculture.[9] Similarly, in the Florida Everglades, some Seminole communities, many of whom had previously maintained a subsistence way of life and avoided settling on reservations, now migrated to reservation communities to work on CCC-ID projects.[10] Depression-era unemployment and racial discrimination beyond the reservation borders, pushed Native people to return home, and federal work programs offered incentives that pulled them back to reservations, interrupting, to some extent, the "seasonal round," they had developed to survive with shrinking resources.

Part of Collier's "Indian New Deal," included the 1935 Indian Arts and Crafts Act, legislation aimed to promote Native artisans and the market for "Indian made" products. Prior to the introduction of Depression-era reforms, local OIA agents and extension workers had devised plans to promote Native craft production to feed a growing market consisting of white, middle-class collectors and their philanthropic organizations. New Deal legislation buttressed those efforts and promoted ways to protect the Native craft market by creating "Indian Made" branding and by trying to rationalize design, materials, and production methods.[11]

Native people were already supplementing their incomes with arts, crafts, and subsistence production, like berrying and wild rice farming, with or without advice from non-Native experts. Weaving rugs and baskets, making jewelry and pottery, and creating other cultural objects to sell in the growing Indian art and crafts market remained economically and culturally important for Native families. For example, Diné women and men created rugs and silverwork to trade for groceries and other supplies at reservation trading posts. Tlingit women sold their baskets to tourists on the waterfront in Sitka and in the hop fields in the Pacific Northwest. Cherokee families wove baskets for their own use as well as to trade within their communities and to sell to a broader market.[12]

Much to the chagrin of OIA officials, many American Indians also found work performing for tourists or in films, carrying on the traditions launched decades earlier in the Wild West show arenas across the country. On several levels, the film and tourist industries were exploiting Native people and creating lasting cultural stereotypes that would reinforce colonial policies well into the late twentieth century. Yet, getting paid "five dollars a week to be regular Indians," appealed to many Native Americans. In addition, that type of temporary, migrant work could find a place in the seasonal round.[13]

The faltering American economy during the 1930s narrowed those options. Unemployment in many non-Native communities started to erode traditional sources of wage labor, particularly in agriculture.[14] In Southern California, in particular, Native workers faced increased competition for jobs from Dust Bowl migrants.[15] In New York, Oneidas, who had worked all over the state, lost their jobs to white workers. As historian Laurence M. Hauptman reports, by 1930, 77 percent of Oneidas were on some sort of public assistance.[16]

Federal work projects, particularly the CCC-ID and the WPA, offered relief and, in the minds of the policy experts, promised to improve the lands and lives of Native people. Indeed, Native people welcomed the income. However, unsurprisingly, those jobs came with strings attached. These programs policed workers' behavior, bolstered men's work at the expense of women's, and reinforced the gendered and racial lessons many Native people learned in boarding schools.[17]

MEN'S RELIEF WORK: THE CCC-ID

The Civilian Conservation Corps, (CCC), one of the most successful New Deal programs (which spawned the CCC-ID), set out to solve interlocking crises of the 1930s: environmental degradation and unemployment. By applying rational, scientific methods to forestry, farming, and the management of watersheds and grazing lands, its architects hoped the program would "rehabilitate" the land and transform workers into productive actors in the struggling US economy.

From 1933 to 1942, CCC crews of young, mostly unmarried men ventured into forests, deserts, mountains, and farmland to build roads, trails, and dams and to generally fortify rural landscapes against natural or human-made environmental disaster. They planted trees and grasses to stop soil erosion; they fought fires, and they created recreational places previously inaccessible to urban Americans. These programs, as historian Neil Maher argues, "embodied the ideals of Progressive Era conservationists" and were meant to make nature profitable—in the long run—rather than reducing

Northern Cheyenne CCC-ID workers, finished with reservoir maintenance, 1941. Quarterly Illustrated Narrative Report of CCC-ID Activities on Tongue River Reservation, April–June 1941. Northern Cheyenne Agency, Lame Deer, Montana, Misc. IECW and CCC-ID Reports, 1933–1942, RG75, Records of the Bureau of Indian Affairs, National Archives and Records Administration, Denver, CO.

it to ruin for short-term economic gain.[18] The programs were supposed to transform the young men, too; their bodies and souls bolstered by the hard work, fresh air, and wholesome lessons they learned laboring outdoors and in the CCC classrooms.[19]

Conservation work was more than a job. Maher argues that the CCC provided space for urban and other downtrodden youth to experience the outdoors, to rebuild and nourish their bodies with hard work and plentiful food, and to restore their manhood with meaningful purpose. Working on a CCC project offered enrollees the opportunity to exercise their economic citizenship. According to Maher, that experience provided a venue for European immigrant men to claim "whiteness," as they created a shared masculine culture of work, mixed with a nationalistic spirit. Part Boy Scout, part farmworker, the CCC enrollees were "playing Indian." "Ironically" Maher continues, "as less-than-white Irish, Polish, Italian, and Jewish boys made their skin as 'brown as Indians' through outdoor labor in the CCC, they were making themselves more . . . American as well."[20]

For American Indians, that process was reversed. The gendered project of making "men" out of Native "boys" was intended to encourage them to emulate, or to assimilate "white" behavior. Non-Native CCC workers would be uplifted by the nature they were supposed to be conserving, but Native Americans needed to be removed from nature itself, or at least, they were to learn to manage it scientifically. Like the lessons learned in Indian boarding schools, managing nature according to settler-colonial priorities was supposed to undermine Native boys' relationship to the land, values and practices linked to their culturally defined ideas about masculinity.[21] Both routes, immersing non-Native working-class boys in nature and removing Native boys and men from it, were supposed reaffirm colonial power structures along gendered lines: alienate Native men from the land and reaffirm non-Native men's racialized authority over it. Making Native men "white" meant undermining their collective relationship to their lands, transforming their workscapes and, ultimately, their tribal sovereignty.

On reservations, CCC-ID projects followed similar land conservation principles as those of the CCC, but they differed in scope and character. The CCC-ID's conservation efforts were supposed to repair rangeland and develop agricultural resources so that Native Americans might establish commercially viable, subsistence farming and ranching economies. More importantly, the camps provided an opportunity to teach Native Americans how to become wage workers and how to fully assimilate into off-reservation society (if they had not already learned those lessons in boarding school), remaking the people and the land on which they lived.[22]

Most federal projects employed men, since many of the initiatives involved construction work—building bridges, government structures, roads, and dams. In 1933, in the first year of the CCC-ID, a total of 14,000 American Indians worked in 200 camps on conservation projects spread across 68 reservations. Approximately 9,000 lived in family camps. Some women participated in the programs as clerks or camp cooks, or they served as home economics instructors at family camps where they taught female family members about nutrition and sanitation. By 1942, when the program ended, 85,200 Native Americans had worked on a CCC-ID project.[23]

According to Collier, the CCC-ID would help Native people rebuild subsistence farming and supplement it with "crafts and secondary industries." This kind of society might offer an answer to the problem of "planless individualism" that brought the United States "to the verge of wreckage." Indian policy offered a potential solution. With great optimism characteristic of the New Deal, Collier predicted, "The Indians and their land can become laboratories and pioneers . . . in this supreme new American adventure now being tried under the leadership of the President." Rebuilding Native communities was part of a "vaster experiment . . . which is intended to bring about a rebirth of the American people."[24] The project, as Daniel Murphy surmised in his official report of the program, "was really work on a life level, supplemented by real instruction which made the work not merely a job but a continuing, progressive learning process."[25]

The CCC-ID seemed to work against Collier's vision of communal, subsistence living, however. Its labor and educational programs taught many of the same assimilationist lessons Native students had learned in boarding schools. For project managers, making Native people into wage workers involved shaping their leisure behavior in addition to teaching them work-related skills.[26] Education programs included lessons on "conduct, dress, meeting people, speech, and table etiquette." They were supposed to develop new social skills at camp-sponsored theatrical productions, sporting competitions, art classes, and socials.[27] Arranging their social lives around such "virtuous" activities was supposed to divert Native men from drinking alcohol and gambling, particularly on payday. Jay Nash, the director of Indian emergency conservation (the predecessor of the CCC-ID), boasted that "because of the wholesomeness of the camps, law violations have been held to a minimum, which reflect very favorably on the quality of our Indian workers."[28] Some directors went further in their efforts to maintain an orderly camp. Leonard Radtke, the superintendent of Hoopa Valley Agency in Northern California insisted on adding a "law and order employee" to the payroll. This person would act as a "liquor officer and . . . maintain order from other offences that may occur." The "law and order employee," Radtke explained to Collier, might "have a commission as deputy sheriff" or serve in some other skilled job. Most importantly, according to Radtke, he "must be a white man."[29] Apparently, racial lessons were also included in the assimilationist, CCC-ID curriculum.

A key social lesson included saving money. Non-Native CCC workers were mostly unmarried young men between the ages of eighteen and twenty-five, from families who were listed on relief rolls. For them, learning how to be financially responsible and sending between twenty-two and twenty-five dollars from their thirty-dollar monthly paycheck home to their families was supposed to be part of becoming a "man."[30] In effect, they were supposedly preparing for their future roles as the breadwinners of their families. American Indian enrollees were also obliged to save a substantial part of their wages.[31] But, unlike its non-Native counterpart, CCC-ID was not simply a youth program. Half of the Native men who participated in a CCC-ID project were more than thirty years old. Many were married and were already raising families. So, instead of preparing them to embrace their role as upstanding, family men, according to the settler-colonial ideal, the program emasculated them by subjecting the men's gendered family role to bureaucratic oversight.[32]

Like the outing program, local superintendents who administrated CCC-ID projects deposited an enrollee's savings in his Individual Indian Money account, a kind of makeshift banking system controlled by agency officials that was supposed to serve the best interests of Native Americans. Data from the 1930s on the operation of the "OIA banks" is notoriously difficult to obtain, so it is unclear whether Native Americans enjoyed full access to their wages. Tribal officials, scholars, and policymakers have discovered so many problems in agency-level accounting, it is safe to assume that the OIA might have mismanaged wages as well. Whether agency superintendents mismanaged wages in the same way they mismanaged other Individual Indian Money accounts remains an open research question. The significance here is that the money filtered into the same paternalistic structure that reinforced Native people's dependency status.[33]

Nevertheless, CCC-ID administrators thought they were helping Native people become independent from government relief, develop their own resources, and learn to manage forests, rangelands, or farms for themselves. Part of that plan included grooming Native men to take on leadership roles in construction and resource management. From the beginning, federal officials instructed project managers to promote Native men up through "the ranks," to foreman and assistant foreman, and to reward their ambition with wage incentives. The average CCC-ID worker received thirty dollars per month in addition to housing and food. Some received a bit more if they commuted from their own homes or if they used their own livestock work teams. Assistant leaders earned thirty-five dollars per month, and leaders received forty-five dollars per month.[34]

Jay B. Nash, the director of Indian Emergency Conservation Work (IECW) (the predecessor of the CCC-ID), thought promoting Indian workers would help advance the project's production goals. More importantly developing Indian leadership was crucial "from an educational standpoint."[35] CCC-ID camps would serve as a kind of incubator for future leaders. E. R. Burton, a personnel supervisor for the OIA reminded his readers that emergency conservation work would end, and "many of the present workers will seek new worlds to conquer." He hoped that many of these Native men might find supervisory positions in the Indian service or in off-reservation industries. Soon, he reported, a placement officer, would be "making a circuit of reservations in the Northwest to interview Indians who have been advanced to the rank of 'Leader' or Assistant Leader' and those who have been appointed to skilled or supervisory salaried positions." Recruits would be evaluated based on the following criteria: "Industriousness, cooperativeness, initiative, trade ability, supervisory ability, and use of leisure time."[36]

In the OIA publication *Indians at Work*, agency superintendents heralded their success promoting men to skilled jobs and leadership positions. In a celebratory headline, the editor cheered: "Indians in the jobs! Indian foremen, Indian camp managers, Indian recreational leaders, Indian cooks, truck drivers, mechanics, blacksmiths and trail locators!" At San Carlos, Apache men were serving as straw bosses, powder men, and truck drivers. At Fort Berthold, the "enrolled Indians [were] doing an excellent job of fence building under their own Indian foreman." Native American men were also serving as foremen at Hoopa.[37]

But most workers performed nonskilled, manual labor. Superintendents favored projects that employed the largest numbers of people. As a result, more men were hoisting picks and shovels, and fewer were operating heavy machinery. Sometimes Native workers did not always see the work as uplifting as its promoters described in the pages of *Indians at Work*. Historian Brian Hosmer, in his study of Wind River relief workers, found that those men who were not placed in supervisory positions did not remember relief work in such grand terms. According to Hosmer, they appreciated earning "A dollar a day" and were "glad to have it." But they did not necessarily see those jobs as particularly "educational."[38]

In the early years, camp superintendents emphasized "on the job training" in the CCC-ID's educational program, and they considered other types of educational efforts, at best, superfluous, at worst, a distraction from the conservation work that needed to be done. Enrollees learned the skills they needed to know to perform their jobs. When Hosmer asked one former enrollee from the Wind River Reservation if he learned anything useful from the experience, he responded, "Damn right I learned how to dig a hole."[39]

But Collier hoped to accomplish broader social goals beyond building roads and digging ditches. He pushed local agency superintendents to teach courses that would prepare Native workers to oversee their own lands when the conservation projects concluded, such as classes on health and safety, masonry, and even forest and range management techniques. At Hoopa Valley, enrollees were learning "Elements of Christianity" and taking vocational courses in carpentry, cooking, and bee keeping.[40] By 1940, project managers had integrated educational programs into CCC-ID projects.[41] Soon thereafter, Native workers studied academic lessons in business English and commercial arithmetic. Some OIA agency officials used the CCC-ID as means to eliminate illiteracy. To get a job, enrollees had to demonstrate the equivalent of fourth grade reading and math skills. If they could not do so, they were obliged to enroll in classes offered at night and on weekends at CCC-ID camps.[42] Native men undoubtedly found some of the training beneficial to them, particularly in English literacy and math. But they were not assuming leadership roles that would help them develop their own initiatives, outside of agency supervision.[43]

In addition to conserving forests, rangelands, and other natural resources, CCC-ID and other relief projects created an infrastructure that would integrate Native American land into the broader US economy. In his accounting of CCC-ID "improvements," D. E. Murphy noted that the CCC-ID crews built 7,522 miles of telephone lines, 23 radio stations, 14 airplane landing fields, 9,709 miles of truck trails, and 1,163 bridges that could accommodate trucks and cars. They fought pests, weeds, and soil erosion. They also built houses, lookout towers, fire breaks, corrals, dams, and irrigation systems.[44]

According to agency officials, developing reservations' infrastructure also advanced the interests of state and national economies. Leonard Radtke, the Hoopa agency superintendent, justified building the Tish Tang trail and truck lines to make it easier for fire crews to travel to the mouth of Tish Tang Canyon. Such development would also allow Native residents to ship their produce out by truck rather than by pack horses. Building telephone lines would expand the agency's phone service, bring them prompter access to medical care and improving "social conditions." Those changes would create a positive ripple effect for the region. He predicted that such development would produce "more wealth for our Indians, and consequently more taxable property for the state and nation."[45] Agency officials may not have considered the forests as a prime commercial asset for Hoopa Valley reservation residents, but protecting those lands was important to preserve the Trinity and Klamath watersheds. Doing so would "make substantial contribution to the Nation," as one production coordinating officer noted, since those water sources were important "to the State of California and the protection of which is clearly in the public interest."[46] By the time the CCC-ID closed in 1942, Native workers had completed projects on 231 reservations and Indian schools.[47]

Agency superintendents boasted about the achievements of former CCC-ID workers when they moved into better paying jobs. For example, Robert A. Miller joined the program at Fort Hall and rose through the ranks to become an assistant clerk for the CCC-ID at Hoopa Valley, earning an annual salary of $1,680—more than four times the pay of the average enrollee.

In 1941, Miller was doing well for himself, compared to what he might otherwise earn as a sawmill worker in Hoopa, which paid approximately $20.31 a week in 1941.⁴⁸ Edward E. Marshall, who made an impressive $5.15 per day as an equipment foreman, was promoted to machine operator and then on to equipment foreman on the roads division in Hoopa. Gilbert Marshall moved from Hoopa, where he started as an enrollee, to become camp foreman at Carson Agency, where he earned $100 per month.⁴⁹

For many Native men, working on a CCC or WPA crew provided welcome income and constituted their initial foray into the waged workplace, even if, as historian Tom Biolsi argues, those jobs created an "artificial economy" where the federal government provided reservation residents with their central source of wealth.⁵⁰ More importantly, by building roads, dams, and buildings Native men were literally beginning to create the infrastructure that would eventually connect their reservations to the larger capitalist market. Indeed, Native men's labor linked their communities to the capitalist economy. Yet, their status, as "men" in that broader economy was suspect. Denied the marker of masculinity—wage work—beyond the reservation, they were at once drawn into the market economy and then subjected to its racialized margins. For some, that experience would later offer a stepping stone into military service or jobs on the home front in the defense industry.

WOMEN'S RELIEF WORK: THE WPA SEWING PROJECT

New Deal–era programs offered women a less secure future in the waged workforce. Women worked too. But, unlike their male counterparts, women's work remained marginal to the bigger story of economic transformation. OIA and county extension agents charged with developing women's relief work folded those initiatives, such as the WPA sewing project, into domestic training programs that were already part of the federal assimilationist curriculum. Native women's labor then became "charity" work, something they did for self-improvement and community welfare, not to earn wages to support their families (even though they received wages, often on par with men's wages). The WPA provided Native women with the opportunity to earn wages and even to acquire vocational training. Yet, those same programs reinforced women's status as non-wage earners, their work indistinguishable from the daily tasks of keeping house and caring for their families.

Collier had been instrumental in extending New Deal programs, including the CCC, Public Works Administration (PWA), and other Emergency

Blackfeet WPA sewing-project workers, 1936. Photo included in the Annual Report of Extension Workers, January 1, 1936, to December 31, 1936, RG 75, Office of the Bureau of Indian Affairs, National Archives and Records Administration, Washington, DC.

Conservation Work (ECW) projects to Indian reservations. Some projects even employed entire families in various types of conservation work, including rodent control, livestock management, and national park maintenance. Yet most WPA, CCC-ID and PWA jobs were reserved for male workers. According to an official accounting, out of approximately 156 WPA projects on Indian reservations, only 11 projects (or 7 percent) were designed to employ women.[51]

Such a skewed gender ratio is not surprising, since non-Native women faced a similar imbalance in work relief programs in their communities. Of the 8,500,000 people employed in WPA projects from its inception in 1935 until the war effort absorbed the program in 1943, only 12 to 18 percent were women.[52] When World War II started to revive the industrial economy, the percentage of women working in WPA programs increased to 27 percent, more accurately reflecting their numbers in the labor market overall. As the need for labor in the defense industries increased, more women moved out of relief work and into permanent industrial jobs. In fact, the New Deal architects envisioned WPA jobs as ladders to the industrial workforce, providing women with the training and work experience needed to move into better-paying, skilled jobs. Eleanor Roosevelt underscored the advantages that women gained with their experience working on a WPA project. After touring a WPA sewing project in Milwaukee, she reported that women in

Building, Digging, and Sewing

these jobs "have an opportunity to work on all types of modern machines, which is a help to future employment."[53]

The mattress project was supposed to provide that same kind of job experience. On August 17, 1934, Aubry Williams, the acting administrator of the Federal Emergency Relief Administration (FERA), another important New Deal agency, announced the development of a mattress-making project to provide jobs to 60,000 women who were on relief roles. The mattress factory project was part of a broader scheme meant to heal the wounded US economy and to solve several interlocking social problems characteristic of the Depression era: commodities without markets, people without jobs, and poor people without decent bedding. Purchasing surplus cotton would aid farmers. Turning that cotton into mattresses would provide jobs for women. Relief agencies would then distribute the products to those in need. According to Ellen S. Woodward, the director of FERA's Women's Work Division, state relief agencies set up 410 such manufacturing units, and 233 more were on the way.[54]

The mattress project was only a small part of a much bigger plan Woodward had imagined for employing women. At Eleanor Roosevelt's urging, FERA administrator Harry Hopkins created the Women's Work Division and appointed Woodward as director. According to historian Martha Swain, Woodward imagined finding jobs for 500,000 women, in a variety of occupations, not simply creating the female version of ditch digging work.[55] But, as Swain demonstrates, many of those programs were eliminated, in Woodward's words, in "the rush to put men to work first."[56] As a result, unemployed women had trouble finding relief work in white-collar, professional, or in other occupational categories usually reserved for men. A woman on relief who wanted a job would most likely find herself behind a sewing machine. During the week ending on April 2, 1938, 56 percent of all women earning WPA wages worked on sewing and other goods-production projects, 41 percent performed various white-collar jobs, and 3 percent found work on construction sites or at other miscellaneous venues.[57]

Unfortunately for Woodward, the mattress project ended almost as soon as it got off the ground. Women's industrial training yielded to corporate pressure. A month before Williams announced plans for the mattress project, industry leaders registered their protest. H. McCain, the president of the Alexandria Bedding Company, argued that such work relief schemes were "obviously impractical and instead of affording relief to labor, will in fact, be a serious detriment to both employers and employees thruout [sic] the country." According to McCain, the program was untenable since it would "rob thousands of mattress factory employees all over the country of what little work there is now available." Instead, McCain thought it was better to create plans "in every State in the Union to preach and teach the unemployed, the feeble, the backward, the timid that correct principle of self-preservation, sacrifice, hard work, how to think and the right of thinking, the development of courage, determination and will power, and demonstrate that there is no place in America for transients, incompetence, indifference, envy and selfishness."[58]

Other businessmen echoed McCain's criticism. They worried about production standards as well as the long-term effect on their industry. It is no surprise that within a month of launching the mattress factory project, Harry Hopkins assured Robert W. Schwab, president of the Southern Spring Bed Company, that the project was not intended to "encourage competing enterprise." In fact, the production process hardly resembled modern manufacturing, since, as Hopkins noted, the "mattresses are made in women's workrooms, provided with simple equipment for hand work only." But he could not convince bedding industry leaders that the project would not threaten their market share. Backing away from his initial goals, he promised Schwab and other bedding industry leaders that the project would end shortly, as soon as one million mattresses were distributed to needy families.[59]

Hopkins faced criticism for setting up sewing rooms in general. In a press conference in October 1934, he tried to quell criticism about such government run "factories." Setting the record straight, he quickly asserted, "They are not factories. They are work rooms. Those people call them factories. I have not seen any that could be called factories. . . . Most of them are just regular working rooms, where a woman can go in and make a dress for her youngster."[60] As much as Hopkins and others tried to downplay the industrial nature of the program, they could not hide the fact that mattresses were commodities, hardly the kinds of items women might make in their own homes for personal use. WPA photographs portray sewing rooms that were closer to the industrial model than to the craft workshop image Hopkins described. Indeed, industrial conditions prevailed in many sewing rooms across the country, even sparking labor unrest, such as the 1937 sewing room strike in Tampa, Florida.[61]

As advocates defended the program, Native women pressured OIA officials to extend the mattress project to reservations.[62] In 1934, Mary B. Salois, a prominent member of the Blackfeet community, wrote to John Collier to express her concern that work relief programs were not reaching the women of her reservation. Salois was president of Blackfeet Indian Welfare, a volunteer organization dedicated to improving educational opportunities and the general well-being of the reservation community. According to Salois, a Blackfeet delegation had visited Washington, DC, a few months earlier to meet with federal officials, but because of so "many important matters pertaining to the needs of the Blackfeet, the question of employment for women was overlooked." Had Mary Salois attended those meetings in Washington, women's issues might have loomed larger on the delegation's agenda. Describing the issue as "real serious," Salois portrayed women's unemployment as a major "social and economic problem confronting us here on our Reservation." There was "no work for the girls and also the women, a great many dependent on their own efforts for a livelihood," she explained. The girls, in particular, were at risk. "There is nothing with which to direct their minds in the right channels in a town like Browning, where all the big business is controlled by whites and an Indian boy or girl is never given a chance to work," Salois maintained.[63]

Some months earlier Salois had discussed these issues, including the possibility of creating a garment factory on the reservation, with the local OIA agent. As the previous director of women's work in the Civil Works Administration (CWA) on the reservation, Salois was convinced that Blackfeet women were ready for waged jobs. "They love to earn and use their earnings for their homes and their children," she boasted.[64] Salois's petition to Collier did not meet with immediate results, however. After briefly consulting with the OIA's Extension Division director, Collier wrote an apologetic letter to Salois, explaining that there were neither the funds nor the personnel to launch such a project.[65]

In 1937, three years after writing her letter to Collier, Mary Salois's demands were finally addressed. Native women, Blackfeet included, found work making mattresses and in other WPA-sponsored sewing projects located in reservation communities. Responding to repeated appeals from concerned philanthropists and activists like Mary Salois, agricultural extension agents expanded the "Indian New Deal" to Native American women.

Native women's work relief resembled the kinds of projects designed for women in other rural and urban areas of the country. Like poor women in Mississippi, New York, or El Paso, Native women were put to work sewing garments, mattresses, and other useful textile goods. And, like their non-Native counterparts, they made products that would be distributed to the needy. Wages, too, would improve their buying power and stimulate the economy. In fact, the sewing rooms in rural counties, both on reservations and off, were similar, employing small groups of women stitching garments by hand. Yet, the size and scope of the sewing projects varied greatly, from industrial-scale garment factories to the more intimate rooms where women fashioned handcrafted linens.

What distinguished Native women's relief work in Cut Bank, Montana, from non-Native women's work in Brooklyn, New York, was neither the products they stitched together nor the tools they used to sew them. The difference centered on the administrative framework itself and the local historical dynamics out of which the OIA and home extension agents interpreted and managed the relief programs and then incorporated them into a system heavily weighted by decades of paternalistic mismanagement. Mary Salois might have imagined the development of a garment industry on the Blackfeet reservation—one that would have ensured young women permanent employment and could have rivaled big business under white control. Instead, what she saw was the outgrowth of the OIA Extension Division's "home improvement" program that taught American Indian women "modern" cooking, sewing, and food preservation techniques. Of course, the difference between learning to sew or to cook new recipes and this program was that woman earned forty-four dollars per month in WPA wages, equal to what men were making building the community centers that housed such domestic projects.[66]

By the time Native women gained access to WPA jobs in reservation communities, projects directed to developing their domestic skills, such as sewing, were already in place and managed by home extension agents. Equipped with the latest research in home economics, extension agents were taking their lessons out of the Indian school classrooms and into the Native women's homes and communities. While the boarding school curriculum may have been aimed at training Native women to become domestic workers in non-Native residences, the extension agents seemed interested in aiding Native women's "improvement" in their own homes—at least as defined by dominant middle-class standards.[67]

With the application of WPA funds to home extension projects, the line between homemaking and wage work was blurred. In fact, the relief work folded into a wide range of home improvement lessons that extension workers were teaching. Extension agents did not make a significant distinction between working for wages sewing mattresses or making new garments out of CCC cast-off clothing and making quilts or making Indian crafts and handmade aprons to be displayed at county fairs. Whether the women were earning wages or not, all the work was done in the name of charity, community uplift, and the appropriate gendered instruction.

Given the kinds of raw materials at their disposal, such as cast-off clothing and army surplus clothing and canvas, the Native women were resourceful. For instance, in April of 1936, Blackfeet women received clothing from abandoned CCC camps including socks, underwear, pants, jackets, shirts, overalls and bedding—all unwashed and in great need of repair. After washing the clothing at the Cut Bank Boarding School's "big laundry," the women set out to rework the clothing into children's garments and other useful items. No piece of fabric was wasted. The extension agent supervisor at Blackfeet, Jessie Donaldson Schulz described the transformation of the soiled CCC castoffs:

> The women then sorted the material into piles for various uses—some to be patched and darned, others to be cut down for little children, etc. The pieces left from cutting down garments were cut into blocks for quilts, and the scraps left from the quilt blocks were used for carpet rags. What wee scraps were still unused were shipped to the Olsen Rug Company to be used by any of the women for new rugs. Hundreds of pairs of old CCC socks were darned and patched. Those unfit for renovation were raveled and dyed and made into hooked rugs with Blackfeet designs. Very attractive.

One woman, whom Schultz described as "ingenious," figured out a way to transform "boxes of large drawers without shirts to match," into knitted dresses. "Some are in one piece, others consist of a skirt and sweatshirt, or an over blouse." According to the extension agent, "These, when dyed are remarkably pretty. . . . The girls are enthusiastic over the dresses and want one or more if they can get them."[68]

Like the New Deal administrator Harry Hopkins, extension agents felt the need to defend these projects as charity, not as economic development. They wrote to Collier, clarifying that the project's goals did not involve turning a profit. "The manufacturing of clothing [was] for relief," as stressed William Donner, the superintendent of the Fort Apache Agency. "The plan is to work up this clothing for orphan children and old people who must be taken care of," he explained. Both the products and the labor "performed by old ladies, cripples, widows" would exist outside of the market, not as part of larger economic development initiatives. Donner continued, "The project will provide relief work for those providing the labor and clothing for those unable to provide for themselves."[69] Consistently stressing the "workshop" quality of these projects, agents were careful to describe the work as charity, not as an effort to develop textile factories that would provide permanent wage work for women on the reservations. Perhaps some of the superintendents shared commercial leaders' suspicion of New Deal programs and worried that government run businesses might compete unfairly with private industry.

The workplace itself seemed to downplay the industrial possibilities of women's work. Agency superintendents used funds reserved for "Indian rehabilitation" to build community centers and canneries. WPA money paid wages to the male construction workers and the women who would eventually work in these facilities. But the buildings were designated as "multi-purpose" and for community use, not for industrial manufacturing. In fact, women completed sewing projects in special sewing rooms, or they spread their work out in general meeting areas or gymnasiums. Extension agents rarely described reservation canneries in industrial terms. Instead, those initiatives were self-help projects in which Native women canned surplus produce for distribution to the poor. They were also places where reservation community members could come and can produce from their own gardens in exchange for a small percentage of their goods which would be distributed to their needy neighbors.

A similar gendered struggle over relief work played out in 1937 on the Crow Reservation. Instead of pleading with OIA administrators to establish sewing projects, Crow women fought with Crow men over the distribution of WPA jobs. Responding to requests from the Crow Indian Women's Federation, the Crow Tribal Council established a small sewing project that employed seven women. Women earned fifty cents an hour and worked ten-day shifts making or repairing clothes for needy children and the elderly who lived on the reservation.[70] Within eight months, Agency Superintendent Robert Yellowtail shut down the sewing project. Writing on behalf of the Crow Indian Women's Federated Club, Executive Secretary Henrietta Crockett argued that Crow women needed this opportunity "for the purpose of enabling them to become self-supporting and responsible members of society." Like Mary Salois, who made a similar argument for Blackfeet women, Crockett worried that "many of their young women, too old to go to school, are running the streets without any supervision." Most importantly, the project needed to be supervised by a Crow woman, "who is in a position to know which of the tribe need the work most."[71]

Indeed, the women's club complained bitterly about Yellowtail, the Crow Agency superintendent who also evaluated individuals for their eligibility to receive WPA relief. The women argued that Yellowtail was not qualified to serve as a case worker since he failed to study the case histories of each worker and spent much of his time away from the reservation. He had also been "discourteous to the WPA women workers, mispresenting facts regarding relief work, etc." Worse still, according to Minnie Williams, he held a "childish attitude against civilization." The Crow Indian Women's Club, like other Native American women's clubs affiliated with the General Federation of Women's Clubs, supported Progressive Era "racial uplift" goals that generally encouraged Native people to embrace "modern" or Anglo-American notions of civilization.[72] Robert Yellowtail, the first Native American to serve as an OIA superintendent, had repeatedly challenged US Indian policy. His family embraced "traditional" Crow cultural practices that included the use of peyote and the resurrection of the Sun Dance. Yellowtail's brother Thomas would become an important medicine man and Sun Dance chief.[73] In 1938 Robert Yellowtail served on the Montana State Appraisal Committee, a body of notable state political leaders, philanthropists, social workers, and labor advocates who evaluated the overall impact of New Deal–era federal relief programs. In that report, he expressed "genuine appreciation for the many benefits received by the Indians through the Federal work relief program . . . and Never in history have the Indians been so fairly treated."[74]

Crow women disagreed. Petitioners accused the Crow superintendent of employing young single men on WPA and CCC projects while neglecting the needs of single mothers. They complained that without sewing work, these women, "must sit home and look longingly at young single men—Crows and other male members of the Crow Indians—work on various projects . . . who are without dependents."[75] To make matters worse, the agency closed the project in the middle of winter, "while white women's sewing projects in Hardin and Billings," towns that bordered the Crow Reservation, continued to operate. The committee members—Kitty Deernose, Laura Covington, Mary One Goose, and Minnie Williams—not only wanted relief, from "the honorable people of Montana," they also wanted an investigation into "the bias, prejudice and discrimination toward all Crow Indian mothers that would work to support their dependents if given a chance." Tired and frustrated, they hoped that their appeal to Senator Murray would improve conditions. According to their petition, "Crow Indian mothers have long born with the attitudes of bias, prejudice and discrimination toward them . . . therefore we have decided to appeal to you to investigate and correct the above-named conditions."

By 1939, the Crow women were still struggling to restore the sewing project. They were angry and fed up with Yellowtail's behavior. According to Williams, he had "decertified" Crow women, making them ineligible for relief jobs. Without suitable workers, there could be no sewing project. Without a sewing project, he could hire more men to work on other "unfinished" WPA projects.[76]

The women's vigilance seemed to pay off. Senator Murray, apparently impressed by the Crow women's committee, sent a telegram to the state WPA administrator Joseph Parker and suggested that the state restart the program and establish a new quota for ten Crow women "willing to work 130 hours for $44 per period."[77] While the women may have succeeded in securing their sewing project, in the end, Yellowtail remained in charge. Perhaps Senator Murray refused to intervene in tribal politics, given Yellowtail's support for the Indian Reorganization Act. It is, in fact, likely that Murray did not want to alienate Yellowtail, since he wielded more political power than the members of the Crow Indian Women's Federated Club.

By sewing mattresses and cast-off clothing women earned an income they were certainly glad to receive. Yet, unlike their non-Native counterparts, many Native women could not bring their experience into the skilled workforce. Such industries did not exist within reach of reservation communities. Later they would have to travel significant distances to find jobs in the defense industry, an option readily available to non-Native women who commonly moved from sewing projects into factory work.

Or perhaps Native women learned that their labor assembling garments, remaking cast-off clothing, or making Native crafts for the tourist market was not "work" at all. Earning wages at the sewing machine seemed to be (at least from the extension agents' perspective) more like volunteer work, a hobby or domestic training rather than industrial employment. Their labor in sewing workshops was not much different from the work they might do in a 4-H club. Indeed, such activity was important to their community and significant for its altruistic achievement. Of course, men's and women's relief work was temporary; sewing quilts and digging ditches were both "make work" projects (as New Deal critics called it) that promised minimal pay for a short period of time. But the meanings attached to men's and women's work differed considerably. By building roads, dams, and economic infrastructure, the men's work drew the broader market closer to reservation communities. Women's labor, by contrast, remained defined or understood as "charity," and it continued to be invisible, on the margins of the capitalist labor market in the 1930s.

New Deal relief programs attempted to elevate Native men's work to conform to the terms of hegemonic masculinity by both increasing the value of men's labor and reducing the visibility of women's labor.[78] By doing so, New Deal administrators hoped to make Native workers into "new men" and proper women and to achieve a racialized middle-class ideal. Indigenous women's work, according to OIA and other government officials, was not

Building, Digging, and Sewing 61

work at all. They earned wages for the mattresses they sewed and the clothing they repaired, but their work remained indistinguishable from what county extension agents taught them about home economics. Consistent with earlier assimilationist programs, federal officials were preparing Native men and women to take different places in the market economy.

Native people needed the jobs, but like the boarding school children, they did not necessarily embrace the policymakers' settler-colonial logic. Notable Native leaders such as Mary Salois, the president of Blackfeet Indian Welfare, and the Crow members of the Indian Women's Federation, struggled for women even to gain access to those programs. They saw relief work for women as a vehicle to alleviate suffering, to challenged gender discrimination within their communities, and to confront racial inequality beyond reservation borders. Native men may have found that serving as CCC-ID camp managers, as Indian service clerks, or as truck drivers prepared them to escape OIA paternalism when they left the reservation to join the military or to take jobs in the defense industries a few years later. These stories, in Gerald Vizenor's words, were acts of "survivance." They survived, despite tremendous political and economic pressure, but they remained an "active presence" in their communities. These acts would help to build the economic and political infrastructures necessary to launch powerful sovereignty movements in the years to come. But, first, Native workers and their communities had more battles to fight.

3

The Limits of "Positive Programming"

AMERICAN INDIANS, GENDER, AND THE POSTWAR URBAN RELOCATION PROGRAM

It's the family man who establishes the reputation that Indian workers are good workers and good citizens.

MAYNARD L. GAGE, RELOCATION OFFICER,
SAN JOSE OFFICE, APRIL 1956

World War II set in motion a new phase in federal Indian policy. Programs specifically aimed at transforming Native Americans into workers dissolved into the country's mobilization for war. John Collier tried to maintain the OIA's influence in Washington, DC. But much to his disappointment, Congress drained most of his resources and thwarted his vision for creating self-sufficient Native American communities that lived and worked, under the guidance of New Deal–era experts, with their cultures intact.

Relief jobs that kept Native Americans on reservations during the Depression era, had largely disappeared, but the need for income did not. For many Native Americans, as for other people of color and Dust Bowl refugees, serving in the US military and work in defense-related industries offered an alternative to agricultural work.[1] As a result, one-quarter of the Native American population in the United States moved to urban areas, igniting a new migration pattern that policymakers would incorporate into postwar relocation plans a few years later.[2]

After the war, Congress renounced the goals of the Collier administration.[3] Instead of trying to improve Native self-sufficiency and support limited self-governance, legislators now attempted to eliminate reservations, for good. As the saying goes, they wanted the federal government to "get out of the Indian business." At the center of this effort was the plan to move Native Americans to urban areas where they could assimilate into the American working class. Labor remained a central tenet of that plan, but it lacked the provisions promised in Indian New Deal projects a decade earlier—provisions that idealistic reformers like John Collier had hoped would grant tribes limited sovereignty.

Drawing from secondary sources, OIA publications, and correspondence from this era, the first part of this chapter traces the shift in Indian policy during and after the war. In the second half of the chapter, Native workers tell a different story. Their words, drawn from OIA survey records, provide evidence that these programs did not always work the way federal officials hoped. Stories gleaned from those sources and other archival records provide a glimpse into the complicated, and often contradictory, results of postwar economic policy.

FROM RELIEF JOBS TO WAR WORK

Starved for funds during the war, Collier found it difficult to reproduce his earlier success extending New Deal programs to Native communities. Instead, he was forced to compromise his vision of American Indian self-sufficiency. Rather than insisting that Native communities develop the resources themselves, Collier approved 800 new oil and gas leases with non-Native operations.[4] He also tried to convince federal officials to create specific Native American units in the military, which would then give the OIA some involvement in the recruitment and training of Native soldiers. Nevertheless, Collier's influence seemed to be waning, and Native men and women who joined the military or were drafted served in integrated units.

Native men and women who had been employed in CCC-ID and WPA projects now found themselves working on projects not necessarily meant to improve reservation infrastructure or support the collective well-being of their communities. They were engaged in industrial training and jobs away from home, meant to mobilize the country's resources for war.

Francisco Castillo, a sixty-two-year-old Navajo medicine man employed as an ammunitions handler at Wingate Ordnance Depot, 1944.
General Photograph Collections, Special Collections and Archives, Cline Library, Northern Arizona University (NAU.PH.2000.45).

In 1940, men from the Mission Indian Agency in Southern California enrolled in a six-week course at the San Diego Vocational School to prepare them for jobs at the Consolidated Aircraft Factory.[5] In December 1941, members of the Akimel O'odham, Tohono O'odham, Diné, Chemehuevi, Quechan, Apache, Hualapai, and Consolidated Ute communities enrolled in the CCC-ID National Defense Training center in Phoenix, Arizona. Job placement, previously arranged by OIA or Indian school officials, was now coordinated by the Arizona Employment Service, the same agency that served the population at large. The men's training included "lathe work, welding, reboring and auto mechanics." In the Northwest, OIA superintendents boasted about their enrollees finding off-reservation work at construction companies in Pendleton and Hermiston, Oregon, and "making good with Boeing Aircraft Corporation in Seattle."[6] In 1942 in Oklahoma, OIA officials reported that "CCC-ID men interested in sheet metal training now work for an aircraft corporation; one who learned stone masonry while in the CCC-ID is now doing masonry on a new powder plant being erected nearby." An Osage CCC-ID tractor operator found work with a construction company at Fort Supply, near Woodward, Oklahoma. Nineteen CCC-ID men from the

Grace Thorpe (Sac and Fox, 1921–2008) at work in General MacArthur's headquarters in Tokyo, Japan, in December 1945. Grace Thorpe Collection, negative box 8, item 19, National Museum of the American Indian Archive Center, Smithsonian Institution, Washington, DC (NMAI. AC.085).

Pawnee Agency found jobs working for aircraft, pipeline, and oil companies. Another man was working on the railroad.[7]

Collier managed to get a handful of schools designated as centers for defense training. But he could not convince Congress to allocate additional money to improve the boarding school curriculum. Instead, schools adjacent to urban areas directly partnered with companies to train the students.[8] For example, the Sherman Institute in Riverside, California, paired with Solar Aircraft in San Diego. According to historian Alison Bernstein, the company trained and hired Native students as welders while they were finishing their schooling, and 95 percent of the school's graduates found good industrial jobs as a result.[9]

Even Native women employed on WPA projects making mattresses found their energies redirected toward mending and repurposing military clothing and sewing curtains and other materials for military recreation centers and facilities."[10] Like Native men, young women enlisted in the military, serving alongside their non-Native counterparts in the Women's Army Auxiliary Corps (WAAC) and Women Accepted for Volunteer Emergency Service

(WAVES). Taking the place of men in noncombat positions, WAACs and WAVES performed clerical work, operated radios, and worked as chemists, cartographers, and in control towers. Some found jobs in ordnance depots, defense industries, and male gendered occupations such as electricians and mechanics much like white women and like other women of color. They also stepped into new jobs at home, becoming teachers and OIA staff, when Native men entered the military.[11]

POSTWAR INDIAN POLICY

After the war, reservation economic landscapes were as desperate as they were in the 1930s. New Deal–era programs that had employed many Native Americans on conservation and public works projects had vanished. Military spending had lifted the rest of the country out of the depths of economic desperation, but the reservations did not share in that prosperity, and Native veterans could not necessarily rely on the GI bill or federal welfare assistance programs.

To address those issues, Congress turned away from the culturally pluralist policies of the New Deal era and unapologetically leaned into assimilationist plans reminiscent of late nineteenth century: termination and relocation. Wrapped in the language of American liberal benevolence that promised prosperity and progress, these policies were supposed to "free" Native people from reservations and terminate federal-tribal relationships, divesting the tribal governments of their political and economic authority. Freedom, from the legislators' perspective, meant American Indians moving to urban areas and leaving their reservation lands, and cultures behind. Like the Indian school curriculum and Depression-era programs, policymakers imagined that wage work would accomplish this transformation.

The OIA had encouraged off-reservation migration and job placement before the 1950s. In fact, the boarding school system might even be seen as the agency's first labor Relocation Program (other than slavery or indenture systems in the nineteenth century and earlier). In 1934, Scott Henry Peters, a Progressive Era Native American leader from Michigan and OIA officer, was placing young women in domestic work and Native American men in industrial jobs in Chicago, Detroit, and Milwaukee. Other agents served as labor contractors for railroad companies and commercial farmers.[12]

Except for Peters's efforts to become a "one man relocation team," OIA officials generally encouraged Native Americans to stay on reservations in the 1930s. They feared that Native Americans would have a difficult time competing against white workers in the tight labor market, and they steered them toward work on conservation projects, such as the CCC-ID or other development initiatives. The postwar Relocation Program reversed that impulse. Instead of encouraging Native Americans to labor at home, BIA (as the OIA was known after 1947) officials launched the Relocation Program to pull people away from reservations and into the labor market as permanent workers.

Framed in civil rights terms, the Voluntary Relocation Program, formally launched in 1952, was supposed to extend the advantages of "economic citizenship" to Native Americans and help them assimilate into the labor market as individuals. According to BIA officials, that process required Native Americans to abandon their traditional lifeways, adopt new gendered behavior, and commit themselves to permanent wage work. Transforming Indigenous people into American workers, according to federal policymakers, would ultimately break down tribal identity. Moving to cities, completing vocational education courses, and finding jobs in industrial or domestic work, would transform them into good American consumers who embraced the gendered and racial norms of society beyond the reservation's borders.

In 1953, a year following the launch of the Relocation Program, Congress passed House Concurrent Resolution 108, which outlined its Indian policy goals of making Native Americans "subject to the same laws and entitled to the same privileges as are applicable to other citizens of the United States."[13] Advocates of termination, which was characterized as part of a larger Indian Freedom Program by Senator Arthur Watkins of Utah, hoped to sever the trust relationship between tribes and the federal government and to incorporate Native people as individuals into American society.[14] That policy, which dominated Indian affairs from the 1940s through 1963, was a devastating attack on tribal sovereignty and dealt a severe blow to those Native American governments, like the Menominee and the Klamath, who had managed to develop successful economies within a reservation context.[15]

A flurry of bills followed, including Public Law 280 that ended federal oversight of tribal affairs and extended the authority of states over specific Indian lands in California, Minnesota, Wisconsin, Nebraska, and Oregon. Termination, as the policy was known, did not sever federal responsibilities to Indian reservations in all states. The law targeted those tribes characterized as the most assimilated and whose members, in the eyes of policymakers, could become independent citizens rather than remaining wards of the government. By 1962, tribes in four more states, including Oklahoma, Texas, Utah, and South Carolina, faced the termination of their tribal governments.

Soon thereafter the public mood shifted, and key architects of the policy yielded to growing criticism and a new Democratic majority in Congress.[16]

Despite the advantages it afforded a small number of American Indians, termination devastated tribal communities. Mostly, tribes objected to the unilateral process that imposed these changes on them without their meaningful consent. Tribes lost access to health, education, and welfare services previously supplied by the BIA. Most notably, the Menominee of Wisconsin and the Klamath of Oregon, relatively prosperous before termination, faced crippling blows to their economies when they saw their trust relationship dissolve. It is telling that Congress targeted those tribal governments *because* they were prosperous. Congress justified this direct assault on tribal sovereignty as a cost-cutting measure, moving tribal lands, resources, and tax dollars into the domain of state governments. Apparently, according to legislators, federal aid was no longer necessary. But the underlying intent of these programs was much deeper. Taken together, termination and relocation would incorporate Native people into the settler-colonial fold as workers and not as sovereign tribal communities. Like the Dawes Act passed in the late nineteenth century, termination meant reducing Native Americans to landless peoples.[17] Earlier policymakers and, to a limited extent, those implementing the Indian New Deal, whittled away at tribal identities by changing Native land use. Postwar Indian policy focused on Native individuals, hoping to break down their tribal affiliations by transforming them into workers.

According to Red Power activists and Indian policy scholars writing in the late twentieth century, the Relocation Program was part of a renewed assault on American Indian sovereignty in the post–World War II era. Activists and scholars have argued that relocating American Indians to alien urban areas, far from family and without much support, was an effort to fully sever American Indian tribal ties and complete the assimilationist program started by the federal government in the nineteenth century. Indeed, some individuals who participated in the program remember it as a disorienting experience. They suffered from homesickness, substandard housing, and poor wages. Adjusting to the challenges of urban living was nearly unbearable without the support of extended family.[18]

More recently, a new generation of scholars, notably Doug Miller and Nick Rosenthal, have complicated that narrative. They emphasize the agency of Native peoples and have sorted out evidence that seems to contradict the earlier, more draconian descriptions of the Relocation Program. In the archives and in the oral histories they have found stories of people who volunteered to "go on relocation" or Native parents who sent their children to boarding schools, like the Intermountain Indian School in Utah, to gain job related skills. Those sources tell a story of people looking for ways to make a living, embracing vocational training programs, even using urban relocation centers as resources to help them find work, negotiate with employers, or track down relatives. As a result, a new picture of relocation—and of Native urbanization—is emerging.[19]

RELOCATION AND NATIVE AMERICAN EXPERIENCE

In 1955, Stanley Thomas, a relocation officer in the BIA's Phoenix Area Office, wrote to his counterpart in Denver to proudly announce "at long last, we have relocatees for you!" He was happy to report that his recruits, David and Elizabeth Williams from the Gila River Pima-Maricopa Reservation (now known as the Gila River Indian Community), were committed to making the trip to Denver.[20] According to Thomas, they had carefully considered their decision. The couple, a twenty-three-year-old Pima (Akimel O'odham) man, David Williams, and his twenty-two-year-old pregnant wife, Elizabeth, had discussed the Relocation Program with Thomas in June. Six months later, Williams dropped by Thomas's office with two of his single buddies to hear more about relocation. "Perhaps, this second time," Thomas reflected, "the words I said sunk in better than they did at first." David then returned with Elizabeth and another couple to hear about relocation for the third time. Finally, they decided to relocate. Williams hoped that his Korean War experience would help his chances at finding a job, preferably as an apprentice in the machine trades. Despite his careful deliberations, he and his family did not move to Denver as they originally planned. By February, ten months after they first contacted the relocation agent, the young family was on its way to California instead.[21]

When Williams arrived in Oakland with his "serious minded and capable" wife, he met their new relocation agent, Brice Lay. Lay arranged housing in a small apartment in North Oakland and a job at the West Coast Soap company, where he would start working as a plant laborer for $1.85 an hour. Undeterred from his original plan, Williams enrolled in night classes in Machine Shop at Laney College. He was determined to gain experience with metal working so that he could eventually become a sheet-metal worker and find a job that provided more security and opportunity for advancement. As a high school graduate and veteran with previous work experience, Williams was particularly well suited for relocation. Better yet, he was a husband and a father. In the minds of the BIA agents, he was the best kind of relocatee.[22]

Native Americans, like the Williams family, volunteered to go on relocation. After all, they needed the money. They were part of a migration of approximately 100,000 Native Americans who moved to cities, including Chicago, Cleveland, Dallas, Denver, Los Angeles, Oakland, Salt Lake City, San Francisco, San Jose, Tulsa, and Oklahoma City between 1952 and 1972. They filled out applications, subjected themselves to their local BIA agent's scrutiny, and boarded buses and trains or drove their own cars to distant cities. They sometimes followed the advice of relocation agents and dutifully showed up for work in defense, steel, or light industries. Others temporarily minded the children and homes of urban middle-class white women.

That effort involved a network of BIA employees to usher Native workers from their reservations into urban labor markets. Agents working out of BIA reservation agency offices recruited and screened potential applicants. They advertised possible destinations and spread the word about the jobs available and what relocatees could expect from city living, hoping to match the applicant's job and location preferences with the demands of a particular labor market. They sorted through market updates circulated by their urban counterparts and tried to steer workers away from areas experiencing large-scale layoffs or strikes. Agents might meet with groups of potential relocatees, advertise relocation information on agency bulletin boards, and talk informally with individuals they identified as good candidates for the program.[23]

Local BIA agents scrutinized a candidate's police records, financial debts, work histories, and physical health to determine the person's eligibility for relocation assistance. Describing the agency's screening procedure, Mary Nan Gamble, the LA relocation services director, explained how a "local agent offered appraisals of [the potential relocatee]. He gets all this information and then, if everything looks pretty good . . . the family is sent to the Public Health Service for a physical examination." In a final assessment of the potential relocatee, Gamble noted that the agent offered "his opinion of the man's sincerity, and of his ability to adapt and adjust to new conditions." Gamble was promoting the program on CBS radio, reassuring potential employers in Los Angeles that Native Americans would meet their expectations.[24] The men needed to be fit, have no outstanding warrants, and no debt. Their wives needed to pass muster, too. Using a common gendered and racialized epithet, Mrs. Streater, the relocation agent in San Jose explained, "The squaw type, women who cling to the old ways," were turned away, along with others "who were unable to make the grade."[25]

David and Elizabeth Williams, the couple who migrated to Oakland, fit the profile of who the BIA expected would "succeed" in the Relocation Program. The program was looking for "family men" with experience living and working off reservation. Married men with children, from the agent's perspective, were more likely to stay put, keep their jobs, and assimilate into American urban society. The BIA assisted single men and women, too, but they strongly encouraged them to relocate in family groups. Reflecting on a Mescalero Apache man who was planning to relocate to Oakland on his own, Brice Lay predicted that the "odds were against him. We feel that eventual success at the point of relocation is dependent on the family moving as a unit."[26]

Relocating Native people as families was a central goal of the program and of the assimilation project as a whole. Agents encouraged parents to bring their children, because as Mary Nan Gamble announced, "It isn't our pattern or wish to divide families. We feel that they should make a change together if they [choose] to make a change."[27] Gamble and her coworkers did not want to separate families, but they did hope that Native workers would conform to a family model that excluded extended networks of relatives. They were reluctant to relocate large families and scolded relocatees for lending money to family and friends or for housing them in their rather modest apartments.[28]

Local agents and school officials carrying out the program also promoted family relocation as a practical matter. Sometimes that effort involved arranging civil marriages for Native Americans who had been married in traditional ways. Agents acquired birth affidavits and followed up with couples to make sure they knew the legal procedures. For example, Intermountain Indian School officials reported that one of their students, Elizabeth Yazzie, was living with her companion, James, and their fourteen-month-old child. Elizabeth reassured the school official that she would obtain a civil marriage "as soon as she has a Saturday off." Making Native people's relationships "legible" in the eyes of the state was just one of the ways that the federal government intervened in the intimate lives of Native American workers on relocation.[29] By doing so, the BIA was hoping to reinforce the patriarchal gender roles that were central to its assimilationist policy, creating small nuclear families, supported by a male breadwinner and with a stay-at-home mother minding the children; it was an expensive model that was beyond the means of many Native men and other working-class families as well.[30]

Single men seemed to create more problems, at least for the agent. The relocation records are full of complaints about single men drinking, brawling, or simply not behaving as the agent expected. One San Jose relocation agent complained, in a rather patronizing tone, that "some of the most difficult and time-consuming matters have been with the single men. A few, behaving like children at a circus—they receive their pay checks and 'settle down,' while others, we wonder if they ever will."[31] Agents spent a considerable amount of their time developing relationships with apartment owners and employers they could count on to place new arrivals. They worried that landlords might refuse to rent to Native workers and that employers would stop hiring them, "spoiling" those contacts for their future clients. The San Jose relocation agent even advocated for diverting relocation funding from single men to families, writing, "It's the family man who establishes the reputation that Indian workers are good workers and good citizens."[32] Maintaining that image was an important public relations issue for a program that continued to defend itself against critics like Oliver La Farge and Native American activists. But agents also felt that family men were easier to manage. In 1960, a relocation agent in Los Angeles complained, "We find that we contribute more service to [three single men] than to the average family unit. This may possibly contribute to the immaturity and lack of sincere interest in making successful relocation."[33]

Worried about Native Americans' "success" in adjusting to the urban environment, BIA officers routinely monitored male and female relocatees' work and personal lives. Seemingly drawing from pre-reform boarding school curricula, they counseled Native relocatees on how to conform to the gendered and class expectations of employers, neighbors, and landlords. That instruction included teaching Native individuals lessons about their appearance and behavior at work, and how they should spend their leisure time. Men were counseled on how to "sell themselves" in a job interview, and how to take initiative at work. BIA agents predicted that Peter Begay, a Navajo who relocated on his own dime with his wife from Gallup, New Mexico, would succeed. The agent noted that Begay had been able to find his own jobs before he contacted the relocation office. But the agent worried, "He does not take well to corrections from superiors, but with counseling maybe able to curb his hot headedness." Other agents wrote encouraging notes to men who earned promotions or who did particularly well in job interviews.[34]

Women's lives were subject to more intimate surveillance. Agents visited married women's homes, unannounced, and offered housekeeping advice. Single women, particularly domestic workers who relocated from boarding schools like Intermountain, experienced closer monitoring by their employers and by Intermountain Indian School staff. Much like outing matrons before the war, Intermountain staff surprised the young women at home, telephoned them, and exchanged follow-up letters with their employers. They were particularly worried about Native women's relationships with men. If a young women stayed out late, dated "strange men," or was discovered drinking on her time off, employers reported her to the BIA and Intermountain staff for "immoral" behavior. Those kinds of transgressions might cost a young woman her job, or at a minimum subject her to humiliating lectures from middle-class white women about maintaining her respectability.35 Native men were exempt from such scrutiny. As long as they managed to stay employed, and paid their rent, BIA officials tended to ignore men's personal behavior.36

It is not surprising that Native American women moved away from domestic work as soon as they could. At Indian boarding schools in the late 1950s, female students studied "Home Service" and spent at least one summer in "on the job training," working in the homes of white middle-class women in Los Angeles, Salt Lake City, Denver, or other relocation cities. Often, after graduation, they returned to those same homes as part of the Relocation Program. But those placements did not last very long. If marriage did not pull them out of the labor market, Native women opted for factory work or other service work as soon as they could. They preferred to assemble electronic parts at the Jennings Radio Company in San Jose, or pack boxes at the Granny Goose Potato Chips factory, or at Max Factor, in Los Angeles, rather than endure close surveillance.37 Reflecting Native American women's job preferences, by 1962, the Los Angeles relocation office opposed the placement of young women in domestic service and was trying to end the Intermountain Indian School's supervision of their former students.38

BIA officials hoped to end domestic work placements and move Native Americans into permanent, full-time jobs. But, working with state employment services, they often placed Native workers in the same type of temporary, low-paying jobs they had been doing before they relocated. Recognizing that contradiction, field agents tried to develop contacts in other industries. In Los Angeles, specifically, BIA agents worried about finding full-time jobs for relocatees in an uncertain, postwar labor market. Some of the best jobs they could find were in the defense industry, at plants like North American Aviation and Northup Industries. When those employers faced strikes or cut back production, agents turned to other options, even casual and agricultural labor to employ Native workers. But even in union shops, Native workers faced seasonal layoffs.39

In the 1950s, students at the Sherman Institute and the Intermountain Indian School in Brigham City (the only boarding school created after World

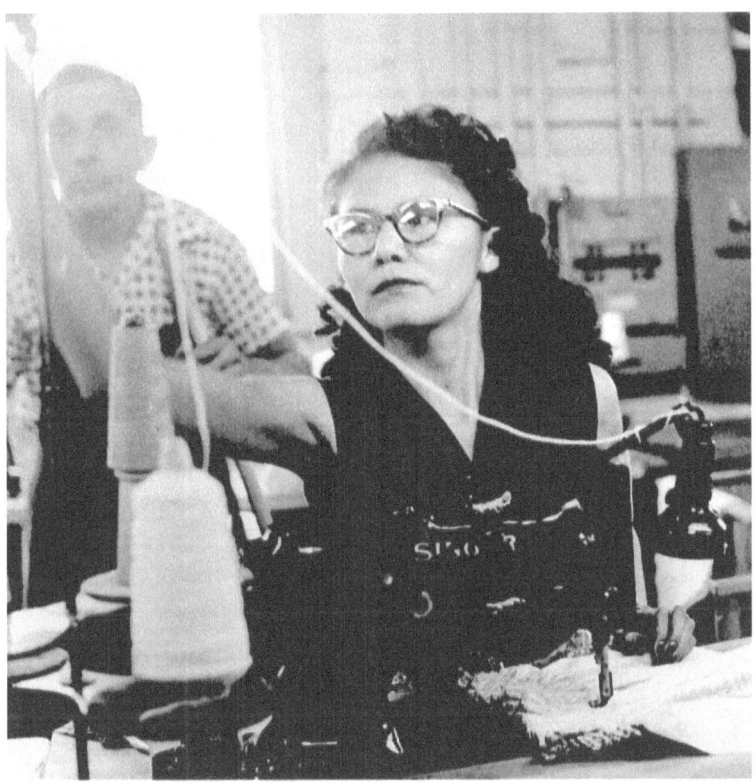

Rena Jones, Diné woman employed at Swimware, Inc., Los Angeles, 1952. Field Employment Assistance Office Files-LA, ccf 1948–62, box 21, file 980½, RG 75, Records of the Bureau of Indian Affairs, National Archives and Records Administration, Riverside, CA.

War II) found themselves routed into domestic service and agriculture, much like their predecessors in the early twentieth century.[40] They could speak their own languages and participate in Indigenous cultural activities at the schools. But, in lieu of studying the kinds of subjects that might occupy their non-Native counterparts in public schools, girls learned "behavioral lessons," such as grooming and poise, and they trained for jobs in housekeeping and other service industries. Students even experienced a postwar version of the old outing system. During the summers, Intermountain officials placed girls in white, middle-class homes in Los Angeles and other cities for "on the job training." When they graduated, many of those young women returned to take jobs as domestic workers, joining the flow of Native migrants who the BIA were relocating to urban areas in the West. Boys enjoyed a broader curriculum that included trades such as auto repair, welding, and carpentry. Yet, most boys trained in agriculture and stayed in Northern Utah to work for area farmers. Those who studied other topics found that their training was not rigorous enough to qualify them for jobs in the skilled trades.[41]

School officials and policymakers at institutions like Intermountain and the Sherman Institute hoped that once students moved to urban areas and found suitable employment, they would be more likely to sever their ties to reservation communities. Moving to the cities was supposed to improve their economic well-being and eventually make reservations irrelevant. According to Senator Arthur Watkins, Termination's architect, once Native people were more self-sufficient, the federal government would be able to terminate reservations, extend control of Native lands to states, and discontinue service and support for Native communities. After completing the five-year program, Watkins believed, Navajos would be prepared to live off-reservation, and eventually the Navajo Reservation itself would dissolve into the states of Arizona, New Mexico, and Utah.

POSITIVE PROGRAMMING, SOVEREIGNTY, AND CIVIL RIGHTS

The American public generally supported the BIA Relocation Program's self-stated, altruistic goals. But significant opposition from Native intellectuals and critics put BIA officials on the defensive. Responding to growing public criticism, BIA officials defended relocation and tried to clear up misconceptions. In a speech before a gathering of state officials, Glen Emmons, the commissioner of Indian affairs, said he wanted to clear up "confusion" and "emotional discussion" about the direction of Indian policy and its implications for preserving Indian culture, assimilation, and integration. As far as he was concerned, cultural issues were "strictly up to the Individual Indian." He thought that such matters were beyond the scope of the BIA. But in a clear articulation of agency philosophy, he stated that tribal governments should stay out of the equation, too. He explained, "All we want to be sure of in this context is that the right of the individual Indian [is] not overridden or sacrificed in the interest of the tribal group. And our primary concern, as reflected in this emphasis on *positive programming*, is to be sure that the individual tribal member really has a free choice and is not condemned to a disgracefully low standard of living through no fault of his own."[42]

Positive programming, as Emmons characterized the Relocation Program, meant moving American Indians out of seasonal work and into permanent, year-round jobs. Emmons's understanding was clearly limited. He failed to comprehend that many Native Americans found work through kin networks; they pooled family resources and maintained subsistence practices depending on where they lived and how much of their traditional workscapes remained accessible to them.[43]

According to policymakers like Emmons, individual rights superseded tribal identities or tribal political authority. Expressing Indianness was fine, but only insofar as it involved a superficial performance of cultural practices and beliefs and did not include, for example, Native claims to collectively control their lands and resources or pursuing culturally defined ways of making a living. BIA leaders were exasperated when critics accused them of forcefully assimilating American Indians or engineering a modern-day Indian removal scheme. They saw their programs as morally neutral and common-sense solutions to the problem of American Indian poverty.

Responding to Oliver La Farge, one of the most vocal critics of federal Indian policy in the 1950s, Secretary of the Interior Douglas McKay directly outlined how termination and relocation policies were meant to protect the civil rights—not the sovereignty rights—of individual Native people and their communities.[44] LaFarge had insisted that American Indian tribes, as part of their distinct history, particularly their history of treaty-making, possessed "special rights." He insisted that Congress should secure a tribe's consent before enacting policies that impacted them. Dumbfounded, McKay disputed LaFarge's definition of American Indians' legal status. Dismissing any claim to sovereignty rights, McKay accused LaFarge of advocating for the right of American Indians to exercise a "special veto power of the legislation which might affect them," a possibility that McKay found ridiculous. The secretary of the interior insisted that Native people were just like other Americans and that no one, except for the president of the United States, could wield such power. McKay, who was officially responsible for Indian policy, was concerned that LaFarge's "principle of Indian consent" would threaten the US Constitution. "With full respect for the rights and needs of the Indian people," McKay continued, "I believe it would be extremely dangerous to pick out any segment of the population and arm its members with authority to frustrate the will of the Congress which the whole people have elected."[45]

McKay was not convinced that economic development programs on tribal land would solve Native American poverty, an initiative that tribes and their supporters advocated. Since their reservation land was inadequate to sustain them, McKay surmised, many Native Americans were already leaving reservations to find work. The Relocation Program was simply an effort "to assist this voluntary movement and guide it along constructive channels." "Detribalization," McKay insisted, was not the BIA's goal. But, by denying Native Americans collective political and economic rights, and by discarding the need for tribal consent, he was clearly advocating a plan meant to support Native Americans as individuals at the expense of their tribal governments.[46]

RELOCATION AND TRIBAL GOVERNMENTS

Tribal government involvement in relocation varied. As historian Doug Miller points out, the Navajos and the Standing Rock Sioux welcomed the program and encouraged their members to work hard and enlist in adult vocational programs. Others such as the San Ildefonso Pueblo and Cahuilla denounced the urban Relocation Program as assimilationist.[47] Even tribal officials who endorsed the program demanded that the BIA improve their training and educational programs and screening procedures to better prepare their kinsmen for city living.[48]

Even as they participated in a program that federal policymakers hoped would weaken tribal affiliations, tribal officials remained critical and actively subverted the program's ultimate goals. For Navajo Nation officials, moving to Los Angeles, San Francisco, or Denver did not mean that their members severed their tribal ties. In 1957, Paul Jones, the Navajo Nation tribal chair sent an open letter to all their migrants and reassured them that their political and economic connections to the Navajo Nation remained intact, whether they were living on the reservation or not. They could continue to own their family homes and livestock, and they could still vote in tribal elections by absentee ballot. Soothing away their concerns, he stated: "You who are away from the reservation are still our people and we are doing our best to safeguard your interests and your property while you are gone." After receiving inquiries from their members, the Navajo Nation organized its own Relocation Committee to evaluate the program.[49]

In January 1957, the Navajo committee members toured the relocation offices in San Francisco, Oakland, San Jose and Los Angeles. They also visited vocational education programs and manufacturing plants where Navajo workers were earning from $1.47 to $2.38 an hour. The committee members were particularly interested in speaking to the Navajo workers directly, and they organized group meetings and house visits to find out how well workers were doing and what they thought of the Relocation Program.[50]

The Navajo committee returned from California impressed by what they had observed. They were satisfied that workers seemed to be earning

Members of the Navajo Nation Tribal Council Relocation Committee visiting Northrup Corporation in Los Angeles, March 1960. Pictured with Northrop official are (*from left to right*) Hoska Cronemeyer, chair; Able Tauchin; and Nat Curley. Field Employment Assistance Office Files-LA, ccf 1948–62, box 1, file 048, Photos, RG 75, Records of the Bureau of Indian Affairs, National Archives and Records Administration, Riverside, CA.

decent wages and living in acceptable housing. According to relocation office memos that documented their visit, the committee members were impressed with one Navajo family's adjustment to urban living. The family regularly attended church, paid fifty-three dollars per month in rent, and reflected positively on the relocation experience. "Joe," the breadwinner of the family, was earning $1.85 an hour and, with overtime, was taking home ninety-seven dollars per week in wages. Asked which he preferred, El Monte or the reservation, Joe picked El Monte. Another relocatee, who was in the process of using a GI loan to buy a house, agreed. He liked LA better, and he appreciated the opportunity to learn cabinet making.[51]

The Navajo Relocation Committee members were particularly impressed with their tour of Northrup and Northern Aviation in Los Angeles. Both plants had hired large numbers of Navajo workers. Hoska Cronemeyer, the chair of the committee, showed particular interest in the jet engine repair station. Enamored with the high-tech environment, Cronemeyer was sure

Byron Chee, Diné worker at North American Aviation, 1960.
Field Employment Assistance Office Files-LA, ccf 1948–60, box 21, folder 980½, RG 75, Records of the Bureau of Indian Affairs, National Archives and Records Administration, Riverside, CA.

that "the brightest" Navajo men needed this sort of training to "successfully compete with the white man." With their own economic development plans in mind, it is likely that Cronemeyer and his committee imagined workers like these men returning home to train their kinsman in a new industrial landscape that they hoped to create for the Navajo Nation.⁵²

THE POLITICAL ECONOMY OF RELOCATION

Signing up for the BIA's program was a deeply personal decision, shaped by an individual's education and previous experience working and living off the reservation. But broader economic forces, beyond the control of an individual, offered a compelling "push" to the relocation agent's "pull" of big city promises. The parents of the Relocation generation had seen their economic resources shrink; their collectively held lands had been carved up into individual allotments and were then eventually lost to non-Native farmers and speculators who had the capital to develop them. Federal policies that were supposed to protect Native economic interests, such as placing allotted lands in trust, made those landholdings almost impossible to develop on a commercial scale. Trust lands could not be sold and they could not be used as collateral for the loans needed to invest in the kinds of technology necessary to succeed as a commercial farmer in the early twentieth century. Allotment inheritance rules sliced landholdings into such small parcels, divided among surviving kin, that the land was almost worthless. The best alternative for many allotted landholders was to lease their lands to white farmers and ranchers and then hire themselves out as laborers.[53]

To understand Native Americans and their tribal government's participation in relocation, it is useful to think about federal Indian policy in the broader context of development policy in the decolonizing world after World War II.[54] BIA policymakers drew from the same pool of ideas and assumptions about development as those designing projects in the postcolonial world. In fact, federal termination and relocation initiatives were the domestic equivalent of "modernization" policies designed by European and American leaders to "uplift" communities that were beginning to emerge from a history of colonial rule and economic exploitation.[55] According to historian Michael Latham, Cold War development officials predicted that foreign policy initiatives such as the Marshall Plan and the Point Four Program would move "'traditional' societies toward the enlightened 'modernity' most clearly represented by America itself."[56]

With its origins in debates about Native poverty in 1947, and the mounting criticism of New Deal programs, including the Indian Reorganization Act, postwar Indian policy allowed BIA officials to apply the lessons they learned from their previous work designing economic uplift schemes for societies in the decolonizing world.[57] Architects of postwar Indian policy embraced initiatives similar to those designed to repair war-torn Europe, stave off communism, and inspire, as historian Paul Rosier notes, "America's liberal social values, capitalist economic organizations, and democratic structures."[58] Indeed, technocrats who administered President Truman's international development and Indian policies overlapped. Dillon Myer, the official in charge of Japanese internment camps during World War II, headed the BIA from 1950 to 1953. His predecessor, John Nichols and other staff moved from their posts at the BIA to positions in the Point Four's Technical

Cooperation Administration in Egypt, Iran, and Latin America. As Paul Rosier notes, they were ready to instruct a "new constellation of people deemed in need of modernity."[59]

How do we understand American Indian choices within a context of such a harsh assault on their collective existence? How do we explain Native American participation in the Relocation Program and the approval of this program, at least in the Navajo case, by tribal governments? To understand Native workers and the fields of power they inhabited, it is useful to think about their participation in relocation as part of a broader story of decolonization, a dynamic moment in which, as Frederick Cooper has observed for post–World War II Africa, "structures of power and the idioms in which power [were] forged and re-forged in relationships."

According to Cooper and scholars in the subaltern studies tradition, peoples struggling within the rubric of decolonization "build diverse networks and combined different cultural idioms, simultaneously engaging with and asserting independence [from] colonial institutions and ideologies." Those "cultural idioms," for postwar American Indian workers (and for tribal leaders as well) included a "universal" notion of what constituted "work," working conditions, and the terms of modernization.[60]

The similarities between postwar European development efforts in Africa and US Indian policy are instructive. As part of a "stabilization" campaign, French and British officials attempted to impose a modernizing project onto Africa, transforming migrant workers into "industrial men." Colonial bureaucrats, according to Cooper, hoped to "create the kind of predictable, known being who could make Africa into the orderly, productive, controllable society that seemed so vital in the post war conjuncture."[61] It was a totalizing effort that ignored cultural differences and distinct histories; the project was highly gendered and attempted to turn migrant male workers into family men and women into their dependents. Women were supposed to abandon the significant roles they played in their village economies and join their husbands in urban areas where they were supposed to "take up the reproduction of the labor force—under the watchful eyes of nurses, teachers, and bureaucrats."[62] Colonial administrators introduced the gendered concept of a "family wage" as a way to control individual agency and transform Africans into modern industrialized workers; but then African trade unions, which emerged out of the western development model, also adopted that demand in their struggle against the colonized state. They may have embraced the idiom of industrial wage work, but African workers and African elites did not become as orderly as colonial officials had hoped.

Using Cooper's framework helps us see how Native workers and their leaders embraced the colonizer's "idiom of development" but not necessarily the colonizer's goals. Even though the underlying goal of relocation and US Indian policy was to weaken the connections between Native peoples and their tribal lands and cultures, many Native workers in the 1950s seemed to welcome the work and the modernization programs. Diné families voluntarily sent their children to the Intermountain Indian School to gain the skills they needed to succeed and get jobs. The Navajo tribal government supported the Navajo Special Program, a curriculum launched at the Intermountain Indian School, the Sherman Institute, and other boarding schools immediately following World War II; it was meant to educate students whose age, family circumstances, and poor English skills made it difficult for them to attend day schools or public schools in reservation border towns.[63] With echoes of the outing system, that program placed Navajo adolescents in domestic service and agricultural labor. The Navajo tribal leadership even participated in the Relocation Program, inspecting job sites in Los Angeles and other relocation centers, and encouraging tribal members to embrace these opportunities. Navajo family members, like the young Native couple I described earlier in this chapter, used relocation offices as employment agencies, even those who had "relocated themselves," returned to them to find work after they were laid off or when they wanted a new job.[64]

Despite the hardship individuals might have experienced when they moved to urban areas, Native workers were enthusiastic participants in the Relocation Program. Even Native leaders such as D'Arcy McNickle called for the creation of development projects like Truman's Point Four Program to solve the problem of reservation poverty.[65] Instead of embracing the settler-colonial goals of the program, Native people incorporated what the programs offered into strategies to broaden their tribal sovereignty and widen the reach of their communities beyond reservation borders.[66]

NATIVE WORKERS' VIEWS OF RELOCATION

Native workers signed up to "go on relocation," but they did not necessarily sever their tribal or family ties on reservations to do so. Navajos who relocated to Los Angeles, for example, held on to grazing permits after they moved to Los Angeles. The permit issue was important enough that Paul Jones felt the need to make a specific appeal to the migrants. He suggested, "If you are not using your grazing permit, you may sell or lease it to some other person, or you may give it to some other member of your family. In this way we will have the use of that grazing permit which we so badly need."[67]

Migrants did worry about losing their political and cultural ties to their reservation communities. They wanted to maintain their formal tribal enrollment status and ensure that they could enroll their children, too, even if they were born off the reservation. Disenrollment was a real concern. Tribes were using a range of criteria to determine tribal membership, including residency, blood quantum, and genealogical connections to ancestors listed on BIA records.[68] In 1957, the Rosebud Sioux passed tribal ordinance 5711, which limited enrollment to those who maintained permanent residency on the reservation. Leaving the reservation for seasonal work or for military service was permitted. But any member who was absent for more than one year was considered a nonresident, and their children were not eligible for enrollment.[69] Other tribes enacted more flexible rules. Crows needed to establish their lineal relationship to an ancestor listed on annuity rolls established by the secretary of the interior in 1943. The Tribal Council of the Three Affiliated Tribes at Fort Berthold insisted that relocation would not impact tribal membership at all. A resolution passed on January 8, 1948, stated: "Children born to members who live away from the Reservation may be enrolled only upon written application to the Tribal Business Council provided the parents of such children were born on the Fort Berthold Reservation."[70]

In 1966, the BIA's Division of Community Services, Branch of Employment Assistance, randomly surveyed Native American workers about their experiences finding jobs and adjusting to city life and recorded their general impressions of the program. Even though the BIA did not officially publish the results of the "TOB Study," as the project was called, its authors circulated a mimeographed report and conducted a follow up study two years later. The statistical data they collected paints a complicated picture of the participants' experience in the labor market, including detailed job histories, wages earned, and the degree to which each individual achieved certain benchmarks of success in mainstream consumer society.[71]

The survey posed a series of "before and after" questions to measure the economic and social impact of relocation. Relocatees were asked if they owned a car, if they maintained savings and checking accounts, and how urban housing compared to where they lived previously, on reservations. Native workers reported the number of bedrooms in their former homes, how much rent they paid, and if those dwellings included indoor plumbing, heat, and electricity. Then, they answered the same questions about their current lodgings. Reminiscent of the classic before and after photos of boarding school students in the early twentieth century, the study's files included photos that compared reservation dwellings to the participants' urban homes. The photos were supposed to demonstrate the program's success, but the contrast between "primitive" and "modern" was often inconclusive. Life in a residential hotel in Cleveland, Ohio, might not look like much of an improvement over a wood-framed house in Clayton, Oklahoma.[72]

The difference between reservation poverty and urban poverty was that in the former, families usually owned their own homes, as modest as they were. Jobs might be more plentiful, and wages might be better in Oakland, San Francisco, and Chicago, but the cost of living was also much higher. On the reservation, individuals did not have to pay rent. In fact, the study's statistical data demonstrates that most Native workers did not experience a great improvement in quality of housing when they moved to urban areas. Thirty-three percent stated that their housing had improved from "substandard" to "standard." But, slightly more, 34 percent, reported that their standard of housing remained the same. Twenty-eight percent experienced similarly "substandard" housing in both locations, and 3.4 percent felt that their living conditions had declined.[73]

The survey also noted other measures of civic life, including whether Native American workers attended church, if they voted in elections, and if they belonged to any social organizations. That data, including details about an individual's social life, the acquisition of consumer goods, and the quality of housing, were used to measure Native Americans' adjustment to urban life and provided key indicators of the program's overall success.

With those criteria in mind, Native workers responded to the interviewers' question: Did they consider themselves "better off" after relocation? In the original study performed in 1966, 41 percent said they were "much better" off, and 26 percent said they were "some(what) better" off; 28 percent felt that they "were about the same," 4.6 percent said their living conditions had declined, and 0.4 percent did not answer the question. When asked if they would do it all over again, 73 percent said yes, 11 percent said maybe, and 9 percent said no. An additional 7 percent were ambivalent.

The survey's design warrants a critical reading of its results. Guiding participants through questions about wages, housing, bank accounts, and voting, the interviewer established the criteria participants were supposed to use to judge what constituted "better off." According to the survey, if their urban housing included indoor plumbing, if they were employed, if they owned their own furniture, and if they were paying taxes, life was "better" than living on the reservation. The survey did not inquire about extended family relationships, ceremonial obligations, or even if the participants felt happy, all of which might have offered a different interpretation of "better off."

From the perspective of the study's authors, returning to the reservation was a sign of the individual's personal failure and an indication that the program had failed as well. Framed in largely negative terms, BIA agents could check a box next to one of the following reasons to explain why a relocatee returned to the reservation: homesickness, failure to adjust, marital problems, drinking, accepting another job, and death in the family. There was no box to check to indicate a participant's preference for rural landscapes, living near family, maintaining livestock or gardens, or hunting and fishing. The study was meant to assess the program's effectiveness and to convince Congress to continue its funding. Whether Native workers and their families were "better off" after relocation was a complicated question not clearly answered with such a poorly designed questionnaire.

Nevertheless, the surveys offer a glimpse into what Native American workers hoped to gain from relocation, and they offer a commentary on whether the program lived up to individuals' expectations. The survey and its supporting documents include interesting data on individual work histories and correspondence from the workers themselves. Often only brief comments, these notes provide insight into how Native Americans used the program to improve their own economic situations. The result is a complicated portrait of Native workers who embraced the program or who used the resources the BIA offered to advance their individual needs. Sometimes their experience corresponded to BIA definitions of "success," and sometimes they subverted the goals of the program.

Unsurprisingly, Native workers who praised the program and said they were "better off" had significantly improved their economic standard of living after relocating. Bill Morley, a Kiowa man from Oklahoma, who earned three dollars an hour working in an Oakland Barber shop, commented that he and his family were doing "obviously better" since they owned their home and furnishings. William Sanders, a Turtle Mountain Chippewa man from North Dakota who relocated to San Jose and who also trained as a barber, told the interviewer he was better off after relocation. He thought he could find better jobs and more opportunities in his new location. As a husband and father of two preschool daughters, he had traded seasonal farm work in North Dakota where he milked cows, plowed fields, and seeded crops and earned forty-two dollars a week plus room and board for a permanent job in San Jose making $3.64 an hour.[74] Jeff Bagley, a Gros Ventre man from Fort

Belknap, Montana, trained at Allied Welding School in Oakland, California, and found a job working in the shipyards that paid $4.50 an hour. He was a union member, and he and his wife were in the process of buying their own home. Marcus Lyon, a Blackfeet man from Yakima, Washington, said relocation and adult vocational training improved life for his family. He worked as an aluminum welder in Tacoma and said he would do it again because now he was "able to provide [his] own food and not live on cornmeal all winter and commodities."75 In fact, he had "done it all again" and gone on relocation twice. The first time he found a job working in the Seattle shipyards. Later he landed a job in aluminum welding in Tacoma making $4.25 an hour.

Like Lyons, other Native American workers expressed support for the program, even though they eventually returned to the reservation, even if just temporarily. Some "returnees," as BIA called them, noted that they found the relocation experience enriching and educational and that they appreciated the new skills they acquired in job training programs. Bob Miller, a Shoshone man from Nevada, had relocated to Cleveland. He commented that he and his family benefited from "city living." The experience increased his family's desire to "have things better." But he found the training courses frustrating because he could not find a job as a welder in Cleveland, and there were no opportunities to use his newly acquired skill on the reservation. Nevertheless, he and his family moved home because his wife "didn't like living in the big city." He finally settled into driving a bus for the BIA in Ibapah, Utah.76

Clinton Wayne, a young Navajo man, responded that he was "doing better" and would "do it again." Growing up around Crownpoint, New Mexico, he had attended school on the reservation up to the seventh grade and then spent four years at Intermountain Indian School in Brigham City, Utah. When he was eighteen years old, he relocated to Dallas but returned to the reservation sometime in 1962 to work at a BIA warehouse driving a truck and doing other types of odd jobs for one dollar an hour. With the help of the BIA, he then moved to Albuquerque to complete a Standard Oil station attendant training course in 1964 that qualified him for a job back at the Crownpoint Chevron Station. In 1968, he went on relocation again, traveling to California to enroll in a new welding course sponsored by the electronics company Philco-Ford at a decommissioned Airforce base in Madera. Finally, after ten years of moving from a boarding school in Utah to relocation offices in Texas, New Mexico, California, and back to the reservation, he finally landed in Denver. There he married and settled into a "good job," as he described it, working for Allied Steel making $3.75 an hour.77

While the majority of those surveyed said they were "better off" and would go on relocation again, many complained about the quality of the training programs. Thirty-eight percent said they would not participate in the same training program again, and 12 percent did not answer the question. Of those who were critical of the training programs, 40 percent were disappointed in the availability of jobs related to their training, and 53 percent felt that they had made the wrong choice and would have preferred another vocational track.[78] Betty Astor, a Pima (Akimel O'odham) woman from Sacaton, Arizona, commented that sure, she would "do it again," since she needed to earn money. But she admitted that she was no better off now than before she relocated to Oakland. Before she left home, she supported herself doing domestic work in private homes in Scottsdale and Phoenix, where she earned between fifty cents and one dollar an hour. A high school graduate and tired of such low wages, she applied to go on relocation to Oakland, where she enrolled in a power sewing course at Oakland City College. But that training did not turn out as she hoped. The work, she explained, was "hard on [my] eyes." She regretted spending her time training for work making casket linings. In hindsight, she would have preferred beauty school. Two years after she had arrived in Oakland, Astor was pregnant, unmarried and heading back to the Gila Reservation in Arizona. At the time of the interview, she was commuting daily from her mother's home to work at the Scottsdale Roadway Inn where she earned $1.50 an hour.[79]

William Paul, a Tlingit man from Alaska, also commented that he was better off after relocation, but he did not attribute his success to the welding program he completed in Los Angeles. Eager to offer his "opinion of the program as [he] experienced it," he added a pointed critique of the BIA at the bottom of the survey form. He believed the program was "built up too much" and poorly managed. Job placement and BIA support for students in between training programs was uneven. After he finished his courses, he "couldn't even obtain a job because every prospective employer wanted an experienced welder." According to Paul, the BIA needed to develop "definite job contacts before a person is trained, with a definite prospective employer." But, most of all, he was upset because the BIA staff did not offer his family financial support when he shifted programs. Paul remembered, "There is one thing that certainly makes me sick whenever I think of it. That is the period between the time I dropped out of RCA training and the time I started the welding course. We practically starved during this time, and the BIA couldn't care less. In other words, my subsistence stopped during this period of two weeks, and this really discouraged both my wife and I. We lived on canned baby food during that time and didn't even have coffee!"

Clearly ambitious, Paul migrated from Yakutat, Alaska, where he had been active in his village council, the Alaska Native Brotherhood, and the Tlingit-Haida organization. His wife had served on the school board. He had previously worked for Alaska Timber and Pulp, making $4.25 an hour, more than many of his fellow Native workers earned in Los Angeles. But a work-related accident left him partially disabled. His left foot had been crushed in a timber accident and had to be amputated. To him, welding seemed like a good option. But, after several months looking for a welding job and not finding one, he returned to Sitka where he found work with the State of Alaska.[80]

Paul was not alone. Many Native workers returned to reservations after living for a year or two in urban areas. While the numbers vary, the initial "Operation TOB" completed in 1966 found that 55 percent of relocatees returned. Even out of those who permanently migrated away from reservations, most did not remain in their initial relocation destination cities. In a 1968 follow up of the 1966 study, the BIA found that only 20 percent of participants still lived in the cities to which they had originally relocated. Those who did not return home migrated to other cities to find work. Anecdotal evidence suggests that their initial experience in the off-reservation labor market helped them find work in other places and increased their mobility and their job prospects. Don Russell, a Tlingit man from Sitka, Alaska, traveled to Los Angeles to train as an airplane mechanic at Northrup Institute of Technology. He had served in the Marine Corps for three years and had worked as a truck driver before deciding to relocate. As he put it, he left Alaska "to better my education in the field I was training in while in the service." He received a job offer after he finished his training program, but he decided to turn it down and move up to San Francisco. At first, he had to work in a warehouse for several months before he found a job working for the Flying Tigers, a military freight company, as an aircraft mechanic. Three years later he moved on to work for Air-California, another aviation firm. When BIA officials interviewed him in 1968, he was living in a two-bedroom duplex in the Laurel Heights neighborhood in San Francisco with his wife and three sons.

One-third of those who relocated to urban areas returned to their reservation communities. Others routinely migrated between those settings, expanding their seasonal round to include places like Los Angeles, Denver and Chicago. Those who stayed in urban areas and who most resembled the BIA's ideal relocatee, did not necessarily embrace the federal agency's social and economic philosophy. In fact, some Native parents raised children in the 1950s who would later form the backbone of the Red Power movement and militantly challenge the relocation policy's assimilationist assumptions and the authority of the federal government itself. Others created new urban Indigenous cultures and transformed places like Los Angeles and Silicon Valley into "Indian Country."[81]

Don Russell and other Native people who repaired airplane engines, minded the children of middle-class white women, harvested beets, worked on assembly lines, or packed boxes, welcomed year-round wage work, but they did not necessarily embrace federal policymakers' assimilationists goals. They might have accepted the terms of the capitalist workforce, and they might have adopted the colonial modernization idiom, but they were also contesting its underlying premise of detribalization. As workers and tribal leaders, they were sorting through the difficult and sometimes contradictory historical process of decolonization. Like peoples in the rest of the decolonizing world, American Indians wrestled with often contradictory impulses and challenges: making a living and creating new economies while at the same time peeling away the layers of colonial power that had controlled their lives on the most intimate levels. Migrating to urban areas did not destroy Native communities, at least not in the ways imagined by reformers. In some ways, that experience created new resources, including wages and opportunities that inspired the next generation to articulate tribal sovereignty in powerful new ways.

4

Jobs and Sovereignty

THE DEVELOPMENT OF THE TRIBAL EMPLOYMENT RIGHTS MOVEMENT

> *He put his ordinance on the table. "This is the law where you have to hire Indian people now. And I'm here to help you do that." The labor relations guy said, "Who the hell do you think you are? Comin' in here like that. We decide who we hire, who we train, and we decide where they work." Navarro responded, "I'm a representative of a sovereign government who has the authority to do this." We all had those experiences with hard core people. A lot of the TERO directors were local Indian people, like me, who were every bit as courageous as Kenny White.*
>
> CONRAD EDWARDS, RECALLING FELLOW CTER
> FOUNDER JOHN NAVARRO'S EARLY CONFRONTATION
> WITH LAKESIDE MINE MANAGEMENT

The ordinance John Navarro placed before Lakeside mine management was the brainchild of the Council for Tribal Employment Rights (CTER), an organization dedicated to improving the lives of Native workers across the United States. Conrad Edwards, member of the Colville Confederated Tribes and CTER's president, fondly remembered Navarro's story of when he, armed with a tribe's Tribal Employment Rights Ordinance (TERO) in the late

1970s, managed to exact concessions from the mining company to extend preference in hiring to Native workers. Even though the company operated just across the reservation's border, the minerals extracted belonged to the tribe. That and other efforts spearheaded by CTER have expanded the terms of sovereignty from control over natural resource rights to the jobs that such development created.[1]

Since the late nineteenth century, the colonial architects of Indian policy imagined wage labor as a solution to the so-called Indian problem.[2] In boarding schools, relief projects, and relocation, Native people endured the machinations of those BIA agents, matrons, and employers who were convinced that making a living required a complete transformation of their cultures and livelihood. But as the previous chapters illustrate, Native workers consistently tested the limits of "positive programming" and thwarted the intent of those policies. By the 1970s, the relationship between work and sovereignty had shifted, particularly on reservation land.

Since the mid-twentieth century, tribal governments have been asserting their sovereignty rights by extending control over natural resources on reservation land: negotiating better leasing terms with multinational corporations; protecting sacred landscapes from industrial pollution; or developing the resources themselves, for the benefit of their tribal economies, including creating jobs for Native peoples. Looking at the history of sovereignty and jobs from the perspective of American Indian workers complicates the story, both in how we assess the impact of economic growth on reservation land and in the ways that workers themselves have redefined the terms of that development.

In assessing the historical repercussions of oil, coal, uranium, and natural gas development, we are left with a story full of mixed results. On the one hand, energy industries provided important opportunities to tribal governments, offering some, like the Diné, with significant royalty revenues that supplied much of the Nation's operating budget. On the other hand, scholars and activists argued that the negative results of energy development clearly outweighed the gains that such revenue generated. Drilling, mining, processing, and storing those resources created a clear pattern of environmental racism. American Indians, who historically wielded little political leverage with states or the federal government, and who faced desperate economic choices, have been saddled with the lion's share of the energy industry's toxic burden.[3] Tribal officials and Native workers faced a difficult balancing act, characteristic of colonial economies, weighing jobs and royalties against their own health and sovereign power to control their own resources. In the case of the energy industries and other economic development projects undertaken in the postwar era, Native workers also expanded the meaning of sovereignty to include jobs as well.[4]

With capital-intensive energy development in the mid- to late twentieth century—whether coal, natural gas, oil, or uranium—came the kinds of jobs that, up to this point, had been largely unavailable in many Native communities. Building and maintaining power plants and pipelines, in addition to mining the resources themselves, created skilled, sometimes unionized jobs that paid better wages than many reservation residents made picking produce, maintaining railroad tracks, or herding livestock for relatives. These jobs also offered some Native workers an alternative to seasonal migrant work, and they were a means to resist leaving their reservation communities for good.[5]

Yet, these jobs were not always open to American Indians, even when the work itself was located on reservation land. Despite their impressive coal resources, for the most part Navajos even found their access to electricity quite limited. The Navajo Nation might supply coal to the massive power plants, but the fruits of such labor remained out of reach for most families, bypassing them overhead on power lines that supplied electricity to the cities beyond the reservation. Jobs too remained elusive. Energy companies and construction firms often brought in their own non-Native workers to build and maintain energy facilities and failed to employ tribal members. So, energy development served as a catalyst for tribal employment rights activists as well as for an emerging nationalist politics. Native workers fought for access to those skilled jobs, and in the process of that struggle, they mobilized a multitribal grassroots movement that would expand the terms of sovereignty itself.[6]

This chapter reconstructs the history of the Tribal Employment Rights Ordinance (TERO), the strategy that Native workers and their lawyers developed in the early 1970s to enforce Indian preference in hiring, agreements that already existed but that had never been adequately enforced. Initially inspired by Navajo construction workers demanding access to jobs at the Navajo Generating Plant, and by Blackfeet activists who insisted on enforcement of Indian hiring preferences in the oil and gas industry, the ordinance quickly outgrew its initial intent.[7] Soon thereafter, tribes throughout the United States—even those without significant energy resources—established TERO offices to enforce Indian hiring preferences in all kinds of companies doing business in Indian country. Since then, TERO officers have enforced Indian preference clauses, transformed their offices into hiring

Jobs and Sovereignty

halls, and served as advocates for Native workers facing racism in a variety of venues, both on and off the reservation.[8]

THE NAVAJO CONSTRUCTION WORKERS ASSOCIATION AND THE NAVAJO GENERATING PLANT

In early 1971, four Navajo construction workers walked into the Tuba City office of Diné be'iiná Náhiiłna be Agha'diit'ahii (DNA), a legal services agency that represented Navajos on civil rights cases and other legal disputes.[9] They were there to complain about discrimination against Navajos working at the Navajo Generating Plant, a massive construction project in Page, Arizona, operated by Arizona Public Service, California Edison, and the Bechtel Corporation. The lease required that the contractors building the plant hire Navajo workers. But union hiring procedures had undermined that contractual obligation, and up to that point, no one had tried to enforce it. The construction workers' unions hired members from their own established list of workers, and it was unlikely that Navajos, as a group, would gain priority. Union workers moving in from other construction jobs in the West often displaced Navajos who did find work at the power plant. Kenneth White, a Navajo man who was a member of the Carpenter's Union and a shop steward at the plant, along with three other activists, were ready to challenge the contractor's practices. The DNA staff quickly referred them to Dan Press, an attorney in the Fort Defiance office, who had more experience with employment law.[10] The struggle that ensued between the Navajo Generating Station and the Navajo workers brought resources and jobs together as two parts of the sovereignty issue. As Press described later, "They were building it on Navajo land and using Navajo water," but not using Navajo labor.[11]

A young, energetic attorney who had just graduated from Yale Law School three years earlier, Daniel Press developed his expertise in Native employment issues by defending Navajo workers in various cases he had filed against the BIA, including a complaint against discrimination at the Gallup Supply Center Warehouse, a facility the Indian service used to store commodity food and other agency supplies. According to Press, in 1970, the warehouse workforce was strictly organized along racial lines. Navajos performed the lowest level of work, while Latinos served as their supervisors, and Anglos occupied the top management positions. Press explained, "There was clear discrimination that went down the ladder. They were searched when they left the building to make sure they weren't stealing anything, and they were limited in all kinds of ways, bathroom breaks, etc." Navajos also

Navajo Generating Station, October 28, 2019, one month before it was decommissioned. Photograph by Eric Kilby. Courtesy Flickr, CC-BY-SA 2.0, https://www.flickr.com/photos/ekilby/49518916178/.

faced layoffs in the summer months, while white supervisors remained on the payroll. When Press filed a lawsuit on the Navajo workers' behalf, BIA officials came out to Gallup to investigate. Six months later, the National Indian Youth Council (NIYC), a militant Red Power organization that got its start in Gallup, brought the case to national attention by picketing the facility.[12] The NIYC's biweekly newspaper, described a bleak situation in which Native people were "only used as beast of burdens."[13] As a result, although without admitting the existence of systematic discrimination, the BIA settled the case. They transferred the offending senior officials to other operations and created ways for Navajos to advance to supervisory roles. In his report on his investigation of the complaint, James Hena, the assistant to the commissioner of Indian affairs, noted that they had removed those officials because, "To term it simply, the supervisors [had] lost their effectiveness to communicate with the employees, or their acceptance by the complainants is ended for all time."[14] Years later, when he came across the workers he had defended in that case, Press noted that "life had gotten much better and some of the employees had been promoted off the bottom level." That effort, according to Press, "was probably some of the first activism in Indian country around employment rights."[15]

What happened next at the Navajo Generating Plant, a case that followed on the heels of the Gallup Warehouse controversy, would have broad and

Kenneth White. White was the founder of the Navajo Construction Workers Association and the first compliance officer for the Office of Navajo Labor Relations. Photograph courtesy of Kenneth White Jr.

long-term implications. The Navajo construction workers initiated a grassroots campaign that sowed the seeds of a national movement and broadened notions of sovereignty. Tribes were beginning to challenge the inequitable terms characteristic of mining leases. To the struggle over royalty rates, pollution, and a legacy of poor resource management, Native workers added their demands for access to jobs that such development created.

A few weeks following the NIYC demonstration at the Gallup Supply Center Warehouse, the struggle over the power plant began to escalate. In June 1971, Press and the Navajo workers he represented, including Kenneth White, Sam Damon, Tom Lincoln, and Kenneth Cody, met with George Vallasis, the Navajo Nation's general counsel, representatives from the construction workers unions, and officials from the firms building the Navajo Generating Station: Bechtel and Morrison-Knudsen. They left that meeting feeling disheartened, since the hiring procedures set in place by the industry and the unions seemed insurmountable. Yet, after a bit of legal research, they discovered that the Navajo hiring preference clause included in the companies' contract with the Navajo Nation offered them the opportunity to argue their case.[16] Consequently, Press filed a lawsuit with the Equal Economic Opportunity Commission (EEOC) and the Office of Federal Contract Compliance.[17]

The Navajo construction workers knew they had to mobilize the community in order to improve conditions at the power plant. They organized the Navajo Construction Workers Association and talked to their friends, family members, and neighbors at chapter house meetings and other gatherings. Slowly, they built momentum. At each meeting, their numbers increased. As Press remembers:

> Each time I'd go out . . . there would be a larger group of both people who were working there and from the community. . . . They lived right there in the shadow of the facility, the Page power plant. When they'd go to the office, they would be told they had to go to Flagstaff, to the union office. So, these folks would scratch whatever couple of pennies they had together to pay for gas to go down there. It was 100 miles away and they'd go down there, and they were told, "I'm sorry all we can do is put you on the 'C' list. We almost never hire off the 'C' list."[18]

Soon they were attracting nearly four hundred people to their meetings and had impressed the members of the Navajo Tribal Council, including its chair, Peter MacDonald. From this point onward, the tribe organized the Office of Navajo Labor Relations (ONLR) and hired Kenneth White as the initial contract compliance officer.[19] Press recalls one skeptic at the meeting who thought the construction workers' efforts were futile. Reportedly, in one of Kenneth White's favorite stories about the organizing efforts, that man said: "See those big red rocks out there, that's where the unions and Bechtel is. They're up there, and we are down here. We are never going to get up there." Later, as Press tells it, when Kenneth White ran into that naysayer again, the man reported that "he was working, his grandson was working, and his son in-law was working." The man turned to White and said, "I think I owe you an apology."[20]

INDIAN HIRING PREFERENCE

By the time he and his fellow workers confronted the energy companies, Kenneth White had felt the full effect of twentieth-century Indian policy. As a young man, he attended the Sherman Institute, the Indian boarding school in Riverside, California. His family had suffered through livestock reduction during the 1930s. He worked at an Army Ordnance Depot in Bakersfield during World War II. After that, he relocated to Los Angeles where he found work in the auto industry. He learned how to survive and adapt to off-reservation workplaces, and he even joined the United Auto Workers union. He likely exemplified the kind of relocatee favored by the BIA agents (see chapter 3). Nevertheless, his life demonstrated the failure of BIA efforts to use wage labor to remove Native people from their lands and assimilate them into the American working class. Kenneth and his family returned to the reservation where he and his fellow Navajo workers ignited a movement that demanded an end to the types of discrimination so characteristic of colonial exploitation of tribal lands. The CTER, an intertribal organization that grew from this conflict, developed a plan to improve working conditions and to guarantee Native workers preference in hiring in industries developed on Native land.[21]

Indian hiring preferences already existed in most federal contracts and private leasing agreements. In fact, as early as 1834, federal officials established the precedent in Section 9 of the Act to Organize the Department of Indian Affairs, requiring that jobs such as interpreters, blacksmiths, and teachers be filled by "persons of Indian descent." According to historian Steve Novak, from the mid-nineteenth century through the 1930s, the OIA mainly employed Native people in lower-level, unskilled positions. Even though the percentage of Native Americans working in OIA jobs began to shrink with the advent of civil service reform and the expansion of the agency, reformers and federal officials held out hope that hiring them would aid their assimilationist program.[22] New Deal legislation reconfirmed this practice, giving preference to Native men and women to work on a variety of development and conservation projects throughout the West, including on the Navajo Reservation.[23] While federal officials may have hoped that jobs might "prevent a return to the blanket," many American Indians saw working on OIA projects as a strategy by which to sustain their communities and cultures.[24] Indeed, wages were important for their survival. But tribal leaders also understood access to jobs in broader terms, as a treaty right. Historian Frank Rzeczkowski quoted a Crow leader making this connection at a ditch council meeting in 1895. The Crow leader said, "This land and this ditch money is ours, and we want to build our own ditches, and get some of our money back." Four years later, Crow headman Plenty Coups continued to demand these jobs when he protested the hiring of white workers on a federal irrigation project on the Crow Reservation.[25] Nearly seventy years later, Title VII of the 1964 Civil Rights Act confirmed Indian preference in hiring.[26]

The problem came in the enforcement of such agreements. According to Dan Press, employers, including the BIA, completely ignored Indian preference clauses. "It was discretionary," Press explained, "they interpreted preference very narrowly."[27] In establishing the ONLR, the Navajo Nation took the bold step of developing a monitoring and enforcement body that was completely independent of any federal agency. It was not a program instituted by Congress or the BIA, nor was it simply an extension of a federal program, such as Housing and Urban Development, or the Indian New Deal. By creating an agency to regulate its own labor policies, the Navajo Nation strongly asserted its sovereignty rights to govern—regardless of federal oversight. Soon, other tribes followed the Navajo example.

In 1972, Dan Press moved to Washington, DC, but he remained active in American Indian law. Inspired by the development of the ONLR, he worked with members of the Native consulting firm ACKCO American Indian Professional Services to develop a new program that would encourage tribes to establish agencies similar to that which the Navajos had created. The result was an initiative funded by an EEOC grant, called the Tribal Employment Rights Ordinance (TERO).[28] Press and the ACKCO consultants produced for tribal officials a model ordinance and a handbook that outlined the legal basis for Indian preference.[29] In April 1977, they gathered representatives from twelve tribes at Kenita Lodge on the Warm Springs Reservation in central Oregon to discuss the idea. Kenneth White, the leader of the Navajo Construction Workers, was the keynote speaker. In his inspirational address, White was quick to remind his audience, "We Native Americans must stand up for what is rightfully ours. Our once poor 'reservations' are filled with large deposits of natural resources. Many private companies have come on our lands, and left the once god given, what we call 'mother earth,' scarred, useless and dry. They have brought pollution, without caring about the land or the people, and many power plants, pipelines, coal mines, etc., have been built, many more are sure to come." Despite the environmental damage wrought by those companies, White did not call for a ban on energy development. He avoided the trap that has often pitted environmentalists and labor activists against each other, particularly in battles over mining, oil drilling, and nuclear waste storage. Instead, he linked the importance of Native people controlling their own resources to ending discrimination in hiring and gaining access to jobs. He continued: "We must stand up for our rights. Our people have been discriminated against in hiring and employment practices for long enough. . . . Indian preference programs aid the average, grassroot Indian worker, and that is what we are striving for. Indian preference also makes the companies that take so much from our lands give a little back by providing us Indian people with much needed jobs."[30]

Making the connection between Native lands and Native labor, White and his fellow CTER activists were expanding the definition of sovereignty, a concept usually associated with governance and culture, to include work. Labor was no longer a tool to remove Native people from the land. Instead, struggling for jobs in industries that used Indigenous resources but not Native labor strengthened tribes' resolve to maintain their tribal homelands.

John Navarro, the human resources manager at Tohono O'odham in Arizona, and Conrad Edwards, the Comprehensive Employment and Training Act (CETA) director for the Colville Tribe near Spokane, Washington, were among the original participants at the Warm Springs conference.[31] Like Kenneth White, both men had been struggling with employment issues in their respective reservation communities. Conrad Edwards was embroiled in a dispute with a lumber mill. He recalled, "The facility was on the reservation, and they were processing tribal timber, yet we had all kinds of problems getting our people hired, keeping them hired and moving them up the ladder." John Navarro was fighting a similar battle on the Tohono O'odham Reservation, trying to get tribal members construction jobs on a Housing and Urban Development (HUD) project.[32]

Edwards and Navarro left the Tribal Employment Rights Conference emboldened with a model TERO ordinance and confident that Indian preference in hiring was a right that could, indeed, be enforced. "After we got together," John Navarro recalled, "we knew immediately that we would go back home, get the ordinance passed, start our TERO programs and have some success."[33]

At first, enforcing Indian preference required great nerve, determination, and significant creativity. One of the original TERO activists, Carl Schildt, the Blackfeet Community Action Project director, was legendary. According to Dan Press, even before they had a TERO ordinance in place, Schildt would approach the foreman on a reservation construction site and tell him: "See that bulldozer over there, if there isn't an Indian on top it tomorrow, the bulldozer isn't going to be found." The next day, there would be an Indian worker operating the equipment. Without any precedents or procedures in place, "Buckles," as Schildt was known, was particularly resourceful for finding ways to ensure contractors' cooperation. Rodney "Fish" Gervais, a member of the Blackfeet Tribal Council and former TERO compliance officer, recalled that TERO was "just a concept," and that the laws were often made "kind of after the fact." When a particular contractor refused to comply, Schildt threatened him with a fine of $500 a day per violation, a figure he simply "pulled out of the sky."[34]

Reflecting on those early TERO officers, Press recalled, "It took a lot of guts for those folks to just walk into an employer and say: 'This is the law, you shall comply, it's going to change the way you hire.'"[35] John Navarro remembered just how confrontational those moments could be. He recalled that he had to resort to a bit of theater to convince one HUD contractor to comply. "When I told him he had . . . to give tribal people preference, he became unfriendly and hostile and said, 'Who in the heck are you?' (he went beyond the heck part, okay)." Navarro had yet to secure support from the Tohono O'odham Tribal Council. But luckily for him, the contractor was unaware of that fact. "So, I went to the telephone and pretended to dial. I pretended I was speaking to the captain of the tribal police force and said, 'Well he's not in right now? Tell him to call me at this number.'" When the contractor asked him to explain, Navarro recalled saying, "I'm calling the police . . . I'm the person that's going to have you removed from this reservation if you don't leave immediately." Apparently, Navarro's ruse worked. After that, according to Navarro, those contractors were much less confrontational and eager to learn how they might comply with the TERO ordinance.[36]

Early TERO activists continued to chisel away at a wall of paternalistic attitudes and bureaucratic practices that had discouraged Native people from challenging employment discrimination in the past. Conrad Edwards remembered confronting the supervisor of a highway project on the Colville Reservation. When Edwards was driving by the construction site, he was disappointed to see few Native workers. When he pulled over to inform the supervisor, that they were in violation of the TERO ordinance, the contractor replied in a rather condescending tone, "Let me tell you something, chief. You see those ribbons tied in those trees over there? That's 22 and a half feet off the centerline of this road. You see that little staple there that's got the same kind of ribbon on it? That's 22 and a half feet on this side. . . . We have a right of way because Indian preference begins on the other side of those ribbons." Feeling defeated, Edwards turned and walked away. "Since I didn't have my ordinance in hand or anything, I headed back to my car," Edwards recalled. "But the more I walked the madder I got, so I turned around and walked back. I tapped him on the shoulder and said, 'Let me tell you something, sir. You see the ribbons on the tree by your pickup? . . . That's where

Conrad Edwards (*left*), president of the Council for Tribal Employment Rights, and Dan Press (*right*), general counsel, December 2007. Photograph by the author.

this project is going to stop until we get a compliance agreement.'" Edwards recommended that the supervisor have his attorney review their contract. Then he warned, "I'm going to come back and remove all this equipment off the reservation. I have the authority to do that." When Edwards returned the next day, the construction site was empty and the supervisor was sitting in his truck outside the TERO office, waiting for him. The contractor had followed Edward's advice and talked with his attorney, who advised him to "settle this right now." After that, Edwards placed a few Native laborers and heavy equipment operators on the job.[37]

Stories such as those told by White, Navarro, Press, Edwards, and Gervais, circulated widely among TERO activists. Retelling those tales seemed to bolster their resolve to keep up the fight. In a recent conversation, Conrad Edwards confessed, "There were so many times that I got frustrated and hit roadblocks and . . . was ready to chuck it all." But at those times, Edwards would find strength in the determination of his fellow TERO activists fighting similar battles across the country. "We were really impassioned about what we were doing. There were times when I would say: 'What would Kenny White do in a situation like this,' you know? These folks were all fighters."

The legendary "Buckles," the Blackfeet TERO officer, was particularly inspiring when he directed the tribal police to seize $28,000,000 worth of mining equipment. Those stories motivated Edwards to say, "Damn it, I'm going to go through with this."[38]

The result of such resolve was the development of tribal institutions responsible for regulating labor conditions on reservation land and protecting the access to jobs that previously might have remained beyond the reach of most Native workers. In this way, their efforts complemented other tribal initiatives that came of age in the era of "self-determination."

In the ten years that followed, TERO expanded significantly, both in the numbers of tribes participating and in its original mission. Between 1977 and 1987, more than one hundred tribes initiated TERO programs. Since then, according to the CTER, the organization that emerged from the 1977 Warm Springs conference, this number has grown to more than three hundred tribes and Alaskan Native villages. These offices are no longer just watchdog operations, although they remain militant enforcers of Indian preference agreements. Some like the Sho-Ban (Shoshone-Bannock) office on the Fort Hall Reservation in Idaho serve as employment agencies and furnish employers with lists of qualified workers.[39] The Cherokee Nation TERO office (like many other tribes) maintains a "skills bank," from which they refer qualified workers to certified employers. Developing the employment referral arm was an important step to enabling TERO officials to enforce the ordinance. As John Navarro explains, "Once we established that we did have the power to make the employer hire Indian people, many of us got caught with our pants down, if you will." When the employer agreed, according to Navarro, "his next comment was okay, I need ten workers tomorrow at seven o'clock in the morning." Pooling their experience and resources, Navarro and Edwards asked Larry Brown, a former union organizer from the Spokane Tribe, to help develop their skills banks, modeling them on union hiring halls. In fact, Navarro recalled, many American Indian workers would refer to TERO as a union, "They got confused, but we tried to take the best ideas we could find from many different sources. We were proactive in preventing problems."[40]

While some TERO offices have remained focused on enforcing Indian hiring preference agreements and administering employment referrals to tribal members, some activists have pushed the original objectives a bit further. For example, Rodney "Fish" Gervais used his position as TERO director for the Blackfeet to raise broader civil rights issues, border town racism, and the problems of unemployment. He was largely concerned about the disparity in unemployment between his community and Cut Bank, a small border town that, while suffering from the decline of the oil and gas industry, still maintained a higher standard of living than what reservation residents enjoy. Gervais, who later served as chair of the Blackfeet Tribal Business Council, was pivotal in organizing a border town racism conference, out of which the Montana Indian Civil Rights Commission developed.[41]

More importantly, TERO was a new way for tribes to assert their sovereignty. According to one *Sho-Ban News* reporter, this was an effort created by the Native people themselves, "There are no federal agencies telling tribes they must adopt such a program, or issuing regulations that impose requirements on how the tribes should run its [sic] program. Instead, each tribe has had the freedom to develop the TERO program only if it wants, at a pace and in a manner that meets its own special circumstances."[42] Assessing TERO's history, Bobby Whitefeather, chair of the Red Lake Band of Chippewa Indians of Minnesota, stated that "Indian preference" is "an important instrument of our sovereignty."[43]

TERO programs have dramatically changed the lives of Native workers. After the Blackfeet developed a TERO ordinance, the numbers of their tribal members working on reservation construction projects tripled. Tohono O'odham workers experienced a similar jump in employment in the copper mine on their reservation.[44] The percentage of Navajos employed on large-scale industrial jobs on their land increased from 10 percent to 60 percent. Kenneth White attributed the ONLR enforcement of Indian preference for the growing numbers of Diné workers employed in highly skilled jobs. Looking back at his efforts, he recalled:

> And after this, a lot of Indian craftsmen got jobs at Peabody Coal. We fought for them. And they trained a lot of people, heavy equipment operators and everything. I went over there, and saw a lot of my people doing heavy equipment. Oh, that really made me happy! I stood up for that. I fought for that. There's a big generating station over here this side of Farmington. Right there, there's a lot of Navajos working there, too. Craftsmen. They train them on the job. All over, all over the country they know how now. That was through this Act, through what we done for the rights, you know. That really made me happy.[45]

At first, trade unions opposed such programs. They were extremely reluctant to give up control over the hiring process. Unions, such as Carpenter's Local 1100 in Flagstaff, Arizona, had exercised that authority at the expense of

American Indian workers. They were slow to realize that granting preference to Native people in union jobs would not destroy the union. They found out that replacing white workers with American Indians created Native union members on Native land.

Eventually, unions began working with the ONLR to include a Navajo preference clause in their collective bargaining agreements. These clauses were similar to those included in leasing agreements that were supposed to give Navajos priority access to jobs on the reservation.[46] As a result of these efforts, the labor movement has become an important advocate for Navajo workers, wielding increasing power in Navajo tribal politics.[47] Unions such as the Carpenters, Laborers International, and Operating Engineers, all of which represent energy industry workers across the United States, have made significant efforts to work with the CTER, offering to train and recruit tribal members for jobs both on and off reservation land. Those unions have even made significant concessions to tribal governments, giving up "union shop" provisions, the cornerstone of a union's power, in exchange for tribal labor agreements.[48]

Comparing CTER with the Council of Energy Resource Tribes (CERT), the better known, multitribal organization, illustrates how institution-building initiatives have expanded tribal sovereignty in different ways. Over the years, the relationship between these organizations has been quite close, since many of CTER's members also belong to CERT. In fact, the two organizations have a history of cooperation. David Lester, who would later become the president of CERT, once helped Navarro and Edwards secure a grant from the Administration for Native Americans, a federal initiative founded in 1974 to aid economic development on Indian reservations. Since then, according to Navarro, the two organizations have demonstrated "reciprocal respect and support for each other." CERT has been helpful in explaining the need for Indian preference when they are negotiating with energy companies.[49]

Both organizations have challenged corporations and the settler state for control over their economies. For CTER, that process has meant ending the discrimination against American Indians seeking jobs or working in non-Native corporations operating on reservation land. CERT leaders have not been as concerned with workers, per se. They want to control the exploitation of their own tribal resources and have demanded an end to leasing practices that undervalued tribal coal, oil, and other mineral reserves. They have also questioned the companies' adherence to, and federal enforcement of, environmental laws.

The organization has been heavily criticized by Native activists as a creation of the Department of Energy or as representing only the most powerful tribes and the interest of Indigenous elites. Yet, despite CERT's limitations, according to journalist Marjane Ambler, its members have successfully created an information clearinghouse on geology, mining, and energy markets that has made them less dependent on federal bureaucracies for technical expertise. CERT has also proved useful as an advocacy organization, representing tribal development interests in Washington, DC.[50]

TERO, by contrast, started through the initiative of Native workers rather than by tribal leaders alone.[51] Like CERT officials, they have challenged the terms of development. But TERO activists have added an additional layer to the sovereignty debate by advocating the rights of Native workers to the jobs those energy industries created. The economic dimension of the multifaceted sovereignty struggle includes workplace issues and access to jobs, in addition to control over the nature of energy development, leasing provisions, and royalty rates.

The TERO case demonstrates the distinctive experience of American Indian workers compared to other workers of color. The collective strategies they employed, like the TERO initiative, set them apart from Black, Asian, and Latino workers. While all people of color have faced discrimination in the workplace, American Indians have found that unions are not particularly sympathetic to their concerns. Alternatively, important Latino and Black leaders emerged from the labor movement, mobilizing workers around broader social justice and civil rights issues.[52] In the case of American Indians' relationship with energy industries, a legacy of treaty obligations and leasing agreements, not constitutional promises, have defined their relationship to US civil society. By challenging the employers' rights, they were redefining sovereignty around the issue of work, thereby renegotiating the terms of capitalist development itself.

During the years since Kenneth White and others assembled at Warm Springs to discuss tribal employment rights, the labor and sovereignty debate has shifted away from non-Native corporations operating on Native land, to tribal governments managing their own enterprises. With the phenomenal success of gaming, labor issues have grown even more complicated. In the 1970s, the relationship between jobs and sovereignty was relatively clear. Non-Native corporations were obligated to employ Indian workers as a condition of developing and exploiting the natural resources on reservation land. But what happens when tribal governments became the employers and non-Native people, the workers? Who manages the largely non-Native workforce? Some tribal leaders see federal labor law as a threat to their rights to govern rather than as legislation meant to protect all workers, Native Americans included.

These issues have complicated American Indians' involvement in unions since at least the 1930s. At best an ambivalent relationship, Native workers and unions have struggled on many fronts to address significant cultural, political, and economic issues. American Indians have had to assert their collective needs as workers and as members of Indigenous nations within a changing political landscape, one that often found unions at odds with emerging tribal governments. In the post-Termination era, tribal governments tried to assert their sovereignty by rescinding federal labor law and resisting the lingering paternalism of the BIA. As some Native labor activists discovered, fighting for sovereignty did not always translate into better working conditions. But American Indian workers have persisted. Navajo workers like Kenneth White gained accommodations from employers, unions, and leaders, and convinced the tribal government to create the ONLR. Other Native workers whom White inspired, like Conrad Edwards and other tribal employment rights activists, created Tribal Employment Rights offices throughout Indian country, initiatives that have encouraged tribes to craft their own labor laws and institutionalized workers' rights.[53]

The story of that movement raises important questions about the role of Native workers in post-Termination sovereignty struggles. Certainly, economic issues, including those related to energy development, have been central to American Indian communities' sovereignty goals.[54] Many of the energy-rich tribes, such as the Navajo, the Blackfeet, and the Three Affiliated Tribes at Fort Berthold in North Dakota, for example, asserted control over the regulation and development of their coal and oil reserves, and struggled to improve the notoriously low royalty rates negotiated by the BIA.[55] Examining that history in light of more contemporary conflicts between unions and tribal governments, and their battles in the federal courts as well as the grassroots campaigns initiated by Native workers themselves, reveals that the struggle toward sovereignty is a complex, multilayered journey. Creating sovereign nations did not simply result from a battle among federal, state, and tribal governments. Neither is the workers' story in this struggle for sovereignty merely a fight between tribal governments and unions. The fight for sovereignty involves all these parties, many of whom are locked in significant conflict over the power to regulate work and jobs on reservation land. The stories of Native workers asserting their rights in relation to their unions, their employers, and federal officials reveal a much more complicated history, one that acknowledges differences between and among Native communities.

5

Labor Rights or Sovereignty Rights?

THE CHALLENGE OF GAMING

> *We always contend the fact that if we're a government, and we're a sovereign government . . . we should have first right of refusal (if you will) to say, "Hey, we'll craft our own labor law."*
>
> DERON MARQUEZ, THE FORMER CHAIR OF THE
> SAN MANUEL BUSINESS COMMITTEE, JUNE 13, 2012

The CTER, as described in chapter 4, got its start as part of a collaboration with the EEOC in the 1970s. With help from an EEOC grant, CTER activists organized their first conference, and developed the TERO, a key tool that tribal governments used to promote the hiring of Native workers in jobs on and around reservations. But after the emergence of the Native American gaming industry in the 1980s, the struggle over the workplace shifted. For a small, but influential group of Native American nations, regulating reservation labor conditions has become the problem of regulating the work of non-Native workers. Tribal governments were no longer simply requiring non-Native controlled industries to hire Native workers. In the gaming industry, tribal governments, facing a largely non-Native workforce, are the owners and operators of the large companies themselves. The TERO movement, which broadened the issue of sovereignty to include jobs, takes on new meaning for gaming tribes. Native American governments are no longer bargaining with employers and the federal government for a part of the profits or for jobs for some of its members in industries they do not control. With casinos, the tribes control the industry. They own the industry; and they accumulate the capital.

The Indian gaming industry significantly shifted how the issue of "work" has shaped the battle for sovereignty. Before the development of the Indian gaming industry, when most of the private employers on reservations were non-Native, the connection between sovereignty and workers' rights seemed clear. According to tribal leaders, neither off-reservation corporations nor labor unions dominated by non-Native people should have the authority to regulate Native economies. With tribal governments as employers managing non-Native workers, the meaning of sovereignty has shifted from the rights to jobs, to the rights to govern the workplace.[1]

Focusing on three notable cases involving the Yuhaaviatam of San Manuel Nation (previously known as the San Manuel Band of Mission Indians) in Southern California, the Mashantucket Pequot Tribal Nation in Connecticut, and the Chickasaw Nation in Oklahoma, this chapter illustrates how successful gaming tribes negotiated that complicated landscape.[2] These stories, which sometimes overlap and which raise recurring questions about the conflict between sovereignty rights and civil rights, show how nations confronted opposition campaigns that reinforced racist stereotypes, withstood shifting political winds in federal and state politics, and maneuvered through internecine legal challenges. These examples suggest that the struggle for sovereignty is layered and uneven and sometimes full of contradictions.[3] These narratives will challenge readers who expect tribal governments to demand labor rights in ways that other workers of color have embraced them, and they will remind readers that American Indian politics cannot be reduced to a progressive/conservative continuum. The goal to exert political and economic power is similar, but tribes have used different strategies and multiple angles to protect and extend their rights even as US partisan politics and the local historical context of settler colonialism frustrated their efforts. These cases illustrate the precarity of sovereignty in the struggle between civil rights and sovereignty rights.

Before the growth of casino gaming on Native lands, tribal governments struggled to gain access to enough capital to develop, operate, and manage their own industries. Complicated legacies of settler-colonial exploitation, including episodic government relief and development programs, reinforced economic dependency and shifted with the political winds in Washington, DC. Meanwhile, non-Native corporations and individuals extracted wealth from Native resources such as minerals and timber, leased Native land as agricultural and grazing lands, and all the while paid royalties at submarket rates. Without significant control over those enterprises, or leasing terms, Native communities suffered significant hardship, including poverty, environmental damage, and dangerous health hazards.[4] Certainly, the wages earned by Native workers might circulate in their communities, but without significant financial infrastructure on reservations, such income hardly provided the capital needed to launch Native owned and operated businesses.[5]

Although reservation communities are still starved for capital, gaming has provided some tribal nations with the significant wealth needed to diversify their economies and stop the cycle of underdevelopment that had previously left them impoverished. That wealth has boosted economic development, decreased unemployment, and strengthened tribal governmental institutions. As a result, Native American incomes in those tribes grew six times the rate of other Americans' incomes, and women's participation in the waged economy also improved substantially. Yet not all tribes experienced similar benefits. In fact, despite the boom in Indian gaming, Native Americans still suffer the highest poverty rates in the country.[6]

Nevertheless, those tribes operating successful gaming industries have enjoyed growing political influence over state and federal officials, improved the educational levels of their tribal members, and stimulated Native cultural innovation and artistic expression. Some tribes have accumulated enough capital to maintain a somewhat stable income, a welcomed departure from the grant based economic schemes often initiated and then abandoned by the federal government in the 1970s.[7] Deron Marquez, a former chair of the San Manuel Business Committee, remembered how gaming transformed his community. "Yeah. I mean, it's the only thing that really created an economy. [Gaming] was the first true operation that created jobs (that had dollar circulation), . . . allowed a lot of people to build homes, or get loans for homes, or [build] some kind of equity to put up against a loan. So, it was the first time that the tribe actually had some means. More importantly, it was the first time we ever had [the money] to hire lawyers. It allowed us, enabled us, and provided the means for defending ourselves."[8]

Remembering the difficulties she and her kin faced growing up on the San Manuel reservation in the 1930s Pauline Ormego Murilio, a San Manuel elder, reflected on how gaming later improved their lives. She wrote, "We are a part of history, as we were once a small reservation trying to survive and now one of the most successful businesses in the state. Sadly, we are fighting to keep it going and trying to educate legislators about our situation so that they might support and help us continue and grow through our casino. Maybe when all my writing is done this will all be resolved. If not, it's up to our younger generation to carry on the battle for tribal sovereignty."[9]

Non-Native workers and their communities have benefited too. Native casinos generate sizable revenue for states, in taxes and direct payments, dispersed according to terms negotiated under the Indian Gaming and Regulatory Act (IGRA). Those "pacts" stipulate that in addition to providing for the general welfare of the tribe, its members, and economy, a percentage of casino profits must be donated to charities and help fund local government agencies.[10] And, of course, gaming facilities and supporting businesses such as hotels, restaurants, spas, sporting and entertainment venues employ workers, many of whom are non-Native. Their wages, plus the money these businesses earn from supplying goods and services to the casinos, create a significant multiplier effect. As a result, gaming has not only revitalized a few previously destitute tribes, casinos serve as a significant economic engine for the states in which they operate. For example, the California Nations Indian Gaming Association reported that between 2010 and 2014, Indian casinos and their associated nongaming services "supported 71,900 jobs" and produced "$43.1 billion in economic output—of which $33.7 billion represents value added to the California economy—$20.6 billion in labor income for California workers, and approximately $2.8 billion in state and local tax revenue."[11] In Connecticut, where only two tribal nations operate casinos, the benefit to the state is even more dramatic. In 2000, only eight years after the Mashantucket Pequot opened their casino, researchers at the University of Connecticut found that the tribe was "contributing 41,000 jobs to the State, with 31,000 of those in New London County, generating $1.2 billion in Gross State Product, and adding $1.9 billion to the State's aggregate personal income." The story is similar in other states, including, but not limited to, Arizona, Florida, and Oklahoma.[12]

Gaming seems like a capitalist success story for Native Americans. But even though tribal gaming operations are immersed in the capitalist market, they do not wield capitalist power, at least not in the world of global finance. As Scott Butera, the former CEO of Foxwoods Casinos, said of the Mashantucket Pequot Tribal Nation (MPTN) to the *New York Times*, their financial world is "sort of like being stuck in no man's land." They do not have the freedom to make decisions like capitalists. In fact, the MPTN seemed to become tethered to the financial industry, which stood first in line for a piece of the casino's profits. Debt payments, in the end, took precedence over per capita payments. And, forced to operate under the terms of IGRA, states now determine how casinos spend their profits. As some critics of gaming suggest, the development of gaming may have ultimately compromised tribes' sovereignty.[13]

In the 1970s and early 1980s, a handful of tribes in Florida and Southern California developed modest, high-stakes bingo and other gambling establishments to make up for the shrinking federal support for tribal economic development. Gambling promised to be lucrative, since the legal structures that governed federal, state, and tribal relationships unwittingly offered Native governments, at least temporarily, a competitive edge by exempting them from state control. That unique legal status dates to the origins of the United States government itself. From its inception, the US Constitution acknowledged American Indian sovereignty by specifically designating Indian policy and treaty-making as a federal responsibility, not subject to the authority of state lawmakers. Although the federal government repeatedly betrayed those principles over the last two centuries, Native people have continued to resist states' efforts to extend their authority over Indigenous land and have demanded that the federal government fulfill its obligations.[14]

Casinos offered a test to the limits of that governing arrangement. Since state laws that prohibited casino gambling and other "vices" were not necessarily applicable to reservation land, tribal governments saw a unique market opportunity.[15] American Indian leaders felt emboldened to establish businesses, like gaming and smoke shops, that sold products usually subject to state regulation and taxation. Without state interference, tribes could sell cigarettes at lower prices and open gambling businesses in regions where they were normally prohibited or strictly limited to seasonal horse racing and state lotteries. Since legal gambling was otherwise mostly limited to Las Vegas and Atlantic City, Native Americans were well positioned to tap an open market.

Establishing a bingo operation required limited capital compared to other types of industries Native people could develop on reservation land.[16] Because of a complicated history of land tenure that started with Indian removal in the early nineteenth century, was exacerbated by the General Allotment Act of 1887, and then further complicated by states extending jurisdiction over Native lands in the termination era, much reservation land was divided up, like a checkerboard, with tangled land titles and trust status. Banks were unwilling to lend money to Native individuals, businesses, and tribal governments since their most valuable asset—land—was inalienable, held in trust, and it could not be mortgaged. Reservations in Southern California were too small to provide a sustainable source of capital, even if Native leaders managed to leverage financing. Gaming offered a viable commercial alternative.[17]

But states did not necessarily agree with tribal sovereignty claims. In 1979, the Seminoles opened a high-stakes bingo operation in Hollywood, Florida, and subsequently faced challenges from the state over regulatory jurisdiction. The Seminoles appealed and, in 1981, won a monumental decision in federal court that restricted states' legal jurisdiction over tribal gaming facilities.[18] Meanwhile, tribes in Southern California were following the Seminole example. The Cabazon band of Mission Indians opened a card club in a single-wide trailer, and the Morongo in Riverside County launched a modest bingo parlor. Like their Florida counterparts, California state and county law enforcement attempted to seize control of those facilities. On February 15, 1983, police and SWAT teams raided the Cabazon card room, confiscated money and equipment, and threatened to arrest everyone in sight. Like the Seminoles, the Cabazon fought back, and eventually, in 1987, won their case in the Supreme Court. The case was seen as a victory for tribal gaming and as a rejection of Public Law 280, passed in 1953, which had subjected the tribes in California, Alaska, Minnesota, Nebraska, Oregon, and Wisconsin to state policing authority on reservation land.[19]

Seminole and Cabazon victories ushered in explosive growth in the Indian gaming industry throughout the United States and, with it, a strong backlash from state and federal lawmakers. Soon after the Cabazon won their Supreme Court case, Congress decided to clarify the legal landscape and passed IGRA in 1988. The legislation allowed casinos on reservation lands if the states where they are located allowed various types of gambling, including a state lottery, horse and dog racing, or off-track betting. IGRA created the National Indian Gaming Commission and defined regulatory categories subject to its jurisdiction. The first, class 1, included traditional games where players won small, relatively insignificant financial prizes; this class was exempt from IGRA oversight. Class 2 games, out of which larger and more lucrative gambling operations grew, included bingo, pull tabs, and lotto and were subject to oversight by the National Indian Gaming Commission. Class 3, which included Las Vegas styled high-stakes gaming, such as slot machines and video poker required states and tribes to negotiate a compact that spelled out the regulatory framework within which tribes and states operate. Those compacts define how tribes might spend their profits and spell out the amount tribes must pay the state. Compacts can differ, state by state, given the political climate in which they were negotiated.[20]

Controversial among Native leaders, the legislation both increased and undermined the sovereignty rights of gaming tribes. On the one hand, IGRA recognized the rights of tribal governments to operate casinos (albeit under a regulatory authority outlined in the legislation) and for some tribes, revenues raised in gaming strengthened the tribal governing institutions and allowed tribes to accumulate the capital they needed to expand bingo operations into larger casinos, diversify their economic portfolios, and develop legal resources they needed to defend their economic and political rights. On the other hand, the legislation opened the door for closer state regulatory authority over Native American economies.[21] Nevertheless, IGRA encouraged Native American governments to explore gaming as an economic opportunity. As Steven Light and Kathryn Rand point out in their seminal study on Indian gaming, the legislation was supposed to be a compromise between states and tribal governments.[22] But, in the end, it may have threatened the sovereignty of Native governments by extending the principals of Public Law 280 beyond the five states originally included in the termination era legislation.

IGRA seemed to clarify the relationship between tribes, states, and the federal government, but the growth of the Indian gaming industry raised new questions about the rights of non-Native employees who work in tribally operated casinos. Workers who cleaned casino hotel rooms, served cocktails to slot machine players, or dealt cards at blackjack tables worried that tribal governments might not enforce federal labor laws. Since tribal governments and casino management overlapped, non-Native workers wondered whether tribal casinos would acknowledge federally guaranteed rights to organize unions and whether they would find protection under tribal antidiscrimination laws. Tribal leaders tried to prevent unions from organizing their establishments; they ardently defended their sovereignty rights, and they rejected claims that state or federal law superseded tribal regulatory authority. A growing and increasingly militant labor movement in the hospitality industry would force the issue as tribes started to develop new plans to expand gaming operations under the terms of IGRA.

Navigating through that legal, racial, and settler-colonial political map, tribes expanded the meaning of sovereignty to include control over the workplaces they created. By the 1990s tribal nations located in densely populated urban areas, such as Southern California, Connecticut, and Central Oklahoma, found themselves on a collision course with unions, state, and federal governments. That conflict created a paradigmatic impasse between sovereignty and civil rights, ideals that framed the social movements important to Native Americans and workers, more broadly. Tribes argued that they had the right to manage their enterprises and that unions were obliged to abide by terms set by tribal law. Non-Native employees, particularly Hotel Employees and Restaurant Employees Union (HERE) and Teamsters disputed those claims and insisted that federal law guaranteed their rights to organize.

The percentage of non-Native workers employed in casinos varies by region. In areas with dense Native American populations and high unemployment, Native workers make up 80 percent of the casino workforce. That percentage falls for casinos located near large urban areas with a majority non-Native population. In 2003, the Harvard Project on American Indian Economic Development reported that 30 percent of the casino workforce in Oklahoma was non-Native. In Southern California casinos, Native workers make up only 10 percent of the casino workforce. According to American Gaming Association data, the two Connecticut tribal casinos employed approximately 26,336 people as of 2023. At the same time, the Mashantucket Pequot Tribe had about 1,100 enrolled members and the Mohegan Tribe about 2,200, for a combined tribal membership of roughly 3,300. The tribes do not publish staff demographics by membership status. But given the large size of the workforce relative to the enrolled population, it is reasonable to infer that tribal members represent a small share of the workforce.[23]

LABOR AND SOVEREIGNTY BATTLEGROUNDS: CALIFORNIA

In the early 1990s, California became the epicenter of this battle. The conflict over Indian gaming during Pete Wilson's terms as governor (1991 to 1999), heightened tensions between tribes and organized labor. Wilson was neither a great friend of the labor movement nor was he interested in complying with IGRA, even though the legislation required him to do so. Nevertheless, the governor made labor a key issue in his opposition to gaming, even though IGRA did not require states to include labor protections in the compacts they negotiated with tribes. Some of Wilson's critics argued that he cynically played tribes and unions against each other to inhibit the negotiating process.[24] Eventually, his refusal to comply with IGRA forced California tribes into court, and when they lost that ruling in 1998, they launched a massive ballot initiative, Proposition 5.[25]

Proposition 5 would have allowed tribes the right to operate class 3—Vegas styled casinos—and would have forced the governor to negotiate a pact. Before they launched this campaign, a few tribes had expanded their gaming operations, including a type of video machine that resembled slot machines. After winning a court battle against the tribes, Wilson's administration threatened to confiscate the machines and shut down their operations. Launching a ballot initiative was the tribes' last resort to maneuver around Wilson and his conservative constituents who wanted to limit their expansion.[26]

The media campaign that followed framed Proposition 5 as a battle between sovereignty and labor rights. The pro-5 forces, the tribes in Southern California who had the most successful gaming establishments, emphasized their sovereignty, and they insisted they had the right to manage their own affairs to insure their own "self-sufficiency." HERE bitterly opposed the initiative and joined forces with an unlikely coalition of religious right-wing conservatives and suburban homeowners.[27] Bankrolled by Nevada gaming interests and organized labor, they disputed tribal depictions of gaming and insisted that the central question was a workers' rights issue, not Native welfare issue. HERE characterized the tribes as anti-labor and as incapable of protecting their employees' rights or ensuring them a safe and equitable workplace. *Los Angeles Times* journalists Hector Tobar and Jenifer Warren characterized the issues surrounding Proposition 5 as a moral trade-off: "How much gaming is enough to guarantee a tribe's self-sufficiency? And if Proposition 5 passes, and Indian gaming becomes an even bigger industry, how much say will non-Native Americans have over crucial issues such as workplace safety and environmental protection?"[28]

The anti 5 media campaign countered the tribes' "self-sufficiency" claims by pointing out the income disparity between other Native Americans and the "rich casino Indians" of Southern California. The notorious TV ad, "The Mansions of San Manuel," insinuated that the tribes were greedy and failed to share their wealth with other, less fortunate American Indians. Placing historical photos of unidentified, impoverished Native people next to contemporary aerial images of the upscale San Manuel homes, nicely landscaped with swimming pools, the "No on 5" commercial implied that gaming tribes were somehow responsible for the poverty of the former. The image implied an underlying question, why should Californians support a system where the minority get rich while "85 percent get nothing." This is an interesting critique of the accumulation of wealth coming from the Nevada gaming industry and conservative Republicans. These images perpetuated a new racial stereotype of the corrupt, "rich Indian," implying, as Alexandra Harmon has described, that wealth was somehow incongruent with Native culture, making them illegitimate or inauthentic.[29] Focusing on San Manuel and other tribes in Southern California, the "No on 5" campaign was trying to undermine the tribes' "social welfare" or self-sufficiency argument. Rich Indians, according to the logic of the campaign, were not worthy of the public's sympathy or support. They certainly were not worthy of "special treatment," as one critic noted. As Ken Ramirez, the vice chair of San Manuel, explained to a *Los Angeles Times* reporter, the ad insinuated that "the only good Indian is a poor Indian."[30] This conflict, fought in the court rooms, the ballot box, and in the media amplifies the disconnect between labor rights, grounded in a civil rights tradition and tribal sovereignty, forged in a settler-colonial context.

This focus on wealth disparity created the perfect opening for the voice of labor to command a legitimate presence. As one of the leading unions in the hospitality industry, HERE was eager to expand. Emboldened by their growing membership, HERE and other unions were ready to organize Indian casinos. But their legal right to do so remained murky. They opposed Proposition 5 because they argued that it did not "sufficiently protect casino workers." Proposition 5 did not mention workers' rights or the rules of collective bargaining at all. Even if voters defeated it, the rights to organize on tribal land would not be settled. That question would not be solved when Californians passed Proposition 5 or when it was later declared unconstitutional. HERE would have to wait for six more years before the union would file a history-making unfair labor practice complaint against the Yaamava' Resort and Casino at San Manuel.

To counter the pro-5 Native welfare argument, HERE's opposition prioritized the rights of non-Native people, often Latino workers, over the sovereignty of wealthy tribes. Calling the initiative "anti-labor," HERE representative Maria Elena Durazo feared that as soon as non-Native people set foot on reservation land, their rights would evaporate. The problem, according to Durazo, was that Proposition 5 did not protect "enforceable rights" of non-Native workers.[31] After all, according to Durazo, "Dishwashers and cooks and housekeepers deserve the same kind of respect for their rights." Allowing tribes to control and regulate their own businesses left non-Native workers vulnerable, without access to state or federal protections. The legendary United Farm Workers leader Dolores Huerta agreed. At a rally to oppose Proposition 5, she explained, "The majority of workers in casinos are not Native Americans.... A large number are Latinos, and they should be protected."[32]

Native American leaders responded with outrage and defended their labor practices. They stressed that their casinos provided jobs that paid better than the market rate, and they expressed their frustration that state officials, particularly Governor Wilson, treated them with contempt, assuming that they were not capable of ethically managing their own companies, and treating their employees with respect.

Reflecting on Proposition 5 and the battle with Pete Wilson, Anthony Pico, chair of the Viejas Band of the Kumeyaay Indians, explained why tribal leaders dug in their heels on the labor issue. Pico thought Wilson and HERE needed to keep in mind that Native people in California had faced their share of racial discrimination in the workplace. He reminded his audience at a California Indian Gaming Summit, "Indians were equally abused by the little guys as well as the rich and powerful. The poor and downtrodden of the world took our lands and our lives as quickly and enthusiastically as any robber baron, Henry Ford, duke, or king." That experience of class and racial discrimination, according to Pico, gave them "greater sensitivity to civil and human rights, feelings and problems of our employees, than most business owner or corporate management." According to Pico, state officials and union leaders simply assumed that Indian casino operators would neglect the welfare of the workers. Beginning negotiations with that assumption, according to Pico, "opens an old wound: The stereotype about how 'Indians can't really do anything as well as Anglos.'"[33]

Tribes tried to keep the focus on the issue on sovereignty rights to counter the argument advanced by the "No on 5" campaign. As George Forman, the leading attorney for the tribes told the Riverside *Press-Enterprise*, "Tribes are not anti-labor." The problem, according to Forman, was the state of California dictating labor policy to "independent tribal governments."[34] David Alvarez, the director of the Yaqui Indian Center, described the problem in grander terms. To a reporter at an Indian youth conference in Fresno, he explained, "Proposition 5 is about self-reliance, sovereignty, privilege, a constitutional right, the freedom to debate and negotiate.... When (outsiders) control gambling, they have control over our lives."[35] Marquez, the former chair of the San Manuel Business Committee, recalled his conversation with a HERE representative at a gaming industry conference. Fondly, he remembered that the union official was "floored" when he told him, "We're not against unions. ... I understand the purpose behind what you're trying to accomplish. We're

Labor Rights or Sovereignty Rights?

just saying, 'Allow us to decide how it unfolds, because it's our sovereign right to do so.' Where is the downside of that?"[36]

Not all unions shared HERE's position. Most notably, the Communications Workers of America (CWA) endorsed Proposition 5 and would soon be the first to sign a collective bargaining agreement with the Viejas Kumeyaay and San Manuel. The CWA developed a reputation as an organization that respected Native Americans and tribal sovereignty. According to Pico, Michael Hartigan, executive vice president of CWA, district 9, treated the tribes with respect, like partners, unlike the HERE organizers, who saw them as adversaries. CWA opposed Governor Wilson's effort to restrict the expansion of gaming. Hartigan told the media that tribes should be able "to expand their operations, just like any other industry." The CWA and Viejas Kumeyaay agreement would serve as a model labor code for other tribes until 2004, when the National Labor Relations Board (NLRB) issued its ruling in response to an unfair labor practice complaint HERE filed against San Manuel.[37]

The conflict between CWA and HERE escalated in the wake of the "No on 5" campaign and sent shock waves throughout Native American communities. Meanwhile, CWA organizers had been meeting with the San Manuel casino workers and encouraging them to sign cards in support of the union. In December 1998, CWA sent a letter to the tribe asking for recognition as the workers' bargaining agent, based on a "card check," a preliminary indicator that a majority of the workers supported the union.[38] Soon thereafter, in January 1999, HERE filed an unfair labor practice lawsuit. The tribe had permitted the CWA to put up a trailer on casino grounds, distribute flyers, and meet with employees during working hours. Since San Manuel tribal officials did not afford similar accommodations to HERE organizers, according to the complaint, the tribe was acting in a prejudicial manner. HERE was not ready to concede ground. As anthropologist David Kamper described, the union participated in a "proactive, aggressive, and innovative labor organizing strategy" that took full advantage of conflicts between tribes and the state government and built on their own momentum from recent success in organizing casino workers in Las Vegas. They had little patience for the tribe's sovereignty argument. Like the United Farm Workers, HERE union campaigns meant more than establishing collective bargaining for employees. Organizing was part of a larger social movement to create a more just society, writ large. Labor rights were akin to civil rights. Sovereignty rights were irrelevant to HERE organizers who, unlike CWA, refused to negotiate with tribal governments on that issue.[39]

San Manuel defiantly responded that they had the right to treat one union differently from another and that the NLRB did not have the jurisdiction to regulate labor relations in tribal enterprises on reservation land. They argued that they had the sovereign rights to create and enforce their own labor laws. Despite their protests and thirty years of case law that had generally supported the autonomy of tribally run enterprises, the NLRB decided against the tribe.[40]

Tribal leaders worried that filing an appeal was risky. Losing in federal court might create a legal precedent that could undermine historic advancements in tribal self-government. And winning the case would validate their sovereignty claims, even though tribal leaders felt their rights were self-evident. Gaming tribes had a lot to lose, given their recent struggle with the California governor. They spent a tremendous amount of money and political capital to gain access to the rights already afforded to them under IGRA. Yet, the political landscape was changing. Californians had elected Gray Davis, a new Democratic governor who was less hostile to tribal needs. He supported an amendment to the state constitution that legalized casino gaming on Native land, and he was beginning to negotiate new state-tribal gaming pacts, albeit, with new labor codes included.

San Manuel had passed its own tribal labor relations ordinances in 1999, which protected workers' rights to join unions and bargain collectively. And, like many states, they instituted a "right-to-work" law that made union membership optional. Most importantly, as summarized in the NLRB ruling, those ordinances "established principles of tribal sovereignty by guaranteeing the primacy of tribal law, ordinances, personnel policies or the tribe's customs and traditions regarding Indian preference in employment, promotion, seniority, lay-offs or retention." The ordinances also established a grievance and dispute resolution procedure. Tribal law protected the rights of workers to strike if the union and management failed to reach an agreement, but it prohibited picketing on reservation land.[41]

Ultimately, the tribe decided to appeal, and in 2007, they lost. The court ruled that labor relations fell under the jurisdiction of the National Labor Relations Act and not under tribal law. What began as a turf war between unions competing for members in 1998 ended in 2007 with a US Court of Appeals decision that significantly challenged the sovereignty of tribal governments to develop and enforce their own labor policies. The implications of the court decision have been profound for non-Native casino employees and tribal governments. Tribal officials see this development as having narrowed the scope of their governing authority. In fact, Judge Janice Brown, in her opinion for the court, asserted a rather restrictive definition of sovereignty. In a somewhat patronizing tone, she acknowledged that the principle of tribal sovereignty "exists as a matter of respect for Indian communities." But, according to Brown, while the federal government intended to give tribal communities some "latitude" in internal affairs, it did not intend to grant tribes "absolute autonomy, permitting [them] to operate in a commercial capacity without legal constraint." To Brown, Native people had the sovereign right "to maintain traditional customs and practices" but not to operate a successful enterprise outside the grasp of US law.[42] Tribal government activities and cultural traditions were distinct from commercial enterprises. Previously, the Cabazon tribe had successfully argued the opposite. They defended their right to operate a gaming establishment to provide funds for the operation of their tribal government. In fact, the tribe argued, gambling had been part of their cultural traditions for centuries.[43]

Like earlier efforts to undermine Native American sovereignty such as by termination, the Dawes Act, and even under the Indian New Deal, when the federal government imposed a governing model on all Native nations, tribal leaders throughout the United States saw this as serious usurpation of their right to govern and to develop their own economies.[44] San Manuel tribal chair Henry Duro worried that this ruling undermined the ability of tribes to provide their members with education, health care, and housing—services that have been largely funded with gaming revenue.[45] But the case clearly highlighted the precarity of sovereignty and the ultimate contradictions in operating a casino under the guidelines provided in IGRA. For Native leaders, casino operations promised to yield significant capital and strengthen their governing institutions. But to do so, they were obliged to cede power to federal and state authorities. After the San Manuel ruling, if they acknowledged the NLRB's jurisdictional claims, they would lose the power to establish their own labor law. If they acknowledged federal authority and conceded some regulatory power to states in gaming pacts, they might see their claims to sovereignty constrained. Waiting in the wings were unions such as the United Auto Workers (UAW), HERE, the Food and Commercial Workers, and the Teamsters who felt encouraged by the ruling and were ready to beef up their organizing efforts in the Indian gaming industry. This case did not resolve the conflict between unions who articulated their rights to organize and tribal governments who maintained their sovereignty rights—their rights to self-governance.[46]

LABOR AND SOVEREIGNTY BATTLEGROUNDS: CONNECTICUT AND THE MASHANTUCKET PEQUOT

In the wake of the San Manuel decision, the reach of federal labor law seemed clear. Workers in some of the largest casinos in Indian country started union organizing drives. In 2007, the Teamsters launched two campaigns in Michigan: at the Little River Casino, operated by the Little River Band of Ottawa Indians, and at the Saginaw Chippewa's Soaring Eagle Resort and Casino. Three years later, the Teamsters would attempt to organize the Chickasaw's WinStar World Casino in Thackerville, Oklahoma. Meanwhile in Connecticut, the UAW, the Laborers International, and the United Food and Commercial Workers Union (UFCWU), responded to workers' complaints at the Mashantucket Pequot Foxwoods Casino. Despite what seemed to be a judicial mandate in California, union leaders discovered that the question of labor rights versus sovereignty rights was far from settled, regardless of court rulings. In the end, the historical context of each battle would play an important role in determining whose rights were protected.

The Mashantucket Pequots had strongly resisted colonial encroachment on their land, and they defended their place in the fur trade in the early seventeenth century. But they were nearly wiped out in 1637 when English colonists and their Native allies set fire to their fortified camp, near the Mystic River. The few who survived were sold into slavery and others dispersed.[47] In the 300 years that followed the massacre, the Pequots persisted, even as their lands were whittled away, confiscated by the state, and neglected by the federal government. By 1972 a single resident, Elizabeth George, a respected elder of the tribe, remained on the last few acres of the original tract of land that had been set aside for the tribe in the mid-nineteenth century. According to popular memory, she maintained the tribe's land claims by simply staying put. There she lived in a dilapidated farmhouse, without electricity and running water, with her dogs for company, and a shotgun for protection. She would not live to see her tribe's renaissance.[48]

In the 1970s a new, energetic generation of Native American activists were ready to test the limits of a shifting federal Indian policy. Richard "Skip" Hayward, Elizabeth George's grandson, embodied that spirit. Elected as president of the Mashantucket Pequot Tribal Nation (MPTN) in 1975, he sued the State of Connecticut for restoration of the tribe's lands, which had been illegally sold in 1856, without the consent of the federal government. The tribe's legal challenges garnered enough leverage that by 1983, they

Foxwoods Resort Casino in Mashantucket, Connecticut, August 2008, as seen from the observation tower of the Mashantucket Pequot Museum. Photograph by Stilfehler. Courtesy Wikimedia Commons.

were able to negotiate a land settlement from the state and secure federal recognition from Congress, bypassing the stultifying federal recognition process.[49] As the MPTN pursued its legal challenges, the tribe was beginning to rebuild their economic base, seeking grants to fund the development of new housing on the reservation, and cultivating small industries including crafts, maple syrup, cord wood, and produce grown in a hydroponic greenhouse. Tribal members built on their success and pursued other business ventures, opening a restaurant, a sand and gravel business, and in 1986, a bingo operation.[50]

Reorganizing their tribal government, rebuilding their community, and accumulating capital from their budding industries, the MPTN was poised to take advantage of IGRA. Like the California tribes, the MPTN had to struggle with a hostile state government that wanted to prohibit Las Vegas– and Atlantic City–style gambling within its borders. Even so, in 1990, the Mashantucket Pequots won their case in federal district court, and the Connecticut governor was obliged to negotiate a state compact. Two years later, the MPTN opened Foxwoods, a massive state-of-the-art casino, considered to be one of the largest in the world.

The casino was a tremendous success and earned the MPTN the reputation as "the Richest Indian Tribe in History."[51] In its first fourteen years, tribal members, the State of Connecticut, and casino workers enjoyed a relatively harmonious relationship. The casino created great wealth for the tribe and for individual tribal members, and it gave a significant boost to the regional economy that had been hit hard by a reduction in defense spending in the 1990s. Entertaining 40,000–70,000 customers a day, the casino inspired new tourist related businesses in the region. The State of Connecticut, which had originally opposed the casino, collected 25 percent of slot machine revenues, banking $1 billion between 1993 and 2000.[52] University of Connecticut economists reported that in its first seven years of operation, Foxwoods directly and indirectly generated 13,000 jobs.[53]

Between 1992 and 2007, the MPTN enthusiastically shared its wealth with its non-Native workforce. Employees enjoyed good wages, health insurance, and worked regular, predictable shifts, a rarity in the food and beverage industry. The casino hosted holiday parties and picnics and handed out complimentary tickets to Six Flags or Lake Compounce (a local theme park), as a way of thanking them for doing a good job.[54] One Foxwoods cocktail waitress fondly remembered recruitment ads that invited workers to "come be part of Foxwoods' family." To her, those words felt sincere. "You really did feel like you were family," she said in an interview with the author in 2012. "You felt like they really, really cared. . . . Seriously, it was an awesome place."[55] She worked "the front of the house," serving cocktails to a regular clientele, six hours a day, five days a week, and made "good money doing it." Most importantly, the job allowed her time to care for her children. She remembered telling her friends, "You will never find a better company to work for than what I have."[56] In fact, working conditions were so good in the early years of the casino's operation that unions struggled to generate interest. When the UAW tried to organize the casino in 1998, they found few takers. Eight years later, that sense of harmony would begin to erode.

The casino continued to enjoy great economic success until "the stinking domino-effect of bad decisions," as described by MPTN communications director Lori Potter, left the tribe drowning in debt.[57] Foxwood's CEO Scott Butera explained to Michael Sokolove, a *New York Times* reporter, "We have six layers of creditors and, within each layer, 20 to 40 institutions." The tribe struggled to meet their debt obligations but could not rely on the usual financial structures that corporations use to satisfy lenders. They could not sell real estate or liquidate their assets, and they were not eligible for Chapter 11 protection. As Butera said, "It was sort of like being stuck in no man's land." To make things worse, customer traffic was down. The economic crisis that started in 2007 cautioned New Englanders from spending their discretionary income on luxury items such as gambling and cultural tourism.[58]

FROM THE FOXWOODS FAMILY TO FOXWOODS TEAM MEMBER

Between 2007 and 2012, the "Foxwoods Family" evolved, according to management rhetoric, into the "Foxwoods team." That shift—from a benevolent to a more corporate philosophy, at least from the workers' perspective—reflected the MPTN's rising economic problems. The MPTN was attempting to address its growing financial stress by hiring a series of management consultants and a revolving door of CEOs (seven between 2007 and 2012) to carry out austerity measures and improve the casino's brand. That meant building a new, glitzy addition to the casino, the MGM Grand Tower, and updating the casino's management style. Gone were the free amusement park tickets, Christmas bonuses, and amiable worker-management relations. Management wanted a more glamorous look in the "front of the house" that would attract a younger, wealthier clientele. Joan Vennoch, a *Boston Globe* reporter, characterized Butera's efforts to attract younger patrons and "bigger spenders," and to not simply cater to the "busloads of senior citizens who show up with walkers and oxygen tanks." Updating the brand was important because, as Butera quipped, "those darn elders don't gamble away enough of their money."[59] Butera, a former executive vice president of Trump Enterprises, was considered a turn-around expert for the casino industry, responsible for restructuring Trump's failing Atlantic City operation. He may have been an expert at restructuring debt, but during his tenure, he managed to spark a senior citizen boycott of the casino, and he gave hospitality workers more reasons to seek the protection of a union.[60]

Even before Scott Butera arrived at Foxwoods in 2010, workers were beginning to lose confidence in management. Three years earlier, when the UAW returned, they found workers much more receptive than they had been in 1998. The workers were beginning to worry that the casino's economic woes were going to translate into cuts in wages, jobs, and benefits. Since the San Manuel decision had seemingly clarified the legal jurisdiction of the NLRB over tribal industries, the door seemed to be open to organize Foxwoods.

In 2007, the table game dealers who made up about one-third of the casino workforce were the first to organize. The cocktail servers and bartenders followed soon thereafter. After a six-month campaign, they voted 1,289 to 852 in support of the UAW, despite protests from MPTN leaders that the NLRB did not have jurisdiction on their land. On August 16, 2007, the tribe enacted the Mashantucket Pequot Labor Relations Law (MPLRL).[61] Closely modeled on the National Labor Relations Act, the legislation guaranteed workers the right to form unions, but it included a type of "right-to-work" provision that that allowed workers to enjoy union benefits without joining the union and paying dues. The law also prohibited MPTN workers from striking or engaging in secondary boycotts—provisions similar to those that limit the rights of state employees throughout the United States—and aimed to prevent work stoppages that might undermine the government's ability to function.[62]

After the election, the union and MPTN continued to struggle over jurisdictional issues. For the next year, MPTN leaders continued to assert their sovereignty rights to establish and enforce labor law, and they refused to negotiate a contract. The MPTN appealed the NLRB's decision to uphold the election, but the NLRB agreed with the UAW; and on September 30, 2008, the NLRB ordered the MPTN to negotiate a contract with the union. The MPTN responded by filing an appeal to the US Court of Appeals, 2nd Circuit. But rather than continuing the fight in court, the tribe and the union found a solution to the impasse. The MPTN recognized the union, and the UAW agreed to negotiate a contract under tribal law, marking a historic moment in union-tribal relations.[63] In the end, they produced a precedent-making compromise that protected MPTN sovereignty and the rights of workers to organize. The union agreed to abide by tribal laws, and the MPTN addressed workers' concerns and created an impartial third-party arbitration panel that could be used to address workers' complaints. MPTN officials and union leaders lauded that agreement as a middle ground that might offer a model for union-tribal relations throughout the country.[64]

That balance did not last long. In January 2008, bartenders and cocktail servers at Foxwoods contacted the United Food and Commercial Workers (UFCW) union. The union had previously attempted to organize Foxwoods in 1998 but at the time had generated little interest among the workers. Their campaign followed a similar story as HERE's, the service workers' union that had successfully organized casino workers in Atlantic City and Las Vegas. HERE representatives told local press that Foxwoods and Mohegan Sun employees were concerned about their lack of control over the workplace. According to HERE organizer Laura Moye, reservations workers were at a disadvantage. They could not rely on federal labor laws to protect their safety and guarantee fair wages. According to Moye, "When you work on the reservation, you don't have that. . . . The power is completely out of proportion."[65] But the union's efforts failed to gather momentum. Keri Hohne, a UFCW organizer, explained that in the mid-1990s, people were thrilled to work at Foxwoods, since the region was suffering from a shutdown of major industries.

"There was [sic] a lot of people out of work," Hohne explained, "and it was a really awesome job for people, you know, very rich health insurance benefits and you couldn't get people in the door fast enough." MPTN leaders reacted strongly and threatened to sue the union and alerted the governor's office. So, the union withdrew.[66]

By 2008, the landscape had changed. The casino's financial problems and questionable management decisions worried workers. Adding more glamour and updating the brand seemed to threaten workers' job security and ignited enough anger to turn reluctant union members into firebrand activists. The San Manuel decision seemed to have settled the NLRB jurisdiction issue, and the UAW's success emboldened the UFCW. So, when the cocktail servers and bartenders at Foxwoods contacted the union, they were ready for the fight.[67] A hapless food and beverage manager provided the catalyst. He pulled one of the older cocktail servers aside and suggested that she move to another type of job. According to Linda Meyer, a fellow cocktail server, the manager then told her, "Well you know, we were thinking for the older gals that we're going to start career counseling, so that we can get you doing something else other than cocktailing."[68] News of that interaction stoked workers' fears that the casino was planning to replace older cocktail servers, many of whom had been working at Foxwoods for twenty years, with younger women. According to Meyer, "They didn't want to see us older gals cocktailing anymore. Well, that was it; when that was let out of the bag, . . . the [union campaign] began again."[69] Up to that point, the waiters had accommodated the managers' plans to update their looks, including wearing bustiers and bolero jackets. Meyer thought that management's introduction of a sexier uniform was meant to force out some of the older workers. But, as Meyer explained to me in our 2012 interview, the women were not deterred. "It doesn't matter. Three hundred-pound girls are wearing them, Meyer laughed." But she and others remained vigilant in their opposition to wearing high heels. Later, when the union won their election, she made shoes a significant negotiating issue.

The workers' fears about job security clashed with the MTPN's concern for protecting its sovereignty. The MTPN continued to insist that the unions respect tribal laws, and they rejected the premise that the San Manuel decision had settled the NLRB jurisdictional question. When the UFCW initially notified the MTPN they were planning to file for an election, the union agreed to hold an election under the new tribal labor laws. But, according to union sources, on the day of the election, the tribe insisted that the union needed to win a majority of the total number of workers in the unit and not simply a majority of those who voted. Counting the people who did not vote as "no votes," the union lost the election.[70]

Their faith in tribal law shaken, the union decided to file again, this time under the NLRB. Meanwhile, the MPTN amended its labor laws. Like the TERO laws the CTER had advocated, the MPTN ordinances provided hiring "preference in employment opportunities . . . first to tribal members, next to spouses of tribal members and third to Native Americans who are not Tribal Members. Generally, employment opportunities include hire, transfer, training, promotion, and retention." To that the MPTN now added, preference in shift assignments.[71] Up to that point, according to union activists, non-Native employees were not troubled by preference laws. They expected tribal members to receive priority in hiring, and as a union organizer recalled, they were not worried about being displaced since there were so few tribal members working in the casino. But they did not expect tribal preference to undermine the seniority system to which the employees (Native and non-Native) were accustomed. Periodically, shifts, hours, and work locations would be opened for "rebidding." Workers submitted their requests, and management accommodated their choices based on each employee's seniority. For those in tip-dependent jobs, Friday and Saturday nights were the most lucrative. Others limited their hours to a schedule that accommodated childcare responsibilities. Older cocktail servers tried to avoid shifts where they worked the slot machine floor, because the volume of service in that area was so physically demanding. The workers with the least seniority might find themselves left with overnight shifts, limited to serving warm milk or coffee, since the casino did not serve alcohol after 2 a.m.[72]

The MPTN's financial problems and floor management decisions increased workers' discontent. Casino managers wanted to move the cocktail servers into full rotation, rather than allowing them to bid for particular work assignments, fundamentally undercutting the seniority system the workers cherished. Then, on July 1, 2010, three weeks before the election, the MPTN announced a plan to end incentive payments (also known as per capita payments) for its members by the end of the year. When that news filtered through the casino workforce and the surrounding community, tribal preference laws suddenly became a key issue in the union's election campaign. If MPTN members were no longer going to receive their part of casino profits, the workers feared, tribal members would begin looking for casino jobs. Since preference laws now included shift choices, union activists believed MPTN members would move ahead of the line and make the seniority system irrelevant.[73]

In the weeks leading up to the election, union activists amplified their concerns on social media and distributed flyers that warned their fellow workers that tribal preference laws and the end of incentive payments threatened their seniority system. For them, the union promised job security.[74] In Facebook posts, union activists warned: "LOOK OUT! Because change is coming. It is going to surely happen to all of us if you do not protect yourself now! . . . Tribal stipends will be cut in January. . . . translation: every one of our jobs are on the line. They will come to work here and are going to take tipped positions like mine and yours. So if you are seniority 20 you may become seniority 40 overnight. They will come in and take your job."[75] Other posts stressed that workers needed a union supported by federal labor laws because they did not feel their interests were protected by the tribe. Stressing the importance of an NLRB-supervised election, one union activist claimed, "Having this protection is our right. We have to abide by federal laws, don't we? We pay federal taxes, don't we?" Even though federal labor laws and the NLRB itself had not always sided with unions, these workers felt that an NLRB election was a right guaranteed to them as US citizens.[76] They saw their right to an NLRB election as extending to them equal protection under the law, a civil right. Workers felt skeptical, at best, that the MPTN could provide that type of protection. As one union activist explained to me, the workers felt they were subject to a legal double standard. As an American, she was subject to the laws and tax responsibilities of the US, but at work, she did not enjoy the legal protection of her government. She simply rejected the notion that a tribe's sovereignty included jurisdiction over her work life. As she related to me, "Basically you're telling me that I work in another country, okay? If I'm working in another country, why am I paying U.S. taxes? We have kids coming in here from Czechoslovakia, Romania, from wherever to work at Foxwoods—they don't pay taxes. So, then I'm coming in from my country too then—why am I paying taxes?"

In the end, casino workers were worried enough to support the union. On July 31, 2010, the union won their election 190 to 145. Shortly after, the MPTN filed an appeal with the NLRB, claiming that the union's use of racially charged rhetoric in the election constituted an unfair labor practice. They argued that Facebook messages and flyers that mentioned tribal preference and incentive payment issues were meant to inflame racial tensions. In particular, tribal attorneys pointed to rhetoric that referred to the tribe as "they" or "them" as a threat to the workers' job security, as evidence of a union-supported racist campaign.

From the perspective of the MPTN, the workers' response might have been reminiscent of the type of backlash the tribe experienced from the surrounding community during the initial struggle to gain recognition and to open Foxwoods. The union activists' words might have seemed reminiscent of anti-Indian rhetoric in popular culture that dismissed Native sovereignty claims as illegitimate. Indeed, their rhetoric may have seemed racist, given the historic racial antipathy directed at MPTN tribal members from surrounding communities. Certainly, echoes of Donald Trump's 1993 remarks at a congressional committee hearing continued to trouble the community. In his characteristically uninformed, rhetorical style, Trump rejected the notion of sovereignty, and wielded racist, age-old blood quantum, language: "If you look at some of the reservations that you have approved. . . . I will tell you right now, they don't look like Indians to me."[77]

A judge evaluating the election rhetoric found no specifically racial references to the MPTN or to Native Americans in general. The tribe found the use of "them, their, and they," to be racially coded, yet similar language might be found in other kinds of labor struggles where workers and management were locked in an adversarial relationship. The judge decided that because of the publicity around the MPTN's plans to end incentive payments, workers had a valid reason to be concerned about their jobs. "They," "them," and "their" might easily refer to bosses rather than Native Americans. In this case, the workers conflated the MPTN with Foxwoods management, and a critique of management became a critique of the tribe. The workers were horrified by the MPTN charges of racism and strongly denied they were using racism to gain support for the union.[78]

After two years of appeals and conversations, the union conceded and filed for a new election under tribal law. Even though they had won the 2010 election, union organizers knew that the MPTN would never agree on the NLRB issue. So, in May of 2011, the union held another election, this time under MPTN labor law. Two years later, they ratified their first contract.[79]

LABOR AND SOVEREIGNTY BATTLEGROUNDS: OKLAHOMA

In October 2010, a non-Native blackjack dealer from the Chickasaw's WinStar World Casino in Thackerville called the Teamsters' office in Oklahoma City. He was hoping he might arrange for an organizer to come out and talk with him and a few of his non-Native coworkers. They were not happy with their work environment at WinStar and did not trust the casino's management to

Winstar World Casino in Thackerville, Oklahoma, September 2012. Photograph by Kym Koch Thompson. Courtesy Wikimedia Commons.

treat them fairly. For example, they complained that the casino was requiring them to work thirty hours per week to maintain their health insurance. If they worked less, they would lose coverage. The workers felt they had little control over the number of hours they worked since the Chickasaw Nation set the schedule and, from their perspective, "played favorites." The blackjack dealers were also upset with the casino's imposition of a new "tote" committee that redistributed tips. The tote committee, which did not include the blackjack dealers, collected all tips and was supposed to divide them up equally among the employees. When the employees received less money than they normally collected on each shift, the workers grew suspicious that the group was skimming off a percentage for themselves. The blackjack dealers, in particular, felt they were earning less money now than they had under the old system that allowed them to take home the tips they earned individually. A teamster organizer explained, "Well at that point they decided they couldn't hardly make a living doing this anymore, like they used to. Things were getting bad."[80]

At their first meeting with the blackjack dealers, in Gainesville, Texas, across the border from the casino, the organizer was surprised to find the workers wearing sunglasses and disguises. They covered their faces with scarves, "and it wasn't that cold that day," remembered one organizer. They asked the union representative to show his credentials, and when they finally started to feel at ease, they revealed their faces. According to the organizer, the workers were terrified that they might lose their jobs if casino management found out they were talking to the union.[81]

The initial group of would-be union activists grew from three or four members to about twenty over the course of two months. Feeling stronger and more confident, they decided to launch a card-signing campaign, an initial effort meant to rally support and gauge the mood of the rest of their coworkers. If they collected enough cards indicating interest in the union, they could request a formal election, overseen by the NLRB, where their fellow blackjack dealers could decide for themselves if they wanted the Teamsters to represent them.[82] But the Teamsters local had a lot of questions. They had never organized casino workers in Oklahoma, and they were not sure if they could legally define the 400 blackjack workers as a bargaining unit. Their biggest question, and one of historical proportions, had to do with the issue of sovereignty and the jurisdictional reach of federal labor law.

They would soon have their answers but not legal clarity. Casino managers responded quickly by questioning employees, singling out workers who had signed cards, and holding captive audience meetings to discourage involvement in the union.[83] The Teamsters then filed unfair labor practice complaints with the NLRB, charging the casino with "unlawful surveillance of union activities, interrogation of employees regarding union activity, and an unlawful no-solicitation policy." Instead of battling it out in a NLRB hearing, as the San Manuel tribe had done, Chickasaw leaders filed a lawsuit in US District Court, requesting an injunction to halt the NLRB's investigation. They asserted that the NLRB did not have jurisdiction over labor issues in tribal enterprises and that, therefore, the board's inquiries were illegal.[84]

That shrewd legal maneuver halted union organizing and achieved what other tribal gaming officials had been trying to accomplish throughout the United States. The court granted an injunction to the Chickasaws, and the NLRB postponed their investigation. Since the San Manuel ruling in 2007, other tribes had resisted union organizing in their casinos and faced courts much less sympathetic than the US District Court in Oklahoma. Two years before the first meeting with the WinStar blackjack dealers, another Teamsters local had tried to organize workers in Michigan, at the Little River Casino and Resort, an enterprise operated by the Little River Band of Ottawa Indians (Gaaching Ziibi Daawaa Anishinaabe). As a prelude to the Chickasaw case, the Teamsters' Local 406 had filed an unfair labor practice complaint. They argued that the tribe's Fair Employment Practices Code contradicted protections afforded workers under the National Labor Relations Act (NLRA).[85]

Meanwhile, as the courts slogged forward, partisan political infighting in Washington, DC, complicated all NLRB business. Another case, also involving the Teamsters but not tribal enterprises, inadvertently called into question pending cases involving the NLRB. In 2010, the NLRB ruled that Noel Canning, a Pepsi distributor in Yakima, Washington, was guilty of an unfair labor practice when it refused to bargain with the union in good faith and to comply with the terms of a collective bargaining agreement. The company protested, arguing that the NLRB's decision was invalid because the board did not have a quorum of legally appointed members. To avoid Republican Party opposition, President Obama had appointed board members while Congress was not in session. Eventually, the US Supreme Court ruled in favor of Noel Canning and declared President Obama's recess appointments between 2010 and January 2012 illegal. Lawyers, businesspeople, and union leaders across the country scrambled to take advantage of the new legal and political landscape, calling on courts to revisit earlier rulings and drafting new appeals to cases under consideration. The fate of workers, their unions, and industries lay in wait as the Republicans attempted to fulfill their promise to stall President Obama's legislative and administrative agenda.[86]

The Little River Band of Ottawa Indians had previously signed labor agreements—under tribal law—with unions including the United Steelworkers.[87] In 2013, under a newly constituted board, the NLRB ruled against the tribe. When the tribe appealed the decision, the 6th District Court of Appeals in Michigan refused to issue an injunction. The tribe was obliged to abide by NLRB rules and follow its administrative process before it could appeal to the federal courts.[88] Appalled at the court's decision, Tribal Council Speaker Steve Parsons told the press, "The federal government should be doing all that it can to protect tribal sovereignty, self-determination and self-sufficiency. This ruling is in utter disregard to the Band's sovereignty and ability to govern its own affairs."[89]

In 2015, after the NLRB appealed the Chickasaws' initial victory in federal court and the fallout of the Noel Canning case was starting to settle, the Chickasaws and the Teamsters were back to arguing their case before a new NLRB panel. The tribe continued to assert that the NLRB did not have jurisdiction. This time they used treaty law to make their case, and the board ruled in their favor. This panel seemed to overturn *San Manuel Indian Bingo and Casino v. NLRB* (2007), the federal court ruling that stressed the "general applicability" of federal law to include reservations, unless otherwise noted. Siding with the Chickasaws, this new NLRB panel argued that specific treaty provisions *protected* the tribe from federal law, instead of including them, *except* for congressional legislation that was intended to apply to Native Americans. Citing the 1830 Treaty of Dancing Rabbit Creek, a notorious removal treaty that required the Chickasaws to cede their lands in Mississippi in exchange for land in Oklahoma, the judges argued that any ambiguity of the law should be decided in favor of the tribe. The court was convinced that applying the NLRA to the Chickasaws would undermine provisions in the treaty including "the right to exclude or place conditions on the presence of those permitted in tribal territory" and "the Nation's treaty rights to self-government." In addition, the 1866 Treaty of Washington, negotiated at the end of the Civil War, secured the Chickasaws the right to be "'secure from and against all laws' except those passed by Congress under its authority over Indian affairs."[90]

Legal experts, tribal officials, and union leaders remained puzzled by the contradictory rulings. Trying to make sense out of the different outcomes, Kaighn Smith, an expert in Native labor law, explained the contradiction as a difference in regional judicial histories. According to Smith, federal courts located in Oklahoma tend to favor tribal sovereignty when laws do not explicitly apply to Native Americans. But in other areas of the country, such as California, the courts tend to be less sympathetic to sovereignty arguments.[91]

Perhaps the strong history of organized labor in Michigan might explain the court's Little River and Soaring Eagle decisions. After all, the militant labor movement that emerged out of the industrial manufacturing industries in Michigan, most notably the auto industry, led to the development of the NLRA in 1935. Even though Detroit's dominance in the auto industry has waned, and the influence of the UAW is not what it used to be, the legacy of labor's importance might seem more familiar to judges and possibly more significant than sovereignty issues. Of course, that is purely conjecture. But it is clear that the Oklahoma judges drew on the history of Chickasaw dispossession and removal as part of their decision. The Little River and Soaring Eagle decision relies largely on labor case law, with little concern for the history of Native peoples in Michigan. These cases demonstrate the precarious nature of sovereignty, which seems to be subject to variances in the historical political climate.

The San Manuel and Little River decisions upheld the jurisdiction of the NLRA, the Chickasaw case seemed to offer a boost to tribal governments who argue that they have the rights to make and administer tribal labor law, beyond the reach of the NLRA. Most observers assumed that the Supreme Court would offer clarity by agreeing to hear those cases. They hoped a Supreme Court decision would solve the split decision between the 6th and 10th US District Courts. Keith Brodie, an expert in labor law, predicted in a 2015 blog post: "The issue of NLRB jurisdiction over Indian Tribes is not going away soon."[92] Indeed, confusion remains. In 2016, the Supreme Court declined to take up the issue.[93] With the courts refusing to weigh in on the tension between labor rights and sovereignty rights, the battle between unions and American Indian leaders moved to the floors of Congress.

THE TRIBAL LABOR SOVEREIGNTY ACT

On January 4, 2005, Arizona congressman J. D. Hayworth tried to offer a solution to the San Manuel problem. He introduced legislation that he claimed would demonstrate to Native people that the United States of America trusts a "sovereign tribal government to treat its employees fairly."[94] HR 16, The Tribal Labor Relations Restoration Act, was meant to override the 2004 NLRB San Manuel ruling that extended its jurisdiction to include Indian-owned and operated businesses on reservation lands. The legislation's title implies that a self-evident sovereignty right, one that protects a tribe's authority to regulate labor conditions, existed prior to the latest NLRB ruling. As a result, according to Representative Hayworth, the legislation would set the record straight and "insert simple but necessary clarification" that tribally owned and operated businesses on reservation land were never meant to be governed under the NLRA.[95]

Many American Indian communities, including the leadership of the National Congress of American Indians (NCAI) joined Congressman Hayworth in denouncing the labor board's decision. Joe Garcia, NCAI president and the governor of Ohkay Owingeh (San Juan Pueblo), registered his support for HR 16 "solely because it confirms the sovereign governmental right of Indian tribes to make and live by their own labor policies based on the economic and social conditions existing on their lands." In his testimony before the House Committee on Education and the Workforce, he reminded committee members that a recent federal district court ruling involving his community affirmed those rights. That case, *NLRB v. Pueblo of San Juan*, established that the tribe did have the authority to enact a "right-to-work" ordinance, a measure enacted by the tribal government to protect itself from disruptive union activity such as strikes and to enforce Indian hiring preferences.[96]

Needless to say, Hayworth's solution was not going to be simple. This was not Hayworth's first attempt at shielding Native communities from federal labor law. Previously, in October 1999, he introduced HR 2992 to amend IGRA, exempting what he called "coerced labor agreements," in tribal/state gaming pacts. Presumably, he was attempting to subvert compromises such as California governor Gray Davis's attempt to broker a deal between unions and tribes by including labor provisions in tribal-state gaming pacts. Like Hayworth's earlier bill, that legislation failed. In 2001 he introduced it again, this time as the Tribal Sovereignty Protection Act, renumbered as HR 103.

Hayworth arrived in Washington, DC, in 1995, as part of new class of uncompromising, right-wing freshmen congressmen who supported Newt Gingrich's "contract with America." Pro-business and hostile to civil rights legislation, Hayworth's connection to Native American issues seemed to have been a purely personal financial concern. With casino interests significantly featured on his list of financial backers, Hayworth was one of the few legislators who refused to return what many of his critics viewed as money tainted by its connection with the notorious lobbyist Jack Abramoff.[97] But the lobbyists did not get their money's worth with Hayworth. In 2006, his congressional career was cut short when he lost his bid for reelection. During his six terms in office, he failed to pass legislation that would exempt tribal governments from the reach of federal labor law.

Congress did little to advance legislation on tribal labor during the Obama administration. While a few Democrats supported legislation like Hayworth's bills, opposition from organized labor generally kept other such bills stalled in committee. In 2015 Senator Jerry Moran of Kansas and Representative Todd Rokita of Indiana introduced the Tribal Labor Sovereignty Act, SB 248 and HR 511, in their respective chambers. They defended their bills as simply extending to tribes the same privileges that state and local governments enjoyed. As Senator Moran explained on the Senate floor in 2015, "This legislation seeks to treat tribal governments no differently than other units of local government, counties, and cities."[98] His bill was supposed to "prevent an unnecessary and unproductive overreach by the NLRB into the sovereign jurisdiction of tribal governments."[99] The bill passed the House, but with President Barak Obama's tacit opposition, Democrats managed to block it in the Senate.[100] In a policy statement, President Obama indicated that he would support a bill that recognized sovereignty and exempted tribes from NLRB jurisdiction "only if the tribes adopt labor standards and procedures . . . equivalent to those in the National Labor Relations Act."[101] Perhaps legislators assumed that the 2007 DC Court of Appeals ruling on San Manuel had settled the issue once and for all. Nevertheless, President Obama's position would prevail, at least for the remainder of his time in office. In fact, several tribal governments such as the Mashantucket Pequot, the San Manuel, and others in Southern California had been developing those types of laws since the struggle over Proposition 5. Yet the conflict between unions and tribal government continued. As of 2025, final reversal of San Manuel remains in limbo, even with a Republican majority in Congress and a president with his own sordid history in the casino industry.

The political landscape during the first Trump administration seemed to pave the way for the Tribal Labor Sovereignty Act. But a stealthy political maneuver, possibly meant to embarrass Democrats and derail Arizona Senator Flake's last months in office, created unforeseen obstacles. Republican House members amended Senator Jeff Flake's bill, S 140, a measure meant to improve reservation infrastructure, to include the text of the Tribal Labor Sovereignty Act. Flake's original bill was much less controversial, unrelated to casinos or labor, and enjoyed bipartisan support. It encouraged American Indian economic development by allowing the Ohkay Owingeh and the Pueblo of Santa Clara to grant 99-year leases on their lands, and it assisted the White Mountain Apache to improve their drinking water. Viewing the new amendment to the original bill as anti-labor, many Democrats voted against it. Congressman Grijalva (D-AZ) condemned the Republicans' act for derailing an important economic development bill with a "political stunt." Nevertheless, the bill passed the House 229 to 173, largely along partisan lines. The bill returned to the Senate, for reconsideration and died.[102]

During Joe Biden's administration, Congress failed to pass a law that would have overturned the San Manuel ruling. Organized labor, one of Biden's major constituencies, managed to rally the votes to defeat a 2018 version of the earlier legislation.[103] Republican Senator Jerry Moran from Kansas and Republican Representative John Moolenaar of Michigan introduced a new version of the bill in 2023. At the time of this writing, the 2023 bill's fate remains unclear, particularly under a second Trump administration.

This is not a traditional labor history story. Tribes are not corporations and unions are learning to navigate a new kind of legal landscape. Tribes are trying to ensure their community's survival and to secure their sovereignty rights, and unions are trying to protect workers' civil rights. Those difficult battles, fought in the anti-colonial terrain of work and the workplace, are part of the long and often-painful process of decolonization that started in the twentieth century. Developing new institutions that preserve collective lands and tribes' distinctive economic and political power is one chapter of a much longer conflict.

What does the conflict over federal labor law jurisdiction have to do with the transformation of work on American Indian lands? What does it have to say about the relationship between jobs and sovereignty? In an early chapter of the book, I tell the story about the movement to gain access to jobs in reservation industries, such as mining, construction, and energy. I argue that Native Americans' efforts to secure those jobs broadened the concept of sovereignty, extending it beyond political and cultural dimensions to include control over work.

This chapter advances the narrative into an era of profound economic development and of American Indian governments' growing political influence. Gaming has strengthened American Indian nations' resolve to establish government-to-government relationships with states and Washington, DC. Whether tribes develop new labor codes that non-Native people will accept remains an open question. Sorting out who controls the conditions of labor on reservation lands predates recent developments of large-scale Indian gaming operations and will undoubtedly take more than a simple revision of the 1935 NLRA.

CONCLUSION

Sovereignty Rights and Work

ANTI-COLONIAL HISTORY IN THE MAKING

We have a lot of work to do.

NATIVE LABOR ORGANIZER ATTENDING A
CTER CONFERENCE, DECEMBER 12, 2012

In December 2012, Jacqueline Berrien, the chair of the EEOC, addressed the annual legal update conference of the CTER in a ballroom of a Las Vegas casino. In the audience were about 300 tribal officials from across the country who were engaged in developing programs and governing structures meant to improve the lives of Native American workers within the reach of their tribal governments. Berrien, an African American woman and an Obama appointee, was there to promote a Memo of Understanding between the CTER and the EEOC. She strongly praised the EEOC's track record in protecting worker's rights and outlined how tribes could benefit from what the EEOC had to offer: workshops for tribal officials on how to enforce federal antidiscrimination laws and help from the EEOC in developing non-discrimination ordinances.

One might have expected an enthusiastic response from a room full of tribal labor officials whose communities had suffered from a legacy of high unemployment and racial discrimination, particularly in towns bordering reservations. Instead, they responded in whispers and moans. Several officials walked into the adjoining hallway and complained to their colleagues about the latest initiative the federal government was trying to shove down their throats.

Berrien appeared surprised by the response. In fact, her attendance at the conference was supposed to be somewhat of an honor for CTER organizers, an indication of increased federal support for their efforts to create new labor protections within tribal governments. Instead, Berrien, a highly respected civil rights lawyer known for her advocacy to end racial and other types of discrimination in the workplace, looked out into a hotel ballroom full of faces that were, at best, skeptical if not outright hostile.[1]

Perhaps Berrien assumed that tribal officials would welcome help from the federal government and see the enforcement of civil rights laws as a great benefit to their communities. But Berrien made a terrible mistake. She failed to acknowledge the sovereignty of the tribal governments whose representatives she had been addressing. Her assumptions about the promise of "civil rights" enforcement as a social justice strategy, which may have been endorsed by her listeners, was lost on tribal leaders whose historical battle has been to resist US colonialism and to assert their sovereignty—culturally, politically, and economically.

Tribal officials who were attending this conference did not see themselves as representatives of the US government responsible for enforcing federal antidiscrimination laws in their communities, nor did they see themselves as social workers who were supposed to help their citizens "know their rights" as Berrien put it. Rather, they were developing, debating, and implementing their own antidiscrimination laws and creating their own institutions to enforce them. To help them do so, CTER leaders introduced a model Workforce Protection Ordinance, which would include antidiscrimination provisions for Native workers on reservation lands and extend to them protections otherwise provided by federal law such as minimum wage requirements, family and medical leave, and Occupational Safety. The model Workforce Protection Ordinance also included a provision that would allow Native workers to meet "their obligations as employees and . . . their tribal culture and religion," by providing leave to attend important cultural events, such as ceremonies and funerals.[2] They hoped its membership would take the model ordinance back to their reservation governments to debate, adopt, and amend.

Perhaps Berrien was unfamiliar with the distinction between sovereignty rights and civil rights. She certainly misjudged her audience. Nevertheless, the incident illustrates the tension between civil rights and sovereignty rights and the growing conflict between federal, state, and tribal governments over who has the right to regulate reservation workforces.

It is clear that the success of gaming enterprises has complicated TERO's role in labor relations. Casinos have introduced new capital into tribal economies but have also brought new problems, including the management of non-Native workers. Since many casino workers are not Native and do not live on reservation lands, the issue of controlling and protecting the workplace has taken on new meaning. While still interested in protecting its members' jobs and rights, sovereignty has become centered on a right to control the workplace itself.

Unfortunately, as Dan Press suggested to me at the 2012 CTER conference, many tribes have been less enthusiastic about adopting the Workplace Protection Ordinance. Some individual tribes, like the Mashantucket Pequot, have adopted their own labor laws. But a tribal version of the NLRA never quite materialized. Instead, the workforce protection model, distributed to its members in 2024, included provisions to include "right-to-work" laws that would guarantee workers at tribally owned and operated businesses, including but not limited to casinos, the "freedom to work without joining a union."[3] Instead of protecting the right to organize, as the Mashantucket Pequot had, some members of the CTER seem to be following the example of states that have enacted laws to discourage unionization. Noticing my discomfort about the debates I was listening to on the floor of the convention, Dan Press took me aside and asked me, "Are you still going to write about Indian workers?" I replied, "Yes, and Native bosses, too."[4]

Unfortunately, the story of "Indian bosses" will have to wait for another historian. Nevertheless, this book here, about Native workers, demonstrates how their struggle over the course of one hundred years has expanded the notion of sovereignty to include control over the nature of work itself. This book explores how federal officials used work to achieve their assimilationist goals from the late nineteenth through the mid-twentieth centuries. From the late nineteenth century through the early 1960s, Native children at Indian boarding schools faced intense pressure to assimilate. OIA educators adamantly believed that preparing students to work in the off-reservation economy—albeit in jobs that reinforced their marginal, racialized status—would eventually bring about total assimilation. OIA leaders believed the children would sever their relationships with their Indigenous communities and that eventually the tribes themselves would cease to exist. Transforming the way individuals made a living, including transforming rural peoples, many of whom lived according to a seasonal round, into urban wage laborers, seemed to be the key to this process.

A global economic depression disrupted that strategy. Instead, federal policymakers changed direction and tried to keep Native workers mostly at home on the reservations, learning the assimilationist lessons of wage labor by working on relief projects. Instead of competing with non-Native people for jobs that they had previously folded into their seasonal round, Indigenous men and women in the 1930s and 1940s earned a living on temporary development projects like refurbishing used clothing, sewing mattresses, digging ditches, and building roads.

From OIA agents' perspectives, those jobs taught lessons similar to what Native people were supposed to learn in boarding schools, including gendered skills and behavior, which would allow them to eventually take their place in the American working class. Some reformers, like John Collier, still held out hope that working on development projects, including soil conservation and road building, would ensure tribal self-sufficiency.

World War II disrupted that effort, at first channeling New Deal–era programs, such as the CCC-ID into defense-related projects and then dissolving those programs altogether. In fact, federal Indian policy, particularly programs meant to buttress tribal economies, remained on the back burner for most of the war years. Nevertheless, Native people, like other Americans, joined the war effort. They enlisted in great numbers, worked in munitions depots, or migrated to cities to find more lucrative jobs in defense industries.

In the aftermath of World War II, Native people found little had changed on reservations. New Deal–era programs had not created permanent jobs or lifted most tribes out of poverty. To make matters worse, Congress and other Indian policy officials dialed back Indian policy goals to the 1880s and launched new efforts to undermine tribal sovereignty. They passed legislation reversing Collier's plans and dismantled some tribal governments. Now more than ever, particularly with a renewed commitment to assimilation via the Relocation Program, work remained a centerpiece of federal Indian policy. Native people participated in those programs. They relocated to urban areas, enrolled in vocational training, and sent their children to boarding schools that promised to prepare them for jobs off the reservation.

Some tribal governments, like the Navajo Nation, embraced these initiatives; and Native workers welcomed jobs, whether that meant migrating to far off cities or doing seasonal agricultural labor. Even so, Native workers did not ultimately embrace the policymakers' goals. Working for wages did not mean letting go of their tribal homelands or turning their backs on their Indigenous identities.

By the 1970s, as Native activists demanded greater control of their communities' resources, governance, and cultures, a social movement emerged to expand the terms of tribal sovereignty to include work, too. Like their counterparts in the Red Power movement, Native workers confronted non-Native employers and their own tribal governments to demand not only an end to discrimination but also greater control over the workplace itself. They created new policy initiatives, tribal institutions, and intertribal organizations to develop and enforce policies that would protect Native workers' rights and ensure their access to jobs on and near reservation land. Their efforts were part of a messy, yet powerful, decolonization process.

Nonetheless, Native people were still working for non-Native employers. It would not be until the rapid growth of the Indian gaming industry, beginning in the 1980s, that tribes would begin to control the workplaces too. The history of labor relations within Native nations, particularly with those communities that developed successful casino operations, offers examples of the contradictions characteristic of the decolonization process. On the one hand, gaming has offered Native governments the capital they need to diversify their economies, gain control over the terms and conditions of work on their land, and acquire more power to influence federal policy. On the other hand, when Native nations mirror the actions of corporations, such as by hiring union-busting law firms to prevent unions from organizing on reservation land and by developing "right-to-work" laws in their tribal labor codes, they may be, as historian Frederick Cooper has pointed out, adopting the cultural idioms of the colonizer. Of course, Indigenous nations in the United States are not corporations. Tribally owned industries, like casinos, operate like nationalized industries in other countries. The wealth belongs to the tribe as a whole and may be distributed as per capita payments to its members or used by tribal governments to buttress the socioeconomic and cultural welfare of its people.[5] Efforts to create tribal labor codes that protect workers' rights, and the right to organize unions, have developed throughout the United States and by Native nations such as the Mashantucket Pequot and the Navajo Nation. Developing conversations within Native American communities about these issues is part of a larger struggle to come to terms with capitalism as it develops within reservations, as those communities begin to dismantle old economies formally dependent on federal grants and resource extraction.

Native people have also seized the opportunity to open new schools that serve their communities' needs and advance tribal sovereignty goals. For example, tribes applied for development funds made available by the BIA and the Economic Opportunity Act, a part of President Johnson's War on Poverty. In 1966, Navajo community members launched the Rough Rock Demonstration School, the first Navajo-controlled school on the reservation and created a curriculum that privileged Navajo language instruction and focused on building a local Navajo economy. The school was, as anthropologist Teresa McCarty describes, "organized around principles of kinship, family, and communalism."6 Peter MacDonald, who served three terms as tribal chair of the Navajo Nation, from 1971 to 1989, stated that Rough Rock students "deviate from just purely learning to speak English, to understand English and to write the English language and to manipulate numbers. They [study] the meaning of culture, the meaning of the whole learning process, how it's weaved into the purpose of life, so that an individual will have the outlook that will provide him with the kind of destiny that will spell to him why he should live and for what reason he should continue trying to exist the next day. [A]nd this is very good. And that's the identity program."7 In 1968, the Navajo Nation also created Navajo Community College, which is now Diné College, a four-year postsecondary educational institution. Like Rough Rock, the institution's mission, *Sa'ah Naaghai Bik'eh Hozhoo*, "is grounded in Navajo cultural traditions."8

Grassroots efforts, emerging from the Red Power movement of the 1960s and 1970s produced alternative educational projects called "survival schools." These schools were part of a broader political and cultural struggle launched by American Indian Movement activists meant to decolonize the settler-colonial educational system. Brenda J. Child describes two survival schools, Heart of the Earth in Minneapolis and Red School House in St. Paul, as products of "women's decades-long work to create culturally and historically meaningful curricula." When the schools closed in 1995 and 2008, respectively, their legacy nonetheless "influenced a new generation of charter schools, language-immersion schools and more mainstream institutions."9

Native leaders and other community members transformed old boarding schools as well. Haskell Indian Boarding School, which started in 1884 as the United States Indian Industrial Training School became Haskell Indian Junior College in 1970 and is now Haskell Indian Nations University, defining itself as a "unique and diverse inter-tribal university committed to the advancement of sovereignty, self-determination, and the inherent rights of tribes."10 The Santa Fe Indian School became the Institute of American

Indian Arts. The Sherman Institute became an accredited high school and transformed its curriculum, which now includes Native American Studies courses. As one of the few boarding schools still in operation, Sherman's students and faculty continue to struggle with its settler-colonial history.[11]

I hope readers do not leave this book thinking that unions and Native workers are mutually exclusive. Granted, the history of the relationship between Native communities and organized labor has been a rocky one. Throughout the twentieth and twenty-first centuries, Native workers have played important roles in organizing unions, like the United Mine Workers, the Alaskan Brotherhood, the United Steelworkers, and the Laborers International Union of North America to improve their working conditions, wages, and access to jobs. Or, like other workers, Native Americans joined unions where they found work when they migrated from rural areas to big cities. But unions have sometimes played a part in excluding Native workers from heavy industrial jobs, like in mining or in the construction industry; while others have organized Native American workers and collaborated with tribal governments to develop apprenticeships and other vocational training programs.[12] In some cases, unions have honored tribal sovereignty claims over controlling the workplace. The relationship between tribal governments and non-Native workers is a history in the making.

Policy crafted in the late nineteenth century has continued to shape Native lives one hundred years later. Even so, putting Native people to work did not erase Native American culture, destroy Native people's relationships to their lands, or completely erode their political power. Only a generation removed from the trauma of the Indian boarding school experience, Native Americans are still here. They have suffered greatly since the republic was established. Through it all, they built social movements and new tribal governments, reclaimed land, remade governing structures, strengthened cultural identities, and engaged the world of wage work on their own terms. Work is no longer an assimilationist tool wielded by the settler-colonial state to extinguish Native American land claims. Instead, jobs and workplaces have become a terrain where Native people and their governments have expanded the terms of tribal sovereignty.

NOTES

ABBREVIATIONS

HVA	Hoopa Valley Agency, Hoopa Valley Administrative Files Relating to CCC-ID Activities, 1933–1943, RG 75, Records of the Bureau of Indian Affairs, National Archives and Records Administration Regional Branch, San Francisco
NARA I	National Archives and Records Administration I, Washington, DC
NARA-Denver	National Archives and Records Administration Regional Branch, Denver, CO
NARA-Riverside	National Archives and Records Administration Regional Branch, Riverside, CA
NARA-SF	National Archives and Records Administration Regional Branch, San Francisco, CA
RG69	Records of the Federal Emergency Relief Administration / Works Projects Administration, National Archives II, College Park, MD
RG75	Records of the Bureau of Indian Affairs
Spilde Papers	Katherine A. Spilde Papers on Native American Gaming, Special Collections, University Libraries, University of Nevada, Las Vegas

INTRODUCTION

1. I use the terms "Native American," "Indigenous people," "American Indians," or "Native" as an adjective, somewhat interchangeably to avoid repetitive prose. Even though "Indian" is a product of the racial dynamics of colonialism and, as such, inaccurate, I include the term when I quote from primary sources to maintain the historical integrity of the documents; and I use the term in the names of institutions and policies, such as "Indian Schools" or "Indian Policy." At the time of this writing, the term "Indian" remains contested and commonly used by many Native people in the United States to refer to an identity derived from their collective historical experience under settler colonialism. The term "Indian Country" conforms to the usage as explained by the National Congress of American Indians (NCAI) as "a general description of Native spaces and places within the

United States, and it is inclusive of the hundreds of tribal nations that occupy these spaces. The term is used with positive sentiment within Native communities, by Native-focused organizations such as NCAI, and news organizations such as Indian Country Today." NCAI press release, as quoted in "Is 'Indian Country' an Offensive Term? Trump Sparks Debate after Tweet Thanking 'Indian Country,'" *Newsweek*, December 27, 2019.

2. R. H. Pratt to H. L. Dawes, April 7, 1880, in Pratt, *Battlefield and Classroom*, 252; Hoxie, *Final Promise*, 85, 94; Adams, *Education for Extinction*, 24.

3. Sitting Bull, "I came here to give some advice, August 22, 1883," 152–53. In this speech, Sitting Bull is most likely using the term "grandfather" in a somewhat ironic way to refer to the US federal government. Normally, grandfather would refer to a highly respected male elder of the community, or ancestor. It is likely that Sitting Bull, like many Native Americans, used the language of kinship in diplomatic negotiations in a way that called upon the United States to fulfill its treaty obligations. For a description of the reservation economy see Ostler, *Plains Sioux*, 112, 128–48. Sitting Bull was well known for his sarcastic oratory. Calcaterra, "A 'Second Look' at Charles Alexander Eastman," 26.

4. Sitting Bull's words were prophetic in many ways. Nineteenth- and twentieth-century federal policy consistently undermined Native people's wealth. Harmon, *Rich Indians*, 171–208.

5. Native American land dispossession is a longer process that started with the arrival of Europeans in the Americas. But for this argument, I am focusing on the removal policy that the United States initiated in the 1830s and on the Dawes Act of 1887, which was meant to undermine Native Americans' collective ownership of land.

6. Histories of Native labor in early colonial America include Brooks, *Slavery, Kinship and Community*; Hackel, *Children of Coyote*; Newell, *Brethren by Nature*. For a discussion of Native Americans' struggles to access the benefits associated with citizenship in the twentieth century, see Klann, *Wardship and the Welfare State*.

The Indian Citizenship Act of 1924 granted citizenship to Native Americans but left their voting rights up to the states to decide. For example, Native people living on reservations in Arizona and Utah were deprived the right to vote until 1948 and 1957, respectively. They suffered racial discrimination and segregation similar to that that faced by Black Americans in the Jim Crow South, particularly in non-Native communities bordering reservations. Such conditions are documented in civil rights commission reports as late as the 1970s. See New Mexico Advisory Committee to the United States Commission on Civil Rights, *Farmington Report*; Minnesota Advisory Committee to the US Commission on Civil Rights, *Bridging the Gap*; Magnuson, *Death of Raymond Yellow Thunder*.

7. "Loafers and Laborers" (illus.), *Puck*, September 29, 1880, 53.

8. O'Neill, *Working the Navajo Way*; Hosmer, *American Indians in the Marketplace*; Raibmon, *Authentic Indians*; Ellis, *A Dancing People*; Littlefield and Knack, *Native Americans and Wage Labor*; Parnaby, *Citizen Docker*; Sangster, *Transforming Labour*; Usner, *Indian Work*; Simonsen, *Making Home Work*.

9. Norrgard, *Seasons of Change*; Bauer, *We Were All Like Migrant Workers Here*; Kamper, *Work of Sovereignty*; Haskins, *Matrons and Maids*; Whalen, *Native Students at Work*; Carleton, *Lessons in Legitimacy*, 192. I am referring to Thomas G. Andrews's use of the term "workscape" in his book *Killing for Coal*, 125.

10. For the civil rights narrative in US labor history see Vargas, *Labor Rights*; Honey, *Going Down Jericho Road*; Korstad, *Civil Rights Unionism*. For a parallel story of feminism

and organized labor see, Kessler-Harris, *Gendering Labor History*; Cobble, *Other Women's Movement*; Gabin, *Feminism in the Labor Movement*; Deslippe, *Rights, Not Roses*.

11. Latinx peoples' experience with colonialism varies considerably. The US-Mexico War, the conquest of California, the different patterns of settler colonialism in Texas and New Mexico, and legacies of US imperialism in the Caribbean imbedded class and racial hierarchies in historically distinct ways, including in practices of land dispossession, racial discrimination, and deportation. For an overview on how settler colonialism offers a useful conceptual approach to understand racism in the United States, see Glenn, "Settler Colonialism as Structure," 54–74.

12. Canadian labor historians have been developing an analysis of settler colonialism in their scholarship on Canadian working-class history. Sangster, *Transforming Labour*; Milloy and Sangster, *Violence of Work*; Lutz, *Makuk*; McCallum, *Indigenous Women, Work, and History*; Parnaby, *Citizen Docker*. See also Burrill's thoughtful critique, "Settler Order Framework," 173–98. Canadian historian Rolf Knight published the first historical monograph on Native labor, *Indians at Work*. Noted American anthropologist Patricia Albers was one of the first scholars to pose the problem of settler colonialism in the development of capitalism. Albers, "From Legend to Land to Labor," 245–73.

13. Sium, Desai, and Ritskes, "Towards the 'Tangible Unknown,'" ii.

14. Tuck and Yang, "Decolonization Is Not a Metaphor,"1–40; Burow, Brock, and Dove, "Unsettling the Land," 57–74. For a discussion of how Native people have contested the definition of citizenship and wardship, see Klann, *Wardship and the Welfare State*.

15. O'Neill, *Working the Navajo Way*; Norrgard, *Seasons of Change*; Raibmon, *Authentic Indians*; Bauer, *We Were All Like Migrant Workers Here*; Hosmer, *American Indians in the Marketplace*; Parham, "'These Indians Are Apparently Well to Do.'"

16. That project involved convincing Native people (either by violence, economic pressure, or other types of intimidation) to surrender their land and adopt settler society's religion, culture, definitions of gender, work, and economic values. Indeed, as interdisciplinary scholar Patrick Wolfe put it, "Settler colonialism destroys to replace." It's a long historical process, as Wolfe observes; it "is a structure, not an event." Wolfe, "Settler Colonialism and the Elimination of the Native," 388; Kauanui, "A Structure, Not an Event."

17. Carlson-Manathara and Rowe, *Living in Indigenous Sovereignty*, 42.

18. There is considerable debate among Indigenous scholars about the use of the term "decolonization." Scholars and activists have generally reaffirmed Tuck and Yang's critical intervention, that decolonization requires Indigenous peoples to regain cultural, political and economic power over their lands. As Paul Berne Burow, Samara Brock, and Michael R. Dove explain, "Decolonization . . . does not simply reflect a swing of the pendulum back to what existed before allotment and white settlement through mirrored, reversed processes of repossession, but is something creatively formed through contemporary struggles around what it means to be Indigenous amid enduring—but not immutable—structures of capitalism and settler colonial domination." Burow, Brock, and Dove, "Unsettling the Land," 68. For a discussion of the interchangeable use of anti-colonialism and decolonization, see Carlson-Manathara and Rowe, *Living in Indigenous Sovereignty*, 43.

19. See classic studies that explore nineteenth-century Indian policy including, Hoxie, *A Final Promise*; Prucha, *Great Father*.

20. The debate over the origins of capitalism is vast. Classic arguments center on the transformation of feudalism, demography, the nature of financial institutions, the modern

nation-state, and the emergence of wage labor. In addition to Marx, *Capital, Volume 1*, see classic texts that fueled this debate, including the collection of essays compiled by Ashton and Philpin in response to Robert Brenner's influential argument about the transition of feudalism, *The Brenner Debate*; Thompson, *Making of the English Working Class*; Wallerstein, *Modern World-System*; Wolf, *Europe and the People Without History*. For foundational work that connects the development of capitalism to slavery, see Williams, *Capitalism and Slavery*. More recent histories of capitalism that center on the United States tend to focus on the development of global markets around specific commodities, such as sugar and cotton. For example, see Beckert and Desan, *American Capitalism*. Regrettably, few scholars have seriously factored Native Americans into the history of capitalism in the United States. On this issue see Harmon, O'Neill, and Rosier, "Interwoven Economic Histories"; see also Harmon, *Rich Indians*.

21. Andrews, *Killing for Coal*, 125.

22. Norrgard, *Seasons of Change*, 4. Steven High has argued that First Nations in Canada incorporated the capitalist economy into their seasonal round as wage workers and independent producers. Those efforts strengthened their traditional economies. High, "Native American Wage Labour," 244. See also Osmond, "'I Was Born a Logger,'" 215–35.

23. Madley, *An American Genocide*; Bauer, *We Were All Like Migrant Workers Here*, 30–57; Phillips, *Vineyards and Vaqueros*; Hurtado, "Hardly a Farmhouse," 245–70. Magliari, "Free State Slavery,"155–92.

24. Mitchell, "Mohawks in High Steel," 20; Blanchard, "High Steel," 43–44; Raibmon, *Authentic Indians*, 77; Arnesen, *Brotherhoods of Color*; Whalen, *Native Students at Work*, 66.

25. Murphy, *Gathering of Rivers*, 80; Rawls, "Gold Diggers," 28–45; Johnson, *Roaring Camp*, 222–23.

26. Norrgard, *Seasons of Change*, 38.

27. Bess, "New Egypt," 491–516; Harmon, *Rich Indians*, 171–208; Allison, *Sovereignty for Survival*, 23.

28. Raibmon, *Authentic Indians*, 98, 78.

29. Bauer, *We Were All Like Migrant Workers Here*, 59.

30. Kersey, *Florida Seminoles and the Indian New Deal*, 36–37; Cattelino, *High Stakes*, 40–42. Some Native communities, like the Pueblos in the Southwest or the Mandan on the Northern Plains, built sedentary lives around agriculture but hosted robust trading fairs that attracted Indigenous peoples from great distances. Fenn, *Encounters at the Heart of the World*; Price and Gebauer, *Last Hunters, First Farmers*.

31. O'Neill, *Working the Navajo Way*, 45; Curley, *Carbon Sovereignty*, 47; Chamberlain, *Under Sacred Ground*; Brugge, Benally, and Yazzie-Lewis, *Navajo People and Uranium Mining*; Iverson, *Diné*, 222–23.

32. Child, *My Grandfather's Knocking Sticks*, 13, 170; Canadian historian Robin Jarvis Brownlie explains that selective engagement in the waged economy was not necessarily the norm. Some Indigenous peoples relied solely on wages to make a living, particularly those who had been displaced from their lands and who could no longer rely on hunting game. Brownlie, "'Living the Same as the White People,'" 44.

33. A notable exception is Brenda J. Child, *Holding Our World Together*. Historians are beginning to think about the relationship between wage work and gender in Native communities. O'Neill, *Working the Navajo Way*; Simonsen, *Making Home Work*; Muszynski,

Cheap Wage Labour; Raibmon, *Authentic Indians*; Raibmon, "Practice of Everyday Colonialism," 23–56.

34. There is an extensive global literature on women, colonialism, and capitalist change. In general, that scholarship shows that capitalist development impacts men and women in highly divergent ways, often favoring the former at the expense of the latter. Such change is quite variable and dependent on the historically specific conditions including class, gender, race, culture, and type of colonial control that ushered in new economic systems. For a foundational book on this topic that examine Native women in early North American colonial history, see note 39 below.

35. Cattelino, "Casino Roots," 72.

36. Weisiger, *Dreaming of Sheep*; Lamphere, *To Run After Them*; M'Closkey, *Swept under the Rug*.

37. Notable Native women activists and intellectuals directly challenged settler colonial policy. See for example, Zitkala-Ša, Helen Peterson, and the women I discuss in chapters 2 and 3, who challenged the terms of New Deal–era relief programs. The term, "everyday acts of resistance," was coined by James C. Scott, in his book, *Weapons of the Weak*, xvii.

38. They found jobs working in commercial agriculture throughout the United States: picking Colorado beets, California citrus, Idaho potatoes, Florida tomatoes, Arizona carrots, and hops grown near the Puget Sound. Others worked on railroad maintenance crews throughout the West or found work in the fish canneries along the Pacific Northwest coast. Mohawks, legendary as "warriors in the sky," built some of New York City's tallest skyscrapers. Most of those jobs required American Indians to migrate away from their reservation homes on a seasonal basis— until the 1930s, when the global economic depression encouraged many of them to stay home and work in a variety of New Deal–era programs.

39. Early scholarship on gender and economic change for Native American women focused on the fur trade and women's role in subsistence agriculture from the sixteenth to the early nineteenth centuries. See Perdue, *Cherokee Women*; Van Kirk, *Many Tender Ties*; Sleeper-Smith, *Indian Women and French Men*; Shoemaker, *Negotiators of Change*; Jensen, "Native American Women and Agriculture"; Etienne and Leacock, *Women and Colonization*.

40. Historians describe this shift in Indian policy as a political and cultural assault on American Indian sovereignty. Indeed, policies such as termination and relocation devastated some Native communities, bankrupting successful tribal economies and shrinking tribal land holdings. Stressing Native American agency, historian Doug Miller demonstrates that American Indians took advantage of the Relocation Program as part of a long-term migration strategy that aided their adjustment to changing economic and political climates. He argues that the program needs to be understood in a broader context of Native urbanization that started in the early twentieth century. Miller, *Indians on the Move*, 8.

41. Burrill, "Settler Order Framework," 173–98; Carleton, *Lessons of Legitimacy*; Ostler, "Locating Settler Colonialism in Early American History," 443–50; Koshy, Cacho, Byrd, and Jefferson, *Colonial Racial Capitalism*; Mills and McCreary, "Which Side Are You On," 133–51; Whiteside, *Proprietary Settler Colonialism*. Much of the focus on the connections between settler colonialism and capitalism in North America comes from critical Indigenous studies. See for example, Coulthard, *Red Skin, White Masks*; Byrd, *Transit of Empire*.

42. Harmon, O'Neill, and Rosier, "Interwoven Economic Histories."

43. Many of those scholars have made a convincing case for abandoning the policy narrative and rejecting the impulse to define Native American history from the colonizers' perspective. Yet, US federal Indian policy provides the thread to weave these stories together, even though Native lives and histories vary considerably in time and space. Examples include Blackhawk, *Rediscovery of America*; Hämäläinen, *Indigenous Continent*; Jagodinsky, *Legal Codes and Talking Trees*; Weisiger, *Dreaming of Sheep*; Miles, *Ties That Bind*; Theobald, *Reproduction on the Reservation*; Ellis, *A Dancing People*; Deloria, *Indians in Unexpected Places*; Denetdale, *Reclaiming Diné History*.

44. See Stoler, *Along the Archival Grain*, for an in-depth meditation on the methodological and ethical challenges of using the colonizer's archive to find the history of colonized peoples.

45. Scott, *Domination and the Arts of Resistance*, 4.

46. I interviewed Deron Marquez, the former chair of the Yuhaaviatam of San Manuel Nation and a key leader in the struggle over Indian gaming in California. I've included contemporary newspaper accounts, legal depositions, and congressional testimony. However, given the controversial nature of gaming and the rather difficult legal issues involved with union organizing on reservation land, my access to Native casino workers and tribal officials was limited. I also interviewed the founders of the Council for Tribal Employment Rights (CTER), including Conrad Edwards, John Navarro, Larry Ketcher, Rodney "Fish" Gervais, and Daniel Press, CTER's lawyer (non-Native).

CHAPTER 1

1. Since the early days of the republic, Native peoples have struggled with federal and state efforts to transform them into sedentary farmers, a scheme meant to undermine their culturally defined relationship to their lands. For a case study of how Ho-Chunks, Menominees, Ojibwes, and Oneidas managed to adapt to the demands of reformers in Wisconsin but reject their assimilationist assumptions during the Progressive Era, see Firkus, "Agricultural Extension," 473–502; Pratt, "Advantages of Mingling Indians with Whites," 46.

2. Keliiaa, *Refusing Settler Domesticity*, 22. See also Littlefield and Knack, *Native Americans and Wage Labor*.

3. Patrick Wolfe's seminal work describes the erasure of Native cultures and the ultimate dispossession of Native people from their lands as central to settler colonialism. Wolfe, "Settler Colonialism and the Elimination of the Native," 396. For a useful review of the debates around the historical specificity of the term settler colonialism for the United States, see Ostler, "Locating Settler Colonialism in Early American History," 446–47. Scott, *Seeing Like a State*, 2.

4. Zitkala-Ša, *American Indian Stories*, 66; Lomawaima, *They Called It Prairie Light*, 49, 66. For broad analysis of how schools fit into the developing capitalist economy, see Littlefield, "Learning to Labor," 43–59.

5. "Survivance," as coined by literary scholar and writer Gerald Vizenor, "is more than survival, more than endurance or mere response; the stories of survivance are an active presence." Vizenor, as quoted in Breinig, "Native Survivance in the Americas," 291.

6. Lomawaima, *They Called It Prairie Light*, 2; Prucha, *Great Father*, 51–53. Using schools as a tool to convert Native Americans and to advance colonial goals was not new, of course. Catholic religious orders and other missionaries had used this strategy since their earliest contact with Native Americans in North America. See also Rubin, *Tears of Repentance*, 7; McKellips, "Educational Practices"; Hollermann, "Where There Was Need"; Dorsey, "Going to School with Savages"; Axtell, "Rise and Fall of the Stockbridge Indian Schools."

7. The historical literature on Indian schools is voluminous. Memories of the boarding school generation remain fresh and vivid and are passed down to younger family members or memorialized in digital exhibits and Native autobiographies. See, for example, the Heard Museum's digital exhibit, "Away from Home: American Indian Boarding School Stories," accessed August 7, 2025, https://boardingschool.heard.org/. Other curated exhibits include Carolyn Marr's illustrated essay "Assimilation through Education"; and "The Carlisle Indian School Project," Muscogee (Creek) Nation National Library and Archives, accessed June 30, 2025, https://mvskokenationallibraryarchive.org/digital-heritage/carlisle-indian-school-project. See also the Carlisle Indian School Digital Research Center, accessed August 2, 2025, https://carlisleindian.dickinson.edu/; and the Genoa Indian School Digital Reconciliation Project, accessed June 30, 2025, https://genoaindianschool.org/. Native leaders, artists, activists, and intellectuals, particularly those who were living in the mid-twentieth century, often include descriptions of boarding school experience in their memoirs. Bennett, *Kaibah*; Zitkala-Ša, *American Indian Stories*; Crow Dog and Erdoes, *Lakota Woman*; Fortunate Eagle, *Pipestone*; Krupat, *Changed Forever*; Nequatewa, *Born a Chief*; Murillo, *Living in Two Worlds*; Qoyawayma and Carlson, *No Turning Back*; Sekaquaptewa, *Me and Mine*; Irene Stewart, *A Voice in Her Tribe*; Talayesva, *Sun Chief*.

8. Indian school scholarship reveals complex histories of Native American struggles with the settler state. Those studies provide a useful measure of Indian policy in its consistent, albeit sometimes contradictory, commitment to assimilation. We know what reformers wanted Native children to learn, and we know what Native students did with that knowledge, whether they accepted the policymaker's goals or not. Indeed, the experience of individual children often varied, even as they struggled with similar types of abuse and exploitation. Much of the scholarship documents the oppressive nature of assimilationist boarding school policy, the most damning of which was the 1928 report by Lewis Meriam. Meriam, *Problem of Indian Administration* (or the *Meriam Report*). See also the following broad studies of Indian education and assimilationist Indian policy: Adams, *Education for Extinction*; and Archuleta, Child, and Lomawaima, *Away from Home*. Case studies of individual schools include Trennert, *Phoenix Indian School*; Coleman, *American Indian Children at School*; Lomawaima, *They Called It Prairie Light*; Ellis, *To Change Them Forever*; Vučković, *Voices from Haskell*; Gilbert, *Education beyond the Mesas*; Haskins, *Matrons and Maids*; Whalen, *Native Students at Work*. Studies that stress Native resilience and agency include Child, *Boarding School Seasons*; and Trafzer, Keller, and Sisquoc, *Boarding School Blues*. The periodical literature is too vast to cite here.

9. Quoted in Kantor, "Choosing a Vocation," 351.

10. Kantor, "Choosing a Vocation," 351.

11. Hoxie, *A Final Promise*, 56.

12. Some white families sent children who were placed with them to public schools. Whalen, "Labored Learning," 153.

13. Pratt did not embrace the more cynical view of Native American academic abilities articulated by Indian Commissioner Francis E. Leupp. See Pratt's scathing critique of Leupp in Richard Henry Pratt, *An Exposure: Address before the Ladies Missionary Societies of the Calvary M. E. Church*, Washington, DC, April 6, 1915, Utah State University Special Collections.

14. For a history of the structural changes in American agriculture that increased production but decreased the number of farmers needed, see Fitzgerald, *Every Farm a Factory*; see also the seminal book on the gendered impact of that transformation, Neth, *Preserving the Family Farm*.

15. US Senate, Committee on Indian Affairs, *Survey of Conditions of the Indians in the United States . . . 1928*, November 19, 20, 22, 23, and 26, 1928.

16. Whalen, *Native Students at Work*, 30–31. By 1890, most people in the United States lived in urban areas. See US Census Bureau, "Increasing Urbanization, Population Distribution by City Size, 1790–1890"; Neth, *Preserving the Family Farm*, 4.

17. On Native power in the early colonial fur trade in North America, see Sleeper-Smith, *Rethinking the Fur Trade*; Stern, *Lives in Objects*. To understand the Comanche's place in the nineteenth century Great Plains horse market, see Hämäläinen, *Comanche*.

18. W. A. Jones, "Uncle Sam's New Schemes to Civilize the Indians," *San Francisco Call*, September 14, 1902, 14.

19. Not all Native Americans who attended boarding schools during the Progressive Era worked in low-waged, racialized jobs. In fact, many members of the Society of American Indians, also known as the "Red Progressives," moved on to attend universities, practice law, become medical doctors, and teach at Indian schools. See Hoxie, *Talking Back to Civilization*, 36–65; Maroukis, *We Are Not a Vanishing People*, 31.

20. Fitzgerald, *Every Farm a Factory*, 107; Neth, *Preserving the Family Farm*, 10–11.

21. Reel, *Course of Study for the Indian Schools of the United States*, 198.

22. Johnson, *Stories of Traditional Navajo Life and Culture*, 39.

23. Nequatewa, *Born a Chief*, 121. Nequatewa attended Keams Canyon School in 1895 for four years; he then went to Phoenix Indian School.

24. Nequatewa, *Born a Chief*, 121.

25. Whalen, *Native Students at Work*, 49.

26. Before 1947, the Bureau of Indian Affairs (BIA) was known as the Office of Indian Affairs (OIA).

27. Rothberg, "Elouise Cobell (Yellow Bird Woman)"; Merjian, "An Unbroken Chain of Injustice," 9; see also Native American Rights Fund, "Individual Indian Money Accounts (Cobell v. Salazar)."

28. Native American Rights Fund (NARF), "Individual Indian Money Accounts (Cobell v. Salazar)," accessed July 17, 2025, https://narf.org/cases/cobell/#:~:text=Accounts%20(Cobell%20v.-,Salazar),trust%20by%20twentieth%20federal%20government.

29. Merjian, "An Unbroken Chain of Injustice," 24.

30. Zitkala-Ša, *American Indian Stories*, 66.

31. Stratton, *Education for Empire*; Leonard, *Illiberal Reformers*; Muhammad, *Condemnation of Blackness*.

32. Lomawaima, *They Called It Prairie Light*, 65–67.

33. Leupp, *In Red Man's Land*, 164.

34. Adams, *Education for Extinction*, 184.

35. Lomawaima, *They Called It Prairie Light*, 5; Adams, *Education for Extinction*, 149, 151; Vučković, *Voices from Haskell*, 185–87. Indian Residential Schools in Canada used a similar system, relying on student unpaid labor to maintain the schools. Carleton, *Lessons in Legitimacy*, 192.

36. Richard H. Pratt to Hon. Thad C. Pound, January 28, 1880, in Pratt, *Battlefield and Classroom*, 249.

37. Joe Lamb's research on Genoa demonstrates a direct connection between the students' work with infected cows and the spread of tuberculosis throughout the school. A school administrator obsessed with his prized dairy herds and a feckless, ethnocentric bureaucracy blamed Native homelife for the disease, and World War I food shortages resulted in the deaths of many children at Genoa. Lamb, "CoughingCows and Utter Disaster," 24–25, 76–78. Boarding school students and their families throughout the United States suffered at greater rates than other populations. Trennert, "Federal Government and Indian Health in the Southwest, 63.

38. *Meriam Report*, 375–76.

39. *Meriam Report*, 385.

40. *Meriam Report*, 386.

41. Fortunate Eagle, *My Life*, 93.

42. Anderson, "Richard Henry Pratt."

43. *Annual Report of the Commissioner of Indian Affairs . . . 1878*, p. xliii. The school's name has changed several times. In this report the school is called the Hampton Normal Institute. It was also called the Hampton Normal and Agricultural Institute, the Hampton Institute, and finally in 1984, it became Hampton University. A historically Black college, Hampton played an important role in the American civil rights movement. Its distinguished alumni include Booker T. Washington. Rosa Parks worked at the school, and Martin Luther King delivered his speech, "The Montgomery Story," there in 1956. MLK's mother graduated from Hampton in 1924. See Hampton University, "History," accessed June 30, 2025, https://home.hamptonu.edu/about/history/.

44. Whalen, *Native Students at Work*, 50–51; Lomawaima, *They Called It Prairie Light*, 2. Historians describe the development of Indian boarding schools, including the outing program, as an outgrowth of the type of educational systems developed for African Americans in the late nineteenth century. Hampton's curriculum, which favored industrial and agricultural training over academic subjects, became the center of a debate between those who favored full and immediate integration of African Americans, such as W. E. B Du Bois, and reformers who advocated the more gradual and practical approach of "racial uplift." For an overview of their viewpoints see Grossman, "A Chance to Make Good," 378–79.

45. Pratt, *Battlefield and Classroom*, 214.

46. Pratt, *Battlefield and Classroom*, 214.

47. Pratt, *Battlefield and Classroom*, 214.

48. Pratt, *Battlefield and Classroom*, 214.

49. Reel, *Course of Study for the Indian Schools*, 189. See also Lomawaima's concise biography of Reel, "Estelle Reel, Superintendent of Indian Schools;" Archuleta, Child, and Lomawaima, *Away from Home*, 31. Haskins, *Matrons and Maids*, 5; Trennert, *Phoenix Indian School*, 73–74. To understand Reel in Indian policy's race, gender, and colonial context, see Cahill, *Federal Fathers and Mothers*, 63–81.

50. Whalen, *Native Students at Work*, 63.

51. Pratt, *An Exposure*, 9.

52. William Torrey Harr is heralded for his work to shift non-Native student learning from rote memorization to a more creative form of inquiry. John, *William Torrey Harris*, 2.

53. Harris, "Civilization and Higher Education," 478.

54. *Annual Reports of the Department of the Interior for the Fiscal Year Ended, June 30, 1901*, 19; Adams, *Education for Extinction*, 126–28.

55. *Annual Report of the Superintendent of Indian Schools to the Secretary of the Interior, 1904*, 32.

56. Haskins, *Matrons and Maids*, 8; Jacobs, "Diverted Mothering," 18; Whalen, *Native Students at Work*, 37; Keliia, *Refusing Settler Domesticity*, 147–76.

57. Whalen, *Native Students at Work*, 37.

58. Jacobs, "Working on the Domestic Frontier," 172–73, 182.

59. In addition to preparing them to work as domestic servants, the curriculum aimed to undermine their culturally defined relationship to the land, particularly their roles in agriculture. Lomawaima, *They Called it Prairie Light*, 86.

60. Jacobs, "Diverted Mothering," 179–92; O'Neill, "Testing the Limits," 584.

61. Trennert, *Phoenix Indian School*, 51–52; Whalen, *Native Students at Work*, 29–30.

62. "Indian Boys and Girls Taking to Domestic Work," *Delta (CO) Independent*, August 29, 1902, 3.

63. *Meriam Report*, 389.

64. *Meriam Report*, 523.

65. Sea beans are large seeds carried into the ocean by freshwater streams and rivers. The polished versions of these seeds were sold as tourist trinkets. Pratt, *Battlefield and Classroom*, 128–29.

66. US Department of Agriculture, Bureau of Statistics, *Wages of Farm Labor*, 31.

67. Pratt, *Battlefield and Classroom*, 129.

68. Leupp, *Indian and His Problem*, 49. Lomawaima and McCarty argue that the Office of Indian Affairs created the Indian Employment Bureau to place boarding school students in the job market. Leupp relied on Dagenett to find employers and negotiate outing contracts. Lomawaima and McCarty, *To Remain an Indian*, 50; Kevin Whalen, email communication with the author, September 24, 2024.

69. Leupp, *Indian and His Problem*, 49.

70. Leupp, *Indian and His Problem*, 49.

71. *Indian Craftsman* (Carlisle Indian School, Carlisle, PA), 1909/1910, 2, 419; *Indian's Friend* 22, November 1909, 3. Douglas Miller describes Dagenett as a rare example of a Native American serving in the "Indian Service's Upper Ranks in the Early Twentieth Century." Miller, *Indians on the Move*, 29–30.

72. *Brooklyn Eagle*, August 31, 1911.

73. Leupp, *Report of the Commissioner of Indian Affairs to the Secretary of the Interior, 1909*, 5.

74. *Brooklyn Eagle*, August 31, 1911.

75. Leupp, *Report of the Commissioner of Indian Affairs to the Secretary of the Interior, 1909*, 5; O'Neil, "Anguished Odyssey," 315–27.

76. Laudenschlager, "Utes in South Dakota," 243; Leupp, *Report of Commissioner of Indian Affairs to the Department of Interior, 1908*, 120.

77. Hoxie, *Talking Back to Civilization*, 36–65; Eastman, "Indian in School," 653–64; Cahill, *Federal Fathers and Mothers*, 104–35.

78. Rejecting a policy-centered approach, historians such as Brenda Child, K. Tsianina Lomawaima, and Kevin Whalen explored the experience of Native students and their families and examined the schools as important sites of Native American resistance and historical agency. Child, *Boarding School Seasons*; Lomawaima, *They Called It Prairie Light*; Whalen, *Native Students at Work*.

79. Scott, *Weapons of the Weak*, 29.

80. Whalen, *Native Students at Work*, 47–50; Child, *Boarding School Seasons*, 85; Jacobs, "Working on the Domestic Frontier," 167; Lomawaima, *They Called It Prairie Light*, 101; Adams, *Education for Extinction*, 252–53.

81. *Annual Reports of the Department of the Interior for the Fiscal Year Ended, June 30, 1904*, 349.

82. Child, *Boarding School Seasons*, 85.

83. Child, *Boarding School Seasons*, 22.

84. Fortunate Eagle, *My Life*, 82.

85. Johnson, *Stories of Traditional Navajo Life*, 64.

86. Johnson, *Stories of Traditional Navajo Life*, 63.

87. Johnson, *Stories of Traditional Navajo Life*, 64.

88. Johnson, *Stories of Traditional Navajo Life*, 64.

89. Johnson, *Stories of Traditional Navajo Life*, 66. In the afterword of Adam Fortunate Eagle's autobiography, historian Laurence M. Hauptman describes him as a "contrary warrior." That term stems from a contrary warrior tradition among Great Plains Native peoples; it was usually used to refer to warriors of exceeding bravery and stubbornness. Fortunate Eagle, *My Life*, 171; Meadows, "Return of the Numu Pukutsi," 190.

90. Since at least the mid-nineteenth century, some American Indian students attended public schools; but their options were often limited by segregationist practices, the availability of public schools near their homes, and state officials. State public school administrators bristled that educating Native children required them to take on an inordinate financial burden, since their parents lived on reservations and did not pay state property taxes. Plus, OIA officials were ambivalent about the quality of education that Native children received in those schools. In 1934, as part of Indian New Deal Legislation, Congress passed the Johnson-O'Malley Act that allowed for the OIA to contract with public schools, underwriting the cost of Native students' attendance. Yet, even with these reforms—like creating day schools for Native students on reservations and backing away from some draconian attacks on Native culture—boarding schools and assimilationist curricula persisted until at least 1960s. For Native students in nonreservation public schools in the post–World War II era, see Amerman, *Urban Indians in Phoenix Schools*. After that some boarding schools, like the Haskell Indian School in Lawrence, Kansas; the Sherman Institute in Riverside, California; and the Diné-controlled day school Rough Rock Demonstration School in Chinle, Arizona, adopted more of a Native-centered approach to education, including teaching Indigenous languages. See Wayne, "Federal Role," 423–30; Prucha, *Great Father*, 948; Szasz, *Education and the American Indian*, 89–105, 156–80.

91. Forgive the anachronism: The quotation is from The Who's "Won't Get Fooled Again" (1971), written by Pete Townshend. According to a federal report released in 2024,

the Department of the Interior documented that "at least 973 documented Indian child deaths occurred across the Federal Indian boarding school system between 1819 and 1969." Newland, *Federal Indian Boarding School Initiative Investigative Report*.

CHAPTER 2

1. Historians have examined the social, economic, and cultural impact of Soil Conservation Service efforts to improve Navajo rangelands by reducing the number of their livestock. See Weisiger, *Dreaming of Sheep*; Parman, *Navajos and the New Deal*; Parman, "Indian and the Civilian Conservation Corps"; Aberle, *Peyote Religion among the Navajo*; Kelly, *Navajo Indians and Federal Indian Policy*; Boyce, *When the Navajos Had Too Many Sheep*; Hall, *West of the Thirties*. There is a growing literature on the impact of New Deal policies on other Indigenous communities in the United States. See Hosmer, "'Dollar a Day and Glad to Have It'"; Biolsi, *Organizing the Lakota*; Rosier *Rebirth of the Blackfeet Nation*; Heaton, *Shoshone-Bannocks*.

2. Before the launch of New Deal programs, Native people living on reservations worked on various reservation projects, often in exchange for rations. Biolsi, *Organizing the Lakota*, 112.

3. Launched in 1935 as part of President Franklin Delano Roosevelt's New Deal, the WPA replaced earlier Depression-era work relief initiatives that offered state, city, and county agencies (as well as charitable organizations) funding to support projects that put unemployed people to work. WPA projects included large-scale public works and scores of historical and cultural preservation efforts. Local agencies received funding from the federal government but largely retained administrative control over the projects they initiated. For other tribal histories that examine the impact of New Deal policies on Native Peoples, see Hosmer, "'Dollar a Day and Glad to Have It'"; Biolsi, *Organizing the Lakota*; Rosier, "'The Old System Is No Success'"; Heaton, *Shoshone-Bannocks*; Reinhardt, *Ruling Pine Ridge*.

4. For a gender analysis of New Deal soil conservation programs on Native lands, see Weisiger, *Dreaming of Sheep*; White, *Roots of Dependency*.

5. The Civilian Conservation Corps (CCC) was a relief program developed during the Great Depression to employ urban youth in land conservation projects. The Civilian Conservation Corps–Indian Division (CCC-ID) was an extension of that program to Indian reservations. The Works Projects Administration (WPA), another New Deal work program, employed people on a variety of largely urban public works projects ranging from building schools and government buildings to creating archives and histories. WPA projects were funded by the federal government but administered by local government officials, often at the county level. Some projects were extended to reservations.

6. Biolsi, *Organizing the Lakota*, 115.

7. According to historian Lawrence Kelly, out of 266 tribes voting, 189 supported the Indian Reorganization Act (IRA) and 77 opposed it. Kelly, "Indian Reorganization Act," 301.

8. Clow, "Indian Reorganization Act and the Loss of Tribal Sovereignty," 131. Vocal Native critics of the legislation worried that tribal governments organized under the IRA would largely serve as puppets to the OIA. Philp, "Termination," 171.

9. Parman, "Indian and the Civilian Conservation Corps," 55.

10. Kersey, *Florida Seminoles*, 102.

11. Bsumek, *Indian-Made*; Mclerran, *A New Deal for Navajo Weaving*, 77, 123–46; Jacobs, "Shaping a New Way," 187–215.

12. Federal efforts to support those efforts waxed and waned depending on the politics of Indian policy in the twentieth century. A significant part of the Indian New Deal included the Indian Arts and Crafts Act of 1935, which was supposed to protect and promote the market for Native American crafts. McLerran, *A New Deal for Navajo Weaving*. Native peoples throughout the United States continue to make a living by blending wage work with crafts and subsistence production. On wild rice farming and berrying, see Child, *My Grandfather's Knocking Sticks*; Norrgard, *Seasons of Change*. On the influence of nonnative experts in American Indian arts in the early twentieth century, see Jacobs, "Shaping a New Way"; Bsumek, *Indian-Made*; Hutchinson, *Indian Craze*; M'Closkey, *Swept under the Rug*.

13. Ellis, "Five Dollars a Week to be 'Regular Indians,'" 184–208; Rosenthal, "Representing Indians," 328–52; Cothran, "Working the Indian Field Days," 194–223, Bunten, "More Like Ourselves," 285–311; Phillips, *Staging Indigeneity*.

14. After the war, when commercial farmers in the Southwest sought substitutes for Bracero laborers, the market for Native American agricultural workers expanded. O'Neill, *Working the Navajo Way*, 98–99.

15. Weber, *Dark Sweat, White Gold*, 131.

16. Hauptman, *Iroquois and the New Deal*, 73. But for some Native people, like the Seminole, the erosion of their subsistence base forced them to seek work as agricultural laborers.

17. Weisiger, *Dreaming of Sheep*, 226. For the gendered dynamics of economic development on the Seminoles, see Cattelino, "Casino Roots." See also Cattelino, *High Stakes*. For analysis of the gendered impact of tourism on Native peoples in the Pacific Northwest, see Raibmon, "Practice of Everyday Colonialism." More recent scholarship on First Nation women and capitalist change includes Kelm and Townsend, *In the Days of Our Grandmother*. More research is needed to understand how settler colonial gender norms, particularly those introduced in boarding schools, continued to influenced craft production during the New Deal Era.

18. Maher, "'Work for Others but None for Us,'" 316.

19. Maher, *Nature's New Deal*, 80.

20. Maher, *Nature's New Deal*, 109.

21. For an overview of Native American gendered practices that predate the 1890s but that offer helpful context, see Slater and Yarbrough, *Gender and Sexuality*, 126–28.

22. Parman, "Indian and the Civilian Conservation Corps," 41. Neil Maher suggests that the CCC sought to remake non-Native men as well. Performing hard manual labor in the forest or the fields was supposed to reaffirm their masculinity and strengthen their bodies and sense of self-worth. The natural landscape was supposed to offer escape from immoral and unhealthy urban environments. Maher, *Nature's New Deal*, 91.

23. *Indians at Work*, September 15, 1933, 6, 15; Murphy, "Final Report of Indian Emergency Conservation Work," 20.

24. *Indians at Work*, September 15, 1933, 3.

25. Murphy, "Final Report of Indian Emergency Conservation Work," 58.

26. See this chapter's epigraph. Letter from M. H. Davis, Forest Supervisor, Hoopa Valley Agency to Claude C. Cornwall, General Enrollee Training Supervisor, March 5, 1941, box 215, folder Enrollees, Hoopa Valley, HVA.

27. Howard W. Oxley, Harry R. Kylie, and Edgar Lancaster, "Memorandum from Professional Committee on CCC Training," June 30, 1941, box 229, folder CCC-ID Misc, HVA.

28. *Indians at Work*, September 15, 1933, 7.

29. Leonard B. Radtke to John Collier, June 14, 1933, box 24, folder Working Plan Reports, L. B. Radtke, HVA.

30. Maher, "New Deal Body Politic," 437.

31. Murphy, "Final Report of Indian Emergency Conservation Work," 6.

32. As historian Laurence Hauptman observed, the CCC-ID often provided a central source of income to support families. According to historian Thomas Biolsi, the CCC-ID provided the largest source of income for Lakota men in 1935. Seventy-five percent of men living on the Rosebud Reservation worked on CCC-ID projects between 1933 until the demise of the program in 1942. Biolsi, *Organizing the Lakota*, 114. Some camps dispensed with the youth camp model entirely and accommodated entire families. Hauptman, *Iroquois and the New Deal*, 117. For a discussion of Native memories of those jobs, see Hosmer, "'Dollar a Day and Glad to Have It,'" 283–307.

33. Scholars have noted that BIA recordkeeping over the last 100 years has "been at best faulty and, at worst, possibly criminal. Poorly staffed, regional BIA offices handled much of the record-keeping and often failed to keep adequate records." Responding to increased criticism and mounting lawsuits, Congress passed the 1994 American Indian Trust Management Act to give Native Americans a full accounting of the funds in their accounts. Unfortunately, this historic audit of Individual Indian Monies was limited to funds deposited after 1987. The Department of the Interior argued that extending the audit back any further would be cost-prohibitive. Oakes and Young, "Reconciling Conflict," 67. Of course, further research on Individual Indian Money accounts is needed. Johansen, "BIA as Banker," 14. Since the 1980s, tribes and individuals have filed lawsuits challenging the BIA's historic management of trust accounts. They have repeatedly demanded a full accounting of the money they earned, but never fully collected, from grazing, oil leases, timber, and other resources. As of this writing, the most recent lawsuit was the Cobell class action case that charged the federal government with mismanaging Native American trust accounts. For a concise overview of the case and its historical implications see Campbell, "Cobell Settlement Finalized after Years of Litigation." In a 1992 report issued by the House of Representatives Committee on Government Relations, Congressman John Conyers admitted that federal mismanagement has cost Native American individuals and their tribes millions of dollars of their wealth. The report notes that corruption and bad accounting dates to at least 1828, when the Office of Indian Affairs was founded. According to H. R. Schoolcraft, one of the first agents to serve in that system, "One would think that appropriations had been handled with a pitchfork . . . there is a screw loose in the public machinery somewhere." Schoolcraft, as quoted in US House of Representatives, Committee on Government Operations, *Misplaced Trust*, 8–9.

34. Murphy, "Final Report of Indian Emergency Conservation Work," 6.

35. *Indians at Work*, September 15, 1933, 7.

36. *Indians at Work*, November 1, 1933, 27–28.

37. *Indians at Work*, October 1, 1933, 28–29; September 15, 1933, 12.

38. Hosmer, "'Dollar a Day and Glad to Have It,'" 290.

39. Quoted in Hosmer, "'Dollar a Day and Glad to Have It,'" 292.

40. Leonard Radtke to John Collier, November 15, 1933, box 224, folder Narrative Reports, HVA.

41. Parman, "Indian and the Civilian Conservation Corps," 47.

42. Howard W. Oxley, Harry R. Kylie and Edgar Lancaster, "Memorandum from Professional Committee on CCC Training," June 30, 1941, box 229, folder CCC-ID Misc, HVA.

43. Established schools operated by the OIA did not necessarily administer these educational programs. Although Indian day schools, developed as part of the New Deal reform, did at times host community-based programs that were connected to various OIA development initiatives. Biolsi, *Organizing the Lakota*, 122. Instructors could be foremen for various projects as could others who served the OIA on an ad hoc basis.

44. Murphy, "Final Report of Indian Emergency Conservation Work," 3.

45. Leonard B. Radtke, "The Narrative Report for the Month of October 1933 of the Indian Emergency Conservation Work at Hoopa Valley, CA," box 24, folder Working Plan Reports, HVA.

46. Lee Muck (Production Coordinating Officer) to John Collier, May 14, 1934, box 224, folder Narrative Reports, HVA. Historians have documented other New Deal conservation programs that were supposed to protect Native Americans' natural resources but that were instead carried out to protect the interests of non-Native people beyond reservation borders. See for example, White, *Roots of Dependency*; Weisiger, *Dreaming of Sheep*. Non-Native communities could also suffer from the development of large-scale environmental conservation programs. See, for example, the local impact of the Tennessee Valley Authority or dam building in the West, where small, rural communities sacrificed their homes in the name of development. For a postwar examination of this issue, see Reinhardt, "Drowned Towns," 149–72.

47. Murphy, "Final Report of Indian Emergency Conservation Work," 56.

48. US Bureau of Labor Statistics, Division of Employment Statistics, *Employment and Pay Rolls*, 19.

49. M. H. Davis, Forest Supervisor, Hoopa Valley Agency to Claude C. Cornwall, General Enrollee Training Supervisor, March 5, 1941, box 215, folder Enrollees, Hoopa Valley, HVA.

50. Biolsi, *Organizing the Lakota*, 115.

51. "Projects sponsored by the Bureau of Indian Affairs, Federal Indian Agency or Reservations," WPA Central Files: General Indian Relief, file 001, box 21, RG69. These number are somewhat skewed, since the document does not include WPA projects for Arizona or New Mexico. For many American Indian men, working in lumber mills and on conservation, road and other construction projects represented a significant shift into the world of wage labor. Hosmer, "'A Dollar a Day and Glad to Have It'"; O'Neill, *Working the Navajo Way*, 2005; Parman, "Indian and the Civilian Conservation Corps," 39–56.

52. US Federal Works Agency, *Final Report on the WPA*, 44; Tidd, "Stitching and Striking," 8.

53. Roosevelt, "My Day: November 12, 1936."

54. Federal Emergency Relief Administration press release, August 17, 1934, FERA Central Files 1933–36: Mattress Projects, box 24, RG69.

55. Swain, "'The Forgotten Woman,'" 204–5, 207–8.

56. Woodward, as quoted in Swain, "'The Forgotten Woman,'" 207.

57. US Federal Works Agency, *Final Report on the WPA*, 44.

58. J. H. McCain, President of the Alexandria Bedding Company to Harold Hopkins, July 16, 1934, box 24, FERA Central Files 1933–36: Mattress Projects, RG69.

59. It is unclear when the project ended, since we have evidence that mattress projects continued on the Fort Hall Reservation until at least July 1941. Industry leaders also worried about production standards. Henrietta K. Burton, Supervisor of Home Extension Work, Supervisor's Report, US Department of Interior, Office of Indian Affairs, Division of Extension and Industry, July 18, 1941, box 175, file 919, Central Classified Files–Fort Hall, 1907–1939, RG75, NARA I; Harry L. Hopkins to Robert W. Schwab, president of the Southern Spring Bed Company, September 19, 1934, box 24, FERA Central Files 1933–1936: Mattress Projects, RG69. Ellen Woodward answered this criticism by insisting that strict quality control would be enforced and that "All mattresses must be constructed in a neat and substantial manner in conformity with the work specifications furnished by this office. Special efforts must be made to avoid lumpiness resulting from careless filling or tufting." Ellen S. Woodward, Director of Women's Work to all State Emergency Relief Administrators, July 6, 1934, box 24, FERA Central Files 1933–36: Mattress Projects, RG69.

60. Harry Hopkins, Work Relief Administration Press Conference, October 8, 1934, Series 737, box 5, RG69.

61. Green, "Relief from Relief," 1012–37; Rose, *Put to Work*, 110.

62. Curiously, while the mattress projects ended in the South and the Midwest, they continued to operate in American Indian communities through 1941. Perhaps bedding industry leaders did not feel threatened by Native women doing the work far from large, commercial markets.

63. In her letter, Salois noted that she had been appointed to serve as a member of the Blackfeet delegation to Washington, DC, but that she had to withdraw at the last minute due to her mother's illness. Mary B. Salois to John Collier, Commissioner of Indian Affairs, August 8, 1934, file 920, Central Classified Files, Blackfeet 1907–1933, RG75, NARA I. Paul Rosier describes Salois as among the most influential women of the Blackfeet Nation. Rosier, *Rebirth of the Blackfeet Nation*, 199.

64. CWA programs were temporary federal relief measures that predated the WPA projects.

65. Internal memo from Huber (no first name indicated), August 16, 1934; handwritten note attached to file signed "Burton," August 15, 1934; and John Collier to Mary B. Salois, September 7, 1934, all in file 920, Central Classified Files, Blackfeet 1907–1933, RG75, NARA I.

66. "Annual Report of Extension Workers, January 1, 1937–December 31, 1937, Blackfeet Indian Reservation, Browning Montana," Central Classified Files, 1907–39, Blackfeet, box 2, file 031, RG75, NARA I. Women and men earned standard wages for people employed on work relief projects throughout the United States. Wages were the same at Fort Belknap. Fred W. Boyd, Superintendent of Fort Belknap Agency, to Commissioner of Indian Affairs, November 5, 1937, box 18, file Fort Belknap, Records of the Rehabilitation Division, Project Records, 1935–1944, RG75, NARA I.

67. Lomawaima, *They Called It Prairie Light*, 81–84; Jacobs, *White Mother to a Dark Race*, 305–7; Child, *Boarding School Seasons*, 81; Littlefield, "Indian Education and the

World of Work," 111–14. Native women were not necessarily the sole audience for these lessons. Agricultural extension agents taught canning, home economics, and scientific farming techniques to rural people in general. While canning and sewing clubs had existed throughout the rural United States since at least the turn of the twentieth century, the passage of the Smith-Lever Act in 1914, helped to create systematic organization of these types of activities and an educational bridge between the scientific research conducted at the land-grant universities to the rural peoples who could apply that information to their lives. Hurt, *American Agriculture*, 256–58; Jensen, "Canning Comes to New Mexico," 201–26.

68. "Annual Report of Extension Workers, January 1, 1936–December 31, 1936, Blackfeet Indian Reservation, Browning Montana," Division of Extension and Industry, Central Classified Files, 1907–39, Blackfeet, box 2, file 031, RG75, NARA I.

69. William Donner, superintendent, Fort Apache Agency, Whiteriver, Arizona, "Self-Help Clothing for Relief," Proposal for Community Improvement Project, Indian Relief and Rehabilitation Fund, April 7, 1937, Records of the Rehabilitation Division, Project Records, 1935–1944, Fort Apache–Fort Belknap, box 18, entry 1007, RG75, NARA I.

70. Kitty Deernose, "A Petition Regarding Employment of Enrolled Crow Indian Women of the Crow Indian Reservation, Crow Agency, Montana," box 271, folder #4, James E. Murray Papers, Archives and Special Collections, Mansfield Library, University of Montana, Missoula.

71. Henrietta Crockett to Senator James E. Murray, July 1, 1937, box 271, folder #4, James E. Murray Papers, Archives and Special Collections, Mansfield Library, University of Montana, Missoula.

72. Tetzloff, "Elizabeth Bender Cloud," 77–115.

73. Hoxie, *Parading Through History*, 329–36.

74. Robert Yellowtail, as quoted in Montana State Appraisal Committee, *Evaluation of the Federal Works Program in Montana*, 29.

75. Kitty Deernose, "A Petition Regarding Employment of Enrolled Crow Indian Women of the Crow Indian Reservation, Crow Agency, Montana," box 271, folder #4, James E. Murray Papers, Archives and Special Collections, Mansfield Library, University of Montana, Missoula.

76. In a letter to Senator Murray, Minnie Williams accused Yellowtail of using his position as a caseworker to dole out political patronage, rewarding family and friends with jobs and denying his political enemies the opportunity to work. She worried that Yellowtail would fire her from her job as a "janitoress" in the CCC office at the Crow Agency if he found out she had written the senator the letter. She was part of a faction on the Crow reservation that favored "civilization" and opposed the use of Peyote. She states that the Crow Indian Women's Federated Club opposed the election of Native American Church representatives to the tribal council. She maintained that those men (referring here to two individuals) did not represent the "Crow people." The women's club supported the Catholic Mission schools on the reservation, not the Native American Church. In the letter she complains that three-quarters of the reservation residents are Peyote addicts. The delegation in Washington was there to lobby for the passage of a law allowing Peyote to be used for religious purposes, and she opposed the practice. Minnie Williams to James E. Murray, July 10, 1939; William Zimmerman to James Murry, April 1, 1939; and Millie Williams to James Murray, March 27, 1939, "A Petition Regarding Employment of Enrolled Crow Indian Women of the Crow Indian Reservation, Crow Agency," all in box

271, folder #4, James Murray Papers, Archives and Special Collections, Mansfield Library, University of Montana, Missoula.

77. Telegram from James E. Murray to Joseph E. Parker, July 13, 1939, box 808, folder 2, James Murray Papers, Archives and Special Collections, Mansfield Library, University of Montana, Missoula.

78. See a useful discussion of the debate over the term hegemonic masculinity in Connell, "Masculinities in Global Perspective," 303–18.

CHAPTER 3

1. Bernstein, *American Indians in World War II*, 73; Miller, *Indians on the Move*, 44–45. World War II inspired the massive internal migration of many Americans. Dust bowl refugees, who traveled to California in search of agricultural work, found jobs in Southern California's defense industry. Many Black workers had moved to northern and western cities in search of industrial jobs in the early twentieth century, and more embarked on a Second Great Migration during World War II. For Black migration to the northern and western United States during World War II, see Effinger-Crichlow, *Staging Migrations*; and Taylor, "Facing the Urban Frontier, 6–27. For Latinx migration north and west during World War II, see Rivas-Rodriguez and Olguín, *Latina/os and World War II*; Durand, Massey, and Parrado, "New Era of Mexican Migration," 518–36; Morales, "Tejano Migrants," 12–24. The Bracero program played a major role in boosting Mexican migration north. See Quintana, *Contracting Freedom*. For Mexican migration during World War I, see Vargas, *Proletarians of the North*. For histories of white workers who moved to the West during the dust bowl migration and who then moved on to work in the defense industry, see Gregory, *American Exodus*.

2. Parman, "Indian and the Civilian Conservation Corps," 53; Howard W. Oxley, Harry R. Kylie and Edgar Lancaster, "Memorandum from Professional Committee on CCC Training," June 30, 1941, box 229, folder CCC-ID Misc, HVA.

3. Frustrated with his waning influence on Indian policy and growing criticism in Congress, Collier stepped down from his position as Commissioner of Indian Affairs. On January 22, 1945, President Franklin Delano Roosevelt reluctantly accepted his resignation. Collier, *From Every Zenith*, 305; DeJong, *Commissioners of Indian Affairs*, 140.

4. Bernstein, *American Indians in World War II*, 65–66; see also Ickes, *Annual Report of the Secretary of the Interior, 1942*, 239.

5. *Indians at Work*, December 1940, 31.

6. *Indians at Work*, December 1941, 31.

7. *Indians at Work*, January 1942, 33. For a discussion of Native workers in Los Angeles, see Rosenthal, *Reimagining Indian Country*, chap. 4.

8. Bernstein, *American Indians in World War II*, 6.

9. Bernstein, *American Indians in World War II*, 72.

10. US Federal Works Agency, *Final Report on the WPA*, 88.

11. Gouveia, "'We Also Serve,'" 153–82.

12. Whalen, *Native Students at Work*, 34–38; Haskins, *Matrons and Maids*, 5; O'Neill, *Working the Navajo Way*, 97. Although Collier originally supported Peters, he eventually decided that his efforts to relocate Native Americans to cities ran counter to official Indian

policy that favored rebuilding reservation economies. LaPier and Beck, "A 'One-Man Relocation Team,'" 29.

13. Text of resolution, as quoted in Prucha, *Great Father*, 1044; US Department of the Interior, *Kapler's Indian Affairs*, 6:614–15. Historians and activists argue that the Relocation Program set the stage for urban Indian activism in the late 1960s. Mankiller and Wallis, *Mankiller*, 69–72; P. C. Smith, *Like a Hurricane*, 16–17.

14. Some Native people on reservations, often the most well-off, supported termination because they saw advantages in lifting federal regulations over the use and exploitation of their resources. Metcalf, *Termination's Legacy*, 6; Philp, *Termination Revisited*, 72–75.

15. O'Neill, "Testing the Limits," 567. For more on relocation and termination, see Miller, *Indians on the Move*; Valandra, *Not Without Our Consent*; LeGrand, *Indian Metropolis*; Rosenthal, *Reimagining Indian Country*; Fixico, *Termination and Relocation*; Philp, *Termination Revisited*; Metcalf, *Termination's Legacy*; Watkins, "Termination of Federal Supervision," 49.

16. Prucha, *Great Father*, 1046–48.

17. Tribes were terminated on an individual basis, each termination requiring an act of Congress. BIA officials categorized tribes as predominately acculturated, semi-acculturated, or predominately Indian. Philp, *Termination Revisited*, 75.

18. The first historical studies of termination and relocation policy and its general impact on American Indian sovereignty include Philp, *Termination Revisited*; Metcalf, *Termination's Legacy*; Fixico, *Termination and Relocation*; Fixico, *Urban Indian Experience in America*; Blackhawk, "I Can Carry On from Here," 16–30; LaGrand, *Indian Metropolis*. Scholars largely examined relocation as a factor shaping the development of pan-Indian activism of the late 1960s and 1970s.

19. Douglas K. Miller is one of the first historians to examine relocation from a labor perspective. Miller, "Willing Workers," 51–76. See also Miller, *Indians on the Move*, 10. Nick Rosenthal's *Reimagining Indian Country* explores the development of the American Indian community in Los Angeles.

20. David and Elizabeth Williams are pseudonyms.

21. Stanley R. Thomas to Stanley D. Lyman, January 27, 1955, Relocation Employment Assistance Case Records, Oakland, 1954, box 4, NARA-SF.

22. Stanley R. Thomas to Stanley D. Lyman, January 27, 1955, Relocation Information Record, 1955; and Brice Lay to relocatee, June 9, 1955, Relocation Employment Assistance Case Records, Oakland, 1954, box 4, RG75, NARA-SF.

23. Miller, *Indians on the Move*, 94.

24. Mary Nan Gamble, field director of relocation services, Los Angeles office of the BIA, CBS radio interview, Field Employment Assistance Office Files-LA, ccf 1948–62, box 1, file 040, Publicity, 1956, RG75, NARA-Riverside. See also, Sorkin, *Urban American Indian*, 26.

25. Jack Calhoun, "Relocation Gives Indian New Hope," *San Jose Mercury News*, February 23, 1956.

26. Brice Lay to Harold Mann, relocation agent for Pueblo Agency, February 21, 1955, Relocation Employment Assistance Case Records, Oakland, 1954, box 4, RG75, NARA-SF.

27. CBS radio interview with Mary Nan Gamble, field director of the Los Angeles office of the BIA, in charge of relocation services. Field Employment Assistance Office Files-LA, ccf 1948-62, box 1, file 040, Publicity, 1956, RG75, NARA-Riverside.

28. Agents opposed relocating large families because they found it difficult to locate adequate housing that the relocatees' could afford on their low wages. Martha H. Quinn, "Report of Visit to Los Angeles Field Employment Assistance Office," October 2, 1962, Field Employment Assistance Office Files-LA, ccf 1948–62, box 21, file 799.4, RG75, NARA-Riverside; Brice Lay to relocatee, February 8, 1955, Relocation Employment Assistance Case Records, Oakland, 1954, box 2, folder 0-55-29, RG75, NARA-SF.

29. Pseudonym used. Phoenix Area Office, Intermountain Indian School, Student Case Files, 1953–63, RG75, NARA-Riverside. For the concept of making the colonized subject legible, see Scott, *Seeing Like a State*, 2, 24; O'Neill, "Testing the Limits," 569.

30. Kessler-Harris, *A Woman's Wage*, 8. The Aboriginal Labour Placement Program in Canada mirrored those same gendered policies and practices. As Joan Sangster describes, the Canadian program was "fundamentally gendered both in the conceptualization of the problem and in the creation of policy solutions." Much like the US program, the Canadian policymakers "assumed a male breadwinner as the ideal. Women were seen as ancillary earners who only worked when they were young and single." Sangster, "Colonialism at Work," 301.

31. Annual Report for Fiscal Year 1960, Los Angeles Field Relocation Office, Field Employment Assistance Office Files-LA, ccf 1948-62, box 16, folder 799.21, RG75, NARA-Riverside.

32. Maynard L. Gage, relocation officer, Monthly Narrative Report, San Jose Sub Office, April 1956, Employment Assistance Service Branch, SF Field Service Office, box 1, folder Narrative and Statistical Reports, 1956; Monthly Narrative Report, San Jose Sub Office, April 1956, Reports and Correspondence, 799.23, box 1; and Monthly Reports, January 1957–December 1957, Relocation Employment Assistance Files, Case Records, Oakland, box 3, all in RG75, NARA-SF.

33. Annual Report for Fiscal Year 1960, Los Angeles Field Relocation Office, Field Employment Assistance Office Files-LA, ccf 1948–62, box 16, folder 799.21, RG75, NARA-Riverside.

34. Relocation Information Record, Relocation Employment Assistance Office, Case Records, Oakland, 1954, box 3, RG75, NARA-SF. Peter and Maria Begay are pseudonyms.

35. O'Neill, "Testing the Limits," 565–92.

36. In a study commissioned by the Intermountain Indian School, Lewis Fish, a graduate student in education at Utah State University, found that "employers . . . did not care what happened [to a young man] after hours as long as he did his work on the job." Fish, "Study of the Reasons for Failure," 30.

37. Monthly Narrative Report, April 1956, San Jose Sub-Office, box 1, folder Narrative and Statistical Reports, 1956, Employment Assistance Service Branch, San Francisco, RG75, NARA-SF; Relocation Employment Assistance files, Case Records, Oakland, 1954, box 1, RG75, NARA-SF; Phoenix Area Office, Intermountain Indian School, Student Case Files, 1953–63, RG75, NARA-Denver.

38. Private individuals and employment agencies continued to contact relocation offices to recruit Native American women into domestic service. But relocation officers redirected their inquiries to state employment offices and boarding schools. Jes Willis and Evelyn Ockerman to Field Relocation Officer, March 21, 1962, Employment Assistance Service Branch, Los Angeles Field Office, RG75, NARA-Riverside; O'Neill, "Testing the Limits," 565–92.

39. Relocation agents paid close attention to labor market issues. Los Angeles Field Relocation Report, Employment Trends and Forecast, June 27, 1958, George Felshaw, relocation officer, Field Employment Assistance Office Files-LA, ccf 1948–62, box 11, folder 721.8, RG75, NARA-Riverside.

40. Despite reformers' efforts in the 1930s, policymakers continued to embrace a curriculum that used work to assimilate Native children (with the goal to eventually transform entire Native societies) well into the 1960s. For a discussion of curriculum in the Intermountain Indian School during the 1950s, see O'Neill, "Testing the Limits," 565–92.

41. O'Neill, "Testing the Limits," 576–78.

42. Address by Glenn L. Emmons, Commissioner of Indian Affairs, before the Governors Interstate Indian Council, Sheridan, Wyoming, August 6, 1956, Field Employment Assistance Office Files-LA, ccf 1948–62, box 1, file 010, Publications, 1948–56, RG75, NARA-Riverside. Emphasis added.

43. Walter V. Woehlke, Area Director, Phoenix Area Office to John Provinse, Assistant Commissioner of Indian Affairs, December 8, 1950, Records of the Phoenix Area Office, box 54, folder 721, RG75, NARA-Riverside; Bauer, *We Were are All Like Migrant Workers Here*, 120; O'Neill, *Working the Navajo Way*, 4; Raibmon, *Authentic Indians*, 109–10; Norrgard, *Seasons of Change*, 25.

44. According to historian Daniel Cobb, in their opposition to termination in 1957, the NCAI argued that Native American rights were not the same as civil rights. D. Cobb, *Native Activism in Cold War America*, 22.

45. Douglas McKay, Secretary of the Interior, to Oliver La Farge, November 30, 1955. Field Employment Assistance Office Files-LA, ccf 1948–62, box 1, file 011, Admin Issuances, 1954–55, RG75, NARA-Riverside.

46. Douglas McKay, Secretary of the Interior, to Oliver La Farge, November 30, 1955. Ardent reformer, writer, and winner of the Pulitzer Prize for the novel *Laughing Boy* in 1930, La Farge argued against termination and relocation in the popular press and in academic journals. For the latter see, La Farge, "Termination of Federal Supervision," 41–46.

47. Miller, "Willing Workers," 64.

48. Hoska Cronemeyer and Savier D. Vaughn, "Report to Navajo Tribal Council of Visits to San Francisco Bay Area January 7–10; San Jose, January 11; Los Angeles January 13–17, 1957," Field Employment Assistance Office Files-LA, ccf 1948–62, box 1, file 064, Navajo Tribal Council, 1956–57, RG75, NARA-Riverside.

49. Paul Jones, "Letter to All Navajo Relocatees," January 4, 1957, Field Employment Assistance Office Files-LA, ccf 1948–62, box 1, file 060, Tribal Ordinances (policy on), RG75, NARA-Riverside.

50. Memo to George M. Felshaw, field relocation officer, March 9, 1960, Field Employment Assistance Office Files-LA, ccf 1948–62, box 1, file 048, Photos, RG75, NARA-Riverside.

51. Memo from Marion E. Henry to Mr. Coffee, assistant field relocation officer, March 18, 1960, Field Employment Assistance Office Files-LA, ccf 1948–62, box 1, file 048, Photos, RG75, NARA-Riverside.

52. Hoska Cronemeyer and Savier D. Vaughn, "Report to Navajo Tribal Council of Visits to San Francisco Bay Area."

53. Cattelino, "Double Bind," 235–62; McLaughlin, "Nation, Tribe, and Class," 108–9. Moore, "Cheyenne Work," 131.

54. Few scholars have compared postwar development strategies in Africa with US Indian policy. Although, some historians have compared earlier colonial histories (most notably, Frederickson, *White Supremacy*), Indigenous critical theory scholars have pointed out the limits of drawing direct parallels between African and South Asian history. As Jodi Byrd and Michael Rothberg have pointed out, those comparisons need to consider the difference in colonial dynamics. The problem of "'fit' between models developed as a response to the colonization of the Indian subcontinent and (to a lesser extent) Africa, on the one hand, and the settler colonies of the Americas, Australia and New Zealand, on the other." Byrd and Rothberg, "Between Subalternity and Indigeneity," 4. But given the lack of scholarship on Indigenous labor and settler colonialism, African scholarship, like Cooper's work, is helpful.

55. Rosier, "Crossing International and Historiographical Boundaries," 955–66. American Indian activists and intellectuals made the connection between their history and de-colonization in the post war world. D. Cobb, *Native Activism in Cold War America*, 27; Latham, *Modernization as Ideology*, 4.

56. Latham, *Modernization as Ideology*, 6.

57. Philp, *Termination Revisited*, 69. As David Wilkins and Heidi Kiiwetinepinesiik Stark suggest, termination plans represented a kind of bipartisan consensus on the solution to America's Indian problem, even though opposing political camps disagreed on its cause. Conservative legislators blamed New Deal policies for "retarding the Indians' Progress as American citizens," and liberals thought that Native Americans suffered discrimination at the hands of the OIA. But a few Indian policy experts feared that many tribes were not ready for modernization and advocated a gradual approach. Wilkins and Stark, *American Indian Politics*, 157–58.

58. Rosier, "Crossing International and Historiographical Boundaries," 955–66.

59. Rosier, "Crossing International and Historiographical Boundaries," 955–66. See also Rosier, *Serving Their Country*, chaps. 4–5; Prucha, *Great Father*, 1030.

60. Cooper, *Decolonization and African Society*, 9–10.

61. Cooper, *Decolonization and African Society*, 2.

62. Cooper, *Decolonization and African Society*, 2.

63. Following World War II, Arthur Watkins steered funding from the Navajo-Hopi Relocation Act to transform the Bushnell Naval Hospital in Brigham City, Utah, into a boarding school for Navajo children who did not have the resources to attend day schools on the reservation. That institution, the Intermountain Indian School, continued to operate until 1984. O'Neill, "Testing the Limits," 565–92. To learn about the students' creativity, see King, Taylor, and Swensen, *Returning Home*.

64. Monthly Narrative Report, April 1956, San Jose Sub-Office, Employment Assistance Service Branch Records, San Francisco, box 1, folder Narrative and Statistical Reports, 1956, RG75, NARA-SF.

65. Even Native leaders such as D'Arcy McNickle, as Dan Cobb points out, called for the creation of development projects like Truman's Point IV program to solve the problem of reservation poverty. D. Cobb, *Native Activism in Cold War America*, 8; Rosier, *Serving Their Country*, 143.

66. For a comprehensive examination of Native urban networks in this period, see Rosenthal, *Reimagining Indian Country*; and Ramirez, *Native Hubs*.

67. Paul Jones, "Letter to All Navajo Relocatees," January 4, 1957, Field Employment Assistance Office Files-LA, ccf 1948–62, box 1, file 060, Tribal Ordinances (policy on), 53–58, RG75, NARA-Riverside.

68. This problem raised enough questions that BIA relocation agents collected data on tribal enrollment requirements. Field Employment Assistance Office Files-LA, ccf 1948–62, box 1, file 063, Enrollment of Indian Children, 1957, RG75, NARA-Riverside.

69. Rosebud Sioux Tribal Ordinance 5711, September 30, 1957, Field Employment Assistance Office Files-LA, ccf 1948–62, box 1, file 063, Enrollment of Indian Children, 1957, RG75, NARA-Riverside.

70. Membership Ordinance, Affiliated Tribes of the Ft. Berthold Reservation, attached Memo from O.K. Walkingstick to Area Director, Aberdeen Area Office, Attn: Area Relocation Specialist, Adopted January 8, 1948, Field Employment Assistance Office Files-LA, ccf 1948–62, box 1, file 063, Enrollment of Indian Children, 1957, RG75, NARA-Riverside. Enrollment criteria shifted dramatically in the twentieth century. Many American Indian governments have been struggling with this issue, given the development of significant mineral and gaming industries on reservations and the difficulties associated with the federal recognition process. For a brief glance into the complicated struggles of one tribe's discussion of enrollment, see Harmon, "Tribal Enrollment Councils," 175–200. On race and tribal enrollment, see Sturm, "Blood Politics," 230–58. For an overview see Wilkins and Lomawaima, *Uneven Ground*.

71. The study's documents fill 28 boxes in Division of Community Services Branch of Employment Assistance, Records Relating to the Operation "TOB" study, 1966–68, RG75, NARA I. For the report generated from these files, see Ola Beckett, director, Dallas Field Employment Assistance Office, "Study of the Effectiveness and Impact of the Voluntary Movement of Indian People: A Study of the Employment Assistance Program," July 1966, mimeograph, Division of Community Services Branch Employment Assistance, Records Relating to the Operation "TOB" study," 1966–68, box 27, folder Miscellaneous Memorandums, RG75, NARA I. A follow-up study was completed two years later. See "1968 Followup [sic] Study of 1963 Recipients of the Services of the Employment Assistance Program, Bureau of Indian Affairs," folder Urban Indians, CFOA 8806, 3 of 4, box 114, White House Central Files: Staff Member and Office Files: Leonard Garment; Richard Nixon Presidential Library and Museum, Yorba Linda, CA. I could not locate an explanation for why the study was nicknamed, "Operation 'TOB'" in the archives or in supporting correspondence. Economist Alan Sorkin relied heavily on that report for his analysis of the relocation program in his book, *American Indians and Federal Aid*.

72. Not all files included before and after photos of the relocatees' housing. Not all photos portrayed a stark contrast between urban and reservation housing. Photos are located in Division of Community Services Branch Employment Assistant Records Relating to the Operation "TOB" study, 1966–68, box 2, folder 8, and box 3, folder 30, RG75, NARA I.

73. Ola Beckett, director, Dallas Field Employment Assistance Office, "A Study of the Effectiveness and Impact of the Voluntary Movement of Indian People: A Study of the Employment Assistance Program," July 1966, mimeograph, Division of Community Services Branch Employment Assistant, Records Relating to the Operation "TOB" study, 1966–68, box 27, folder Miscellaneous Memorandums, RG75, NARA I.

74. Division of Community Services Branch of Employment Assistance, Records Relating to the Operation "TOB" study, 1966–68, box 2, folder 17, RG75, NARA I.

75. Division of Community Services Branch of Employment Assistance, Records Relating to the Operation "TOB" study, 1966–68, box 5, folder 53, RG75, NARA I.

76. Division of Community Services Branch of Employment Assistance, Records Relating to the Operation "TOB" study, 1966–68, box, 2, folder 19, RG75, NARA I.

77. Division of Community Services Branch of Employment Assistance, Records Relating to the Operation "TOB" study, 1966–68, box 6, folder 77, RG75, NARA I; *Madera Daily Tribune*, May 31, 1962, 1–2.

78. Ola Beckett, director, Dallas Field Employment Assistance Office, "Study of the Effectiveness and Impact of the Voluntary Movement of Indian People: A Study of the Employment Assistance Program," July 1966.

79. Division of Community Services Branch of Employment Assistance, Records Relating to the Operation "TOB" study, 1966–68, box 6, folder 74, RG75, NARA I.

80. RCA is the acronym for the former Radio Corporation of America. Division of Community Services Branch of Employment Assistance, Records Relating to the Operation "TOB" study, 1966–68, box 1, folder 4, RG75, NARA I.

81. Rosenthal, *Reimaging Indian Country*, chap. 6; Ramirez, *Native Hubs*, chap. 3; O'Neill, *Working the Navajo Way*, 97.

CHAPTER 4

1. CTER cofounders Conrad Edwards and John Navarro and General Counsel Dan Press discussion, video. Coal and other types of mining as well as large-scale energy development projects located off reservation land provided Native workers with jobs, too. Navajos migrated to the coal mines in Colorado for work as early as the 1920s. Yaqui and Apache men worked in the copper mines in Southern Arizona. See O'Neill, *Working the Navajo Way*; Meeks, *Border Citizens*, 136; Rogge, McWatters, Keane, and Emanuel, *Raising Arizona's Dams*, 143–49.

2. For an in-depth analysis of the origins of the term, "Indian Problem," see Hays, *Editorializing "The Indian Problem,"* 1.

3. Powell and Long, "Landscapes of Power," 231–62. For a clear outline of health problems Navajos faced because of working in uranium mines, see Johnston, Dawson, and Madsen, "Uranium Mining and Milling," 111–34; Brenda Norre, "Energy Genocide, Backlash Yield New Peoples' Movement in the Americas," *Indian Country Today*, July 24, 2006, 1; Lewis, "Skull Valley Goshutes," 304–42; Dawson, "Navajo Uranium Workers," 389–97; Brugge, Benally, and Yazzie-Lewis, *Navajo People and Uranium Mining*; Eichstaedt, *If You Poison Us*; Ishiyama, "Environmental Justice," 119–39.

4. For a more in-depth discussion of the literature on American Indian history, labor, and colonialism, see O'Neill, *Working the Navajo Way*, 5–11, 142–60.

5. O'Neill, *Working the Navajo Way*, 138–39; Curley, *Carbon Sovereignty*, 63–65.

6. Glaser, "'Absolute Paragon of Paradoxes,'" 161–202; Needham, "'Piece of the Action,'" 203–30.

7. Gervais interview by author.

8. John McGill, "BCC Conference to Focus on Discrimination and Racial Profiling," *Glacier Reporter*, May 19, 2004.

9. *Diné be'iiná Náhiiłna be Agha'diit'ahii* translated into English means "attorneys who work for the revitalization of the people." Iverson, *Diné*, 238. See also DNA People's Legal Services, accessed May 5, 2024, www.dnalegalservices.org.

10. O'Neill, *Working the Navajo Way*, 138.

11. Dan Press interview by Sylvia Danovitch.

12. The Gallup Supply Warehouse stored supplies for distribution to BIA facilities on reservations in the Gallup area, such as to the Navajo and Zuni; Press interview by author *Americans before Columbus: Newsletter of the National Indian Youth Council*, April–July 1970, 1. Thanks to Sterling Fluharty for bringing this source to my attention. Shreve, "Red Power Rising." See also Fluharty, "For a Greater Indian America."

13. "Testimony of Gerald Wilkinson and Bill Pensoneau of the National Indian Youth Council before the National Council on Indian Opportunity, January 8, 1979," *Americans before Columbus: Newsletter of the National Indian Youth Council*, December 1969–January 1970, 6.

14. James Hena, assistant to the commissioner of Indian Affairs to the Commissioner of Indian Affairs, August 7, 1970, Records of the Office of the Commissioner of Indian Affairs, Office Files of Commissioner Louis R. Bruce, 1969–72, entry #180-V, box 11, folder Field Trips, RG75, NARA I.

15. Press interview by author.

16. Press interview by author.

17. Press interview by author.

18. Press interview by author.

19. Robbins, "Navajo Participation in Labor Unions," 10.

20. Press interview by author.

21. White interview by author; "A Look Back at the Birth of TERO, Part I: The Ken White, Sr., Story," Council for Tribal Employment Rights, accessed July 3, 2025, https://cter-tero.org/2017/10/11/a-look-back-at-the-birth-of-tero-part-i-the-ken-white-sr-story/.

22. Prucha, *Documents of United States Indian Policy*, 70; Novak, "Real Takeover of the BIA," 640–46.

23. Novak, "Real Takeover of the BIA," 642.

24. Novak, "Real Takeover of the BIA," 651; Hosmer, "'Dollar a Day and Glad to Have It,'" 294. See also the historical literature that shows American Indians using wage work (in addition to working for the BIA) to sustain their cultures rather than simply assimilating the values and behavior of the dominant society. Meeks, "Tohono O'odham"; Raibmon, *Authentic Indians*; Bauer, *We Were All Like Migrant Workers Here*; Hosmer, *American Indians in the Marketplace*; O'Neill, *Working the Navajo Way*; Littlefield and Knack, *Native Americans and Wage Labor*.

25. Unidentified Crow spokesperson, as quoted in Rzeczkowski, "Reimagining Community," 260. Rzeczkowski points out that in 1895, another Crow leader, Cold Wind, was also concerned that non–Crow Indians would take their jobs.

26. In 1973 non-Native BIA employees filed a class action lawsuit in the US District Court in New Mexico, charging that the Equal Employment Opportunities Act of 1972 nullified provisions that protected Indian preference in Title VII of the 1964 Civil Rights

Act. That judgment, however, was overturned the following year by the US Supreme Court in *Morton v. Mancari*. In that landmark case, the court found that hiring preferences were specifically protected: "The purpose of these preferences, as variously expressed in the legislative history, has been to give Indians a greater participation in their own self-government; to further the Government's trust obligation toward the Indian tribes; and to reduce the negative effect of having non-Native people administer matters that affect Indian tribal life." *Morton v. Mancari*, 417 U.S. 535 (1974). Legal scholars have interpreted this ruling as a precedent for viewing "Indian" as a political rather than a racial category. Baca, "American Indians, the Racial Surprise," 975.

27. Press interview by author.
28. ACKCO are the initials of the founders of this consulting firm.
29. Press, *Indian Employment Rights*. Press interview by Danovitch.
30. "Appendix B: Kenneth White, keynote speech delivered at the first Indian Employment Rights Conference, Kenita Lodge, Warm Springs, Oregon, April 1977," in Press, *Indian Employment Rights*, B-1.
31. CETA (Comprehensive Employment and Training Act) was a federal program that funded various employment programs throughout the country, aimed at disadvantaged populations. John Navarro and Conrad Edwards would then go on to create the Council for Tribal Employment Rights (CTER). Navarro served as CTER's president until 2007. When he retired, Conrad Edwards took over his responsibilities.
32. Edwards, president, Council for Tribal Employment Rights, and Navarro, founding president of Council of Tribal Employment Rights, interview by author.
33. Edwards and Navarro interview by author.
34. Gervais interview by author.
35. Press interview by author.
36. Edwards and Navarro interview by author.
37. Edwards and Navarro interview by author.
38. Edwards and Navarro interview by author.
39. "From One to 100: A Decade of TERO," *Sho-Ban News*, January 29, 1987, 4.
40. Edwards and Navarro interview by author.
41. Gervais interview by author.
42. "TERO Promotes Tribal Self-Sufficiency," *Sho-Ban News*, September 3, 1987, 2.
43. Quoted in John Kozlowicz, "TERO Celebrates 25 Years," *Hocak Worak, Newsletter of the Ho-Chunk Nation*, July 10, 2002.
44. "From One to 100: A Decade of TERO," *Sho-Ban News*, January 29, 1987, 4.
45. White interview by author.
46. Testimony of Thomas H. Brose, in US Commission on Civil Rights, *Hearing before the United States Commission on Civil Rights, Window Rock, Arizona*, October 22–24, 1973.
47. In 2003, Joe Shirley, who served as president of the Navajo Nation from 2003 to 2011, appointed Lawrence Oliver, a former president of the United Mine Workers local in Window Rock and chairman of *Naalnishí* (the Navajo Labor Federation), as head of the division of Human Resources.
48. Author's notes on a Laborers International presentation at the Council for Tribal Employment Rights' 2006 Legal Update and Indian Preference, Imperial Palace Hotel and Casino, Las Vegas, Nevada December 6–8, 2006.
49. Edwards-Navarro interview by author.

50. For a detailed examination of CERT's beginnings and its critics, see Ambler, *Breaking the Iron Bonds*, 73–117; Fixico, "Understanding the Earth and the Demand on Energy Tribes," 21–34. See also Fixico, *Invasion of Indian Country*, 159–75.

51. Once established, TERO offices quickly became institutionalized within tribal governments.

52. A. Philip Randolph, president of the Brotherhood of Sleeping Car Porters, and Cesar Chavez, president of the United Farm Workers Union, were both important civil rights leaders in addition to their roles as union presidents.

53. This is not to say that the Navajo Nation government is unabashedly pro-union. The tribal government's position on organized labor (like that of other governments) varies with the political climate. For how organizing campaigns reveal tensions between tribal leaders and Navajo labor activists, see Kamper, *Work of Sovereignty*. With the status of coal mining on the reservation in flux, United Mine Workers of America (UMWA) members sometimes found themselves in conflict with Navajo environmentalists. Jim Maniaci, "Black Mesa Worker Graymouth: Enviros Not Real Grassroots People," *Gallup Independent*, June 17, 2005. Curley, *Carbon Sovereignty*, 185.

54. I am using the term "movement" here since those who created TERO offices did so with an activist strategy and passion. I observed members of CTER use the term themselves at their Legal Update meeting in Las Vegas, December 6–8, 2006, and December 5–7, 2007.

55. Ambler, "Three Affiliated Tribes at Fort Berthold," 195; "Court Opens Window for Navajo Nation Trust Suit," Indianz.com, October 27, 2003, https://indianz.com/News/archives/002205.asp; Barry Meier, "Navajo Lawsuits Contend U.S. Government Failed the Tribe in Mining Royalty Deals," *New York Times*, July 18, 1999.

CHAPTER 5

1. This is not to say that Native casino workers are necessarily anti-union. American Indian workers have joined unions throughout the United States. See Kamper, *Work of Sovereignty*, 101–200; Weitzman, *Skywalkers*, 65; O'Neill, *Working the Navajo Way*, 140–41. These studies are useful, but no complete portrait of Native union membership is available. The US Bureau of Labor Statistics does not categorize union membership by ethnicity. See the AFL-CIO website highlighting Native union activists.

2. On April 16, 2025, the San Manuel Band of Mission Indians adopted the name Yuhaaviatam of San Manuel Nation to reflect their name in their native language. They trace their ancestral lands to what is now Southern California, the area spanning the Mojave Desert and the Inland Empire. See their website, https://sanmanuel-nsn.gov/. Also see Victoria Ivie, "Why the San Manuel Tribe Is Going Back to Its Original Name," *San Bernardino (CA) Sun*, May 1, 2025. I am using the name San Manuel when I refer to historical documents, including legal cases, and media accounts about specific labor conflicts and initiative campaigns that predate 2025.

3. These contradictions are the product of settler-colonial expectations. See Jessica Cattelino's use of "expectation" in her analysis of Native wealth. Cattelino, "Double Bind," 237. In this case, I use the term "expectation" to describe settler expectations of Native political views. Deloria, *Indians in Unexpected Places*.

4. Powell, *Landscapes of Power*, 53. For the environmental impact of energy of resource extraction on the Diné people, lands, and sovereignty, see Brugge, Benally, and Yazzie-Lewis, *Navajo People and Uranium Mining*; Anderson, *Unlocking the Wealth of Indian Nations*; and Allison, *Sovereignty for Survival*.

5. See tribal financial leaders' testimony in US Senate, *Accessing Capital in Indian Country*, 3, 51. Since the turn of the twenty-first century, Native entrepreneurs have created lending institutions that cater to reservation communities. Even so, Native communities remain, "unbanked," and Native-owned and operated small businesses represent a tiny minority in the United States overall. Yet small businesses that produce a variety of products and services (ranging from wild rice, beauty products, clothing, skateboards, to traditional arts and crafts) have been growing, especially those that benefit from online marketing. See, for example, businesses listed in the Native American Student Assembly's "Native Owned Business Directory," accessed June 30, 2025, https://usg.usc.edu/nasa/native-owned-businesses-directory. As of 2025, there were twenty Native American–owned banks and eleven credit unions in the United States. Brian Edwards, "Native Banks Deliver Outsized Impact Despite Undercapitalization, New National Bankers Association Report Finds," *Tribal Business News*, May 24, 2025, https://tribalbusinessnews.com/Sections/Finance/15152-Native-Banks-Deliver-Outsized-Impact-Despite-Undercapitalization-New-Report-Finds; National Congress of Native Americans, "Securing Our Futures" (policy paper).

6. Akee, Spilde, and Taylor, "Indian Gaming Regulatory Act," 186; Shannon Shaw Duty, "Working Together: Tribal Partnerships Bring Regional Jobs: Osage Nation Joins with City, County for Economic Development Projects," *Indian Country Today*, April 13, 2022.

7. The economic impact of gaming on tribes varies according to the tribe's size, proximity to urban markets, management experience, and its relationship with state government officials. Akee, Spilde, and Taylor, "Indian Gaming Regulatory Act," 94. As of 2024, there were 245 tribes in 29 states operating 527 gaming establishments. National Indian Gaming Commission, *NIGC FY 2023 Gross Gaming Revenue Report*.

8. Marquez interview by author.

9. Murillo, *Living in Two Worlds*, 51.

10. National Indian Gaming Commission, "The Commission: FAQs," accessed June 30, 2025, www.nigc.gov/commission/faqs. Each tribal nation negotiates individual compacts with states, so the terms and percentages vary.

11. California Nations Indian Gaming Association, *2016 California Tribal Gaming Impact Study*, 5.

12. Carstensen et al., "Economic Impact," 24; Nykiel, "Assessment of the Many Contributions," 51–56; Stevens, "IGA Report."

13. Michael Sokolove, "Foxwoods Is Fighting for Its Life," *New York Times Magazine*, March 14, 2012; Light and Rand, *Indian Gaming and Tribal Sovereignty*, 43.

14. Deloria and Wilkins, *Tribes, Treaties, and Constitutional Tribulations*; Light and Rand, *Indian Gaming and Tribal Sovereignty*, 39.

15. Cattelino, *High Stakes*, 54.

16. In 1976, the Oneida Nation in Wisconsin opened a modest bingo operation that would later grow into a lucrative recreation, hospitality, and gaming business. Hoeft, *Bingo Queens of Oneida*.

17. Way, "Raising Capital in Indian Country," 167–200; Lofthouse, "Institutions and Economic Development," 227–48.

18. Cattalino, *High Stakes*, 1, 14.

19. Suzette Brewer, "Cabazon: The Raid that Changed Gaming History," *Indian Country Today*, February 24, 2017; *California v. Cabazon Band of Mission Indians*, 480 U.S. 202 (1987); Gordon, *Cahuilla Nation Activism*, 95–96.

20. Light and Rand, *Indian Gaming and Tribal Sovereignty*, 43.

21. Legal scholars and tribal officials have debated whether the development of the Indian gaming industry undermines or supports tribal sovereignty. For a good overview of the issue and the struggle over Indian casinos in California, see Goldberg and Champagne, "Ramona Redeemed?," 43–63.

22. Light and Rand, *Indian Gaming and Tribal Sovereignty*, 43.

23. In 2009, the National Indian Gaming Association reported that out of 250,000 casino employees in tribal gaming establishments nationwide, 75 percent were non-Native. Gordon, "Nation, Corporation or Family?" 1–12. For the Indian gaming impact on non-Native communities, see Spilde and Taylor, "Economic Evidence on the Effects of the Indian Gaming Regulatory Act"; Grant, Spilde, and Taylor, "Social and Economic Consequences of Indian Gaming in Oklahoma"; "State of Play" (interactive infographic), American Gaming Association, accessed August 4, 2025, www.americangaming.org/research/state-of-play-map/?state=connecticut; and "Mohegan Federal Recognition," Connecticut History, https://connecticuthistory.org/mohegan-federal-recognition/.

24. Anthony R. Pico, "Organized Labor and Tribal Governments," remarks delivered at the Indian Gaming Summit, Palm Springs, CA, March 20, 2000, MS-00092, box US News: Labor Unions, 1988 August–2001 March 2/3, Spilde Papers.

25. For a comprehensive analysis of the conflict between tribes, the state of California and unions over gaming, see Kamper, *Work of Sovereignty*, chaps. 2–3.

26. Rossum, *Supreme Court and Tribal Gaming*, 234.

27. For the sake of clarity, I will simply refer to the Hotel Employees and Restaurant Employees Union as HERE, since the organizing campaign at San Manuel started before the merger with UNITE. During the organizing campaign and San Manuel court battle, HERE merged with UNITE, an amalgamation of garment workers unions, to form UNITE-HERE. The merger fell apart in 2009, as the union's leadership struggled in what Alec MacGillis, a staff writer for the *Washington Post*, called an "ill-fitting marriage." Other labor journalists described the conflict between HERE and UNITE, and the Service Employees International Union's (SEIU) intervention, as a tragic personality conflict between charismatic union leaders. Alec MacGillis, "SEIU and UNITE HERE End 18-Month Feud," *Washington Post*, July 27, 2010; Peter Dreier "Divorce—Union Style: Can the Labor Movement Overcome UNITE HERE's Messy Breakup?," *The Nation*, August 12, 2009; Kamper, *Work of Sovereignty*, 234.

28. Hector Tobar and Jenifer Warren, "UCLA Session Touches on Impacts of Tribal Casinos, but Frequently Strays into Emotional Outbursts and Finger-Pointing," *Los Angeles Times*, October 21, 1998, A-3, MS-00092, box 28, folder US News: Labor Unions 1991 October–1998 July 1/3, Spilde Papers.

29. Harmon, *Rich Indians*, 392.

30. Tom Gorman, "TV Ad Charges Casinos Profit Only the Rich," *Los Angeles Times*, October 27, 1998, 3. For an analysis of similar types of racial dynamics in Florida see Cattelino, "Tribal Gaming and Indigenous Sovereignty," 193; Cattelino, *High Stakes*; Kamper and Spilde, "Legal Regimenting of Tribal Wealth," 1–29.

31. In 2021, leading up to its eventual name change in 2025, the tribe changed the San Manuel Casino's name to Yaamava' Resort and Casino at San Manuel. This jurisdictional conflict is like the problem of law enforcement on tribal lands. As established by the Major Crimes Act of 1885, it is the federal government, not the states, that maintains the power to prosecute Native and non-Native perpetrators of felonies and other serious crimes on reservation lands. Tribal governments may prosecute misdemeanors and less serious crimes, but their jurisdiction over non-Native perpetrators is limited. These types of jurisdictional disputes continue to shift the relationship between states, tribes, and the federal government. *McGirt v. Oklahoma*, 140 S Ct.2452, 2459 (2020). For an analysis of how the Major Crimes Act of 1885 impacts violence against Native women, see Deer, *Beginning and End of Rape*; Prucha, *Documents of United States Indian Policy*, 166.

32. Dion Nissenbaum, "Gaming Initiative Alliances Unusual," *Press-Enterprise*, August 30, 1998, MS-00092, box 28, folder US News: Labor Unions, 1991 October–1998 July 1/3, Spilde Papers.

33. Pico, "Organized Labor and Tribal Governments."

34. John Taylor, "Indian Youth Show Support for Prop 5 at Education Meeting: Students Say the Initiative Is Needed to Preserve Self-Reliance," *Fresno Bee*, October 31, 1998.

35. "Indians, Unions in Clash of Interests: Labor Wants a Place in the Casino Industry. Tribes Say Sovereignty Is the Issue," *Press-Enterprise* (Riverside, CA), February 21, 1999.

36. Marquez interview by author. As historians Suzanne E. Mills and Tyler McCreary point out, tribal governments face conflicting interests. As employers they may espouse anti-union views like their settler counterparts. But they also represent the interest of their communities as a whole and must act on an "anticolonial desire for economic self-reliance and a mistrust of settler dominated institutions including unions." Mills and McCreary, "Which Side Are You On?," 146.

37. See Kamper, *Work of Sovereignty*, chap. 3; Michelle DeArmond, "Viejas Indians Sign Agreement to Let Union Organize a Casino," *Associated Press*, August 8, 1998.

38. According to NLRB procedures, a union can be established by a "card check," where the employer recognizes the union if cards circulated by employees constitute majority support for the union. Or the employer can insist that an election be held to determine the outcome of workers' preferences. Unions prefer the former. Employers often insist on elections as a stalling tactic to undermine the union's organizing momentum and erode workers' enthusiasm.

39. Kamper, *The Work of Sovereignty*, 34.

40. *San Manuel Indian Bingo and Casino*, 341 NLRB 1055 (2004); "First Contract Was 'In the Cards' for San Manuel Casino Workers," *CWA News*, November 1, 2000, www.cwa-union.org/news/entry/first_contract_was_in_the_cards_for_san_manuel_casino_workers; Kamper, *Work of Sovereignty*, chap. 2; Gordon, "Nation, Corporation or Family?," 4–5.

41. *San Manuel Indian Bingo and Casino*, 341 NLRB 1055 (2004).

42. *San Manuel Indian Bingo and Casino v. NLRB*, 475 F.3d 1306 (D.C. Cir. 2007), 15; "California Tribe Loses Major Sovereignty Court Case," Indianz.com, February 12, 2007, https://indianz.com/News/2007/000860.asp.

43. Rossum, *Supreme Court and Tribal Gaming*, 142.

44. The San Manuel case was a focal point of discussion among tribal officials at CTER conferences I attended in 2006 and 2012. The San Manuel decision was also on the minds

of tribal officials who attended a union busting workshop at the 2012 Oklahoma Indian Gaming Convention I attended in Oklahoma City.

45. Erica Werner, "Indian Casinos Bound by Labor Law, Court Says Sovereignty Not a Trump Card," *Hartford Courant*, February 10, 2007.

46. At the December 6, 2006, CTER meeting in Las Vegas, the Laborers International and the United Brotherhood of Carpenters presented proposals that expressed their willingness to work with tribes, even conceding their rights to strike or closed shop provisions in their collective bargaining agreements. Author's observation.

47. The attack ended protracted conflict between English colonists and the Pequots in the 1630s. Many Native American and North American colonial historians have studied the Pequot War and massacre at Mystic Fort in 1637. Classic monographs include Cave, *Pequot War*; and Salisbury, *Manitou and Providence*. See "Our History," Mashantucket Pequot Tribal Nation, accessed June 30, 2025, www.mptn-nsn.gov/history/. For an environmental analysis of the war, see Grandjean, "New World Tempests," 75–100.

48. Brett D. Fromson, "Pequot Uprising," *Washington Post*, June 21, 1998.

49. Light and Rand, *Indian Gaming and Tribal Sovereignty*, 107; Campisi, "New England Tribes," 185; Campisi, "Emergence of Mashantucket Pequot Tribe," 138.

50. See "Our History," Mashantucket Pequot Tribal Nation, accessed June 30, 2025, www.mptn-nsn.gov/history/.

51. Fromson, *Hitting the Jackpot*.

52. The state collects 25 percent of slot machine revenue according to the terms of the gaming pact negotiated with the Mashantucket Pequot Tribal Nation. Carstensen et al., "Economic Impact," 1.

53. Carstensen et al., "Economic Impact," 3.

54. Hohne interview by author.

55. Anonymous Foxwoods worker interview by author.

56. Anonymous Foxwoods worker interview by author.

57. Potter, "Domino-Effect of Really Bad Decisions."

58. Sokolove, "Foxwoods Is Fighting for Its Life."

59. Joan Vennochi, "Have Mass. Casinos Become a Risky Bet?," *Boston Globe*, May 24, 2012.

60. Jean Falbo-Sosnovich, "Derby Seniors Boycotting Foxwoods over CEO's Reported Remarks," *New Haven Register*, July 20, 2012; Lore Croghan, "Scott Butera, the 37-Year-Old EVP of Trump Hotels and Casino Resorts, Has Tall Order—Building Trust Between Bondholders and Donald Trump," *Hotel Online: News for the Hospitality Industry*, April 12, 2004.

61. *Mashantucket Pequot Gaming Enterprise d/b/a Foxwoods Resort Casino . . .*, Decision and Direction of Election, 14.

62. Gale Courey, "Mashantuckets to Challenge NLRB Union Win," *Indian Country Today*, December 5, 2007, A1, A3.

63. Ghan, "Federal Labor Law and the Mashantucket Pequot," 531; Gale Courey Toensing, "Mashantucket-UAW in Groundbreaking Agreement to Negotiate Under Tribal Law," *Indian Country Today*, November 12, 2008, 3; *Mashantucket Pequot Gaming Enterprise d/b/a Foxwoods Resort Casino . . .*, Decision and Direction of Election.

64. The UAW campaign did not necessarily open the door for other unions. Other campaigns launched by the UAW and the Operating Engineers the following year were

not as successful. A summary of previous union campaigns at Foxwoods can be found in *Mashantucket Pequot Gaming Enterprise d/b/a Foxwoods Resort and Casino . . .*, Decision and Direction of Election.

65. Andrew Julien, "Union Considers Organizing at Casinos," *Harford Courant*, June 20, 1997.

66. Hohne interview by author.

67. "UAW Withdraws after Foxwoods Employees Reject Second Union Vote," *Indian Country Today*, June 11, 2008.

68. The name Linda Meyer is a pseudonym. Anonymous Foxwoods' worker interview by author.

69. Anonymous Foxwoods worker interview by author.

70. Hohne interview by author.

71. Mashantucket Employment Rights Office, "Mashantucket Pequot Tribal and Native American Preference Law (Preference Law)—Title 33 M.P.T.L.," accessed June 1, 2023. www.mptnlaw.com/MERO/MERO.htm.

72. Anonymous Foxwoods' worker interview by author.

73. The Mashantucket Pequot Tribal Nation did not publicly report the amount individuals received in incentive payments. It is nearly impossible to state exact figures given the range of numbers circulated in the press. Newspapers usually reported estimates based on unnamed tribal sources that cannot be corroborated with official reports. Brian Hallenbeck, "Mashantuckets to End Incentive Payments," *The Day*, July 10, 2010; *Mashantucket Pequot Gaming Enterprise d/b/a Foxwoods Resort Casino . . .*, Hearing Officer's Report; "Pequots' Financial Problems Mount," *Global Gaming Business Magazine*, Aug 2, 2010.

74. Brian Hallenbeck, "Tribe Contests Legitimacy of Union Vote at Foxwoods," *New London Day*, September 23, 2010.

75. *Mashantucket Pequot Gaming Enterprise d/b/a Foxwoods Resort Casino . . .*, Hearing Officer's Report, 1.

76. Indeed, their faith in federal law might have been misplaced. It is common knowledge among labor organizers that labor law and the NLRB often protect employers in labor conflicts. Scholars have shown that the NLRB reflects the ideological worldview of the presidential administration that appoints its practitioners. Some labor law scholars have argued that the original intent of the National Labor Relations Act (NLRA), and the legislation the NLRB has been tasked with administering, has eroded since the NLRA's passage in 1935. Cooke and Gautschi, "Political Bias in NLRB," 539–49; Alder, "Further Reasons for the NLRB's Inability."

77. Cramer, "Common Sense of Anti-Indian Racism," 315; US House of Representatives, Subcommittee on Native American Affairs, *Implementation of Indian Gaming Regulatory Act*, 242.

78. Anonymous Foxwoods worker interview by author.

79. Hohne interview by author; Brian Hallenbeck, "Contract Vote Ahead for Beverage Workers at Foxwoods Resort Casino," *The Day*, December 14, 2013.

80. Cobb and anonymous Teamster organizer interview by author.

81. Cobb and anonymous Teamster organizer interview by author.

82. Not all union campaigns work this way. In some cases, unions ask for recognition based on a simple card check rather than holding an election.

83. A captive audience meeting favors the employer since workers are required to attend and these meetings are usually held at the workplace.

84. *Chickasaw Nation v. National Labor Relations Board*, No. CIV-11-506-W, slip op. at 13 (W.D. Okla. July 11, 2011); Guss, "Gaming Sovereignty?," 1653.

85. In a related lawsuit in Michigan, the Saginaw Chippewa who operate the Soaring Eagle Resort and Casino, faced a similar ruling in 2015. Plumer, "Overriding Tribal Sovereignty,"131–32.

86. Maya Jackson Randall and Melanie Trottman, "GOP Keeps Appointments on Hold," *Washington Post*, December 19, 2011; Robert Barnes, "Supreme Court Rebukes Obama on Recess Appointments," *Washington Post*, June 26, 2014.

87. Fletcher, "Little River Band"; Linda Stephan, "Little River Casino Agrees to Second Union Contract," Interlochen Public Radio, March 3, 2012, www.interlochenpublicradio.org/2012-03-22/little-river-casino-agrees-to-second-union-contract.

88. *NLRB v. Little River Band of Ottawa Indians Tribal Government*, 788 F.3d 537 (6th Cir. 2015). Decided June 9, 2015.

89. "NLRB Overrules Little River Band of Ottawa Indians Concerning Labor Laws at Casino. Next Move Being Considered," *Ludington Daily News*, March 21, 2013.

90. *San Manuel Indian Bingo and Casino . . .*, 341 NLRB 1055 (2004), enforced by *San Manuel Indian Bingo and Casino v. NLRB*, 475 F.3d 1306 (D.C. Cir. 2007); *Chickasaw Nation d/b/a Winstar World Casino and International Brotherhood of Teamsters Local 886, affiliated with The International Brotherhood of Teamsters*, 362 NLRB 942 (2015).

91. Smith, "NLRB and Indian Gaming Three Ways."

92. Brodie, "NLRB Jurisdiction over Indian Tribes."

93. Robert Iafolla, "Supreme Court Won't Consider Labor Board over Indian Casinos," *Reuters*, June 27, 2016.

94. Hayworth, "Statement of Hon. J. D. Hayworth."

95. Wilkins and Lomawaima argue that "tribal rights are based in the doctrine of inherent sovereignty" as established through treaties, congressional action, and constitutional and federal case law that dates to the early republic. It seems unlikely that Hayworth is referring to the same doctrine. Wilkins and Lomawaima, *Uneven Ground*, 8; Hayworth, "Statement of Hon. J. D. Hayworth."

96. Garcia, "Statement of Hon. Joe Garia." See also National Congress of American Indians, "Congressional Clarification of Treatment of Indian Tribes as Governments for Purpose of the National Labor Relations Act," The National Congress of American Indians, Resolution #MOH-04–028, accessed April 22, 2024, https://ncai.assetbank-server.com/assetbank-ncai/action/viewAsset?id=2782; *NLRB v. Pueblo of San Juan*, 276 F.3d 1186 (10th Cir. 2002) (en banc).

97. Michael Wines, "Politics: Congressional Memo: Fervor of Freshman Wanes as Re-Election, Nears Time," *New York Times*, March 24, 1996, sec. 1, p. 1. The Center for Responsive Politics listed Hayworth as the highest recipient of individual campaign contributions from Jack Abramoff. Philip Shenon, "In Congress, a Lobbyist's Legal Troubles Turn His Generosity into a Burden," *New York Times*, Dec. 19, 2005, sec. A, p. 22; "Hayworth Will Keep Tribal Gifts," *Arizona Republic*, December 23, 2005, sec. A, p. 1; *NAACP Civil Rights Legislative Report Card*, accessed August 27, 2006, www.naacp.org/wpcontent/uploads/2016/04/109thCongress.pdf.

98. Unanimous Consent Request, S. 248, 114th Cong., 2nd sess., *Congressional Record* 161, no. 184 (December 17, 2015), S8776–S8777, www.govinfo.gov/content/pkg/CREC-2015-12-17/html/CREC-2015-12-17-pt1-PgS8776.htm; Smith and Williams, "Native Americans, Tribal Sovereignty, and Unions," 22–23, 28.

99. Jack Katzanek, "Why Inland Tribes Declined Exemption That Would Have Made Unionizing Harder," *Press-Enterprise*, September 25, 2016.

100. Tribal Labor Sovereignty Act of 2015, H.R. 511, 114th Cong., 2nd sess., *Congressional Record* 161, no. 169 (November 17, 2015).

101. US Office of Management and Budget, "Statement of Administration Policy H.R. 511—Tribal Labor Sovereignty Act of 2015," November 17, 2015, http://src.bna.com/7K.

102. Bill to Amend the White Mountain Apache Tribe Water Rights Quantification Act of 2010 to Clarify the Use of Amounts in the WMAT Settlement Fund, S. 140, 115th Cong., 2nd sess., *Congressional Record* 164, no. 6 (January 10, 2018); "Republicans Stir Drama by Adding Controversial Tribal Labor Sovereignty Act to Unrelated Bill," Indianz.com, January 11, 2018, www.indianz.com/News/2018/01/11/republicans-add-controversial-tribal-lab.asp.

103. Noam Scheiber, "Bill to Curtail Labor Rights on Tribal Land Falls Short," *New York Times*, April 17, 2018, B5.

CONCLUSION

1. Author's observation notes, from the CTER, 2012 Comprehensive Tribal Employment Law and Legal Update Conference, Las Vegas, Nevada, December 12, 2012; Bart Barnes, "Jacqueline Berrien, Former EEOC Chairwoman, Dies at 53," *Washington Post*, November 12, 2015.

2. CTER, "Model Tribe/Nation Workforce Protection Ordinance," September 8, 2022, https://cter-tero.org/wp-content/uploads/2022/09/Model-Tribal-Workforce-Protection-Act.pdf.

3. CTER, "Model Tribe/Nation Workforce Protection Ordinance."

4. Conversation between the author and Dan Press at the Council for Tribal Employment Rights (CTER), "2012 Comprehensive Tribal Employment Law and Legal Update Conference," Las Vegas, Nevada, December 12, 2012.

5. Observations of the author, who attended a union busting workshop at the 2012 Oklahoma Indian Gaming Association in Oklahoma City, Oklahoma, August 14, 2012. Cooper, *Decolonization and African Society*, 9–10; Champagne, "Tribal Capitalism and Native Capitalists," 323.

6. McCarty, *A Place to Be Navajo*, 73, 86.

7. MacDonald interview by O'Neil, Doris Duke Oral History Collection.

8. Szaz, "Path to Self Determination, 97; Diné College, "The Educational Philosophy of Diné College," accessed March 26, 2025, www.dinecollege.edu/about-us/educational-philosophy/.

9. Child, *Holding Our World Together*, 158. For an in-depth study of the survival schools, see Davis, *Survival Schools*. By the 1970s, The Intermountain Indian School had added significant academic subjects and more up to date vocational programs. Students were

no longer routed into domestic service and agricultural labor. When the school closed in 1984, students protested. Tonnies, "Away for the Homeland."

10. "Mission Statement," Haskell Indian Nations University, accessed August 5, 2025, https://haskell.edu/about/vision/.

11. Hyer, *One House, One Voice, One Heart*; "Making History: Celebrating 60 Years of IAIA and 50 Years of MoCNA," Institute of American Indian Arts, accessed August 5, 2025, https://iaia.edu/making-history-celebrating-60-years-of-iaia-and-50-years-of-mocna; Hilary Beaumont, "'We're Still Here': Past and Present Collide at a Native American Boarding School," *The Guardian*, May 22, 2022.

12. O'Neill, *Working the Navajo Way*, 140; Curley, "T'ááá hwó ají t'éego and the Moral Economy," 71–78; Doran, "Ganienkeh"; Norrgard, "Indigenous Unions."

BIBLIOGRAPHY

PRIMARY SOURCES

Manuscript Collections

Archives and Special Collections, Mansfield Library,
    University of Montana, Missoula, MT
  James E. Murray Papers
Library of Congress, Washington, DC
  Prints and Photographs Division
Navajo Nation Museum, Window Rock, AZ
National Archives and Records Administration I, Washington, DC
National Archives and Records Administration II, College Park, MD
National Archives and Records Administration Regional Branch, Riverside, CA
National Archives and Records Administration Regional Branch, Seattle, WA
National Archives and Records Administration Regional Branch, Denver, CO
National Archives and Records Administration Regional Branch, San Francisco, CA
National Museum of the American Indian Archive Center,
    Smithsonian Institution, Washington, DC
Richard Nixon Presidential Library and Museum, Yorba Linda, CA
  White House Central Files: Staff Member and Office Files: Leonard Garment
Special Collections, J. Willard Marriott Library, University of Utah, Salt Lake City, UT
Special Collections, University Libraries, University of Nevada, Las Vegas
    Katherine A. Spilde Papers on Native American Gaming
Special Collections and Archives, Cline Library,
    Northern Arizona University, Flagstaff, AZ
  General Photograph Collections
Special Collections and Archives, Merrill-Cazier Library,
    Utah State University, Logan, UT

Government Documents

Annual Report of the Commissioner of Indian Affairs to the Secretary of the Interior for the Year 1878. Washington, DC: Government Printing Office, 1878. https://archive.org/details/usindianaffairs78usdorich/page/n3/mode/2up.

Annual Report of the Superintendent of Indian Schools to the Secretary of the Interior, 1904. Washington, DC: Government Printing Office, 1904. Hathi Trust Digital Library. https://babel.hathitrust.org/cgi/pt?id=nyp.33433081680401&seq=180&q1=1904.

Annual Reports of the Department of the Interior for the Fiscal Year Ended June 30, 1901, Indian Affairs. Part I: *Report of the Commissioner, and Appendixes.* Washington, DC: Government Printing Office, 1902.

Annual Reports of the Department of the Interior for the Fiscal Year Ended June 30, 1904, Indian Affairs. Part I: *Report of the Commissioner, and Appendixes.* Washington, DC: Government Printing Office, 1905.

Bill to Amend the White Mountain Apache Tribe Water Rights Quantification Act of 2010 to Clarify the Use of Amounts in the WMAT Settlement Fund, S. 140, 115th Cong., 2nd sess., *Congressional Record* 164, no. 6 (January 10, 2018).

Garcia, Joe. "Statement of Hon. Joe Garia, Governor, Pueblo of San Juan, New Mexico." In *Hearing before the Subcommittee on Employer-Employee Relations of the Committee on Education and the Workforce, US House of Represenatives, 109th Congress, 2nd Session, July 20, 2006* (Serial 109–48), 25–30. Washington, DC: US Government Printing Office, 2006. www.congress.gov/109/chrg/CHRG-109hhrg28809/CHRG-109hhrg28809.pdf.

Harris, William Torrey. "Civilization and Higher Education." In *The Annual Report of the Commissioner of Indian Affairs, 1901,* 478–79. Washington, DC: Government Printing Office, 1901.

Hayworth, J. D. "Statement of Hon. J. D. Hayworth, a Representative in Congress from the State of Arizona." In *Hearing before the Subcommittee on Employer-Employee Relations of the Committee on Education and the Workforce, US House of Representatives, 109th Congress, 2nd Session, July 20, 2006* (Serial 109–48), 5–15. Washington, DC: US Government Printing Office, 2006. www.congress.gov/109/chrg/CHRG-109hhrg28809/CHRG-109hhrg28809.pdf.

Ickes, Harold. *Annual Report of the Secretary of the Interior, 1942.* Washington, DC: Government Printing Office, 1943.

John, Walton C., ed. *William Torrey Harris: The Commemoration of the One Hundredth Anniversary of His Birth. Bulletin 1936.* Bulletin 1936, No. 17. Washington, DC: US Department of the Interior, Office of Education. https://archive.org/details/ERIC_ED542456/page/n1/mode/2up.

Leupp, Francis E. *Report of Commissioner of Indian Affairs to the Department of Interior, 1908.* Washington, DC: Government Printing Office, 1908.

Leupp, Francis E. *Report of the Commissioner of Indian Affairs to the Secretary of the Interior, 1909.* Washington, DC: Government Printing Office, 1909.

Meriam, Lewis, comp. *The Problem of Indian Administration: Report of a Survey Made at the Request of Honorable Hubert Work, Secretary of the Interior, and Submitted to Him, February 21, 1928.* Baltimore, MD: Johns Hopkins University Press, 1928.

Minnesota Advisory Committee to the US Commission on Civil Rights. *Bridging the Gap: A Reassessment.* January 1978. Hathi Trust Digital Library. https://babel.hathitrust.org/cgi/pt?id=osu.32435009892910&seq=1.

Montana State Appraisal Committee. *An Evaluation of the Federal Works Program in Montana*. March 1938. Hathi Trust Digital Library. https://catalog.hathitrust.org/Record/102193246.

Murphy, D. E., "Final Report of Indian Emergency Conservation Work and U.S. Civilian Conservation Corps-Indian Division Program, 1933–1942." Typescript. US Department of Interior Library, 1943.

Newland, Brian. *Federal Indian Boarding School Initiative Investigative Report*. Vol. 2. Washington, DC: United States Department of the Interior, July 2024. www.bia.gov/sites/default/files/media_document/doi_federal_indian_boarding_school_initiative_investigative_report_vii_final_508_compliant.pdf.

New Mexico Advisory Committee to the United States Commission on Civil Rights. *The Farmington Report: A Conflict of Cultures*. July 1975. Hathi Trust Digital Library. https://babel.hathitrust.org/cgi/pt?id=uiug.30112045537286&seq=7.

Reel, Estelle. *Course of Study for the Indian Schools of the United States*. Washington DC: Office of Indian Affairs, Government Printing Office, 1901.

Report of the Superintendent of Indian Schools to the Secretary of the Interior, 1904. Washington, DC: Government Printing Office, 1904. Hathi Trust Digital Library. https://babel.hathitrust.org/cgi/pt?id=nyp.33433081680401&seq=181&q1=1904.

US Bureau of Labor Statistics, Division of Construction and Public Employment. *Employment and Pay Rolls*. Serial No. R. 1300. Washington, DC: Government Printing Office, 1941.

US Census Bureau. "Increasing Urbanization: Population Distribution by City Size, 1790–1890." Infographics and Visualizations, July 19, 2012. www.census.gov/dataviz/visualizations/005/.

US Commission on Civil Rights. *Hearing before the United States Commission on Civil Rights, Window Rock, Arizona, October 22–24, 1973*. Vol. 1: *Testimony*. Washington, DC: Government Printing Office, 1973.

US Department of Agriculture, Bureau of Statistics. *Wages of Farm Labor*. Bulletin 99. Washington, DC: Government Printing Office, 1912. https://ia800301.us.archive.org/23/items/wagesoffarmlabor99holm/wagesoffarmlabor99holm.pdf.

US Department of the Interior. *Kappler's Indian Affairs*. Vol. 6: *Laws and Treaties*. Compiled, annotated, and edited by Charles J. Kappler. Washington, DC: Government Printing Office, 1979.

US Federal Works Agency. *Final Report on the WPA Program, 1935–43*. Washington, DC: Government Printing Office, 1947. www.loc.gov/resource/gdclccn.47032199/?sp=7&r=-0.551,0.037,2.103,1.356,0.

US House of Representatives, Committee on Government Operations. *Misplaced Trust: The Bureau of Indian Affairs' Mismanagement of the Indian Trust Fund. Seventeenth Report*. 102nd Cong., 2nd sess., H. Rep. 102–499. Washington, DC: US Government Printing Office, 1992.

US House of Representatives, Subcommittee on Native American Affairs. *Implementation of Indian Gaming Regulatory Act and Related Law Enforcement Issues, October 5, 1993*. Serial No. 103–17, Part V. Washington, DC: Government Printing Office, 1994. https://ia801207.us.archive.org/12/items/implementationof05unit/implementationof05unit.pdf.

US House of Representatives, Subcommittee on Native American Affairs. *Implementation of Indian Gaming Regulatory Act: Oversight Hearing Before the Subcommittee on Native American Affairs of the Committee on Natural Resources, House of Representatives One hundred Third Congress, First Session on the Implementation of Public Law 100–497, the Indian Gaming Regulatory Act of 1988.* Washington, DC: Government Printing Office, 1993.

US Senate. *Accessing Capital in Indian Country: Hearing before the Committee on Indian Affairs.* 114th Cong., 1st sess., 2015. www.govinfo.gov/content/pkg/CHRG-114shrg97306/html/CHRG-114shrg97306.htm.

US Senate, Committee on Indian Affairs. *Survey of Conditions of the Indians in the United States. Hearings before a Subcommittee of the Committee on Indian Affairs United States Senate. Seventieth Congress, Second Session Pursuant to S. Res. 79 A Resolution Directing the Committee on Indian Affairs of The United States Senate to Make a General Survey of The Condition of The Indians of The United States Part 2 San Francisco, Calif, Riverside, Calif, and Salt Lake City, Utah, 1928.* Washington, DC: Government Printing Office, 1929.

Legal Cases and Materials

California v. Cabazon Band of Mission Indians, 480 U.S. 202 (1987).

Chickasaw Nation d/b/a Winstar World Casino and International Brotherhood of Teamsters Local 886, affiliated with The International Brotherhood of Teamsters, 362 NLRB 942 (2015).

Chickasaw Nation v. National Labor Relations Board, No. 5:11cv506W (W.D. Okla. July 11, 2011). https://turtletalk.blog/wp-content/uploads/2011/07/chickasaw-judge-west-order-07-11-2011.pdf.

Mashantucket Pequot Gaming Enterprise d/b/a Foxwoods Resort Casino, Employer, and United Food and Commercial Workers Union, Local 371, Petitioner, and Mashantucket Pequot Tribal Nation, Intervenor. Decision and Direction of Election. National Labor Relations Board, Docket of Activity. October 14, 2010. www.nlrb.gov/case/34-RC-002392.

Mashantucket Pequot Gaming Enterprise d/b/a Foxwoods Resort Casino, Employer, and United Food and Commercial Workers Union, Local 371, Petitioner, and Mashantucket Pequot Tribal Nation, Intervenor. Hearing Officer's Report. National Labor Relations Board, Docket of Activity. November 3, 2010. www.nlrb.gov/case/34-RC-002392.

McGirt v. Oklahoma, 591 U.S. 894 (2020).

Morton v. Mancari, 417 U.S. 535 (1974).

NLRB v. Little River Band of Ottawa Indians Tribal Government, 788 F.3d 537 (6th Cir. 2015).

NLRB v. Pueblo of San Juan, 276 F.3d 1186 (10th Cir. 2002).

San Manuel Indian Bingo and Casino and Hotel Employees and Restaurant Employees International Union, AFL–CIO, CLC and Communication Workers of America AFL–CIO, CLC, Party in Interest and State of Connecticut, Intervenor, 341 NLRB 1055 (2004).

San Manuel Indian Bingo and Casino v. NLRB, 475 F.3d 1306 (D.C. Cir 2007).

Newspapers, Magazines, and Newsletters

Americans before Columbus: Newsletter of the National Indian Youth Council
Arizona Republic
Boston Globe
Brooklyn Eagle
Communications Workers of America News
Delta (CO) Independent
Fresno (CA) Bee
Gallup (NM) Independent
Glacier Reporter (Browning, MT)
The Guardian
Harford (CT) Courant
Hocak Worak, Newsletter of the Ho-Chunk Nation
Indian Country Today
Indian Craftsman (Carlisle Indian School, Carlisle PA)
Indians at Work
Indian's Friend
Los Angeles Times
Ludington (MI) Daily News
Madera (CA) Daily Tribune
The Nation
New Haven (CT) Register
New London (CT) Day
New York Times
New York Times Magazine
Reuters
Press-Enterprise (Riverside, CA)
San Bernardino Sun
San Francisco Call
San Jose Mercury News
Sho-Ban News (Fort Hall, ID)
Tribal Business News
Washington Post

Autobiographies, Memoirs, and Published Speeches

Bennett, Kay. *Kaibah: Recollections of a Navajo Girlhood*. Los Angeles: Westernlore Press, 1964.
Collier, John. *From Every Zenith: A Memoir and Some Essays on Life and Thought*. Denver, CO: Sage Books, 1963.
Crow Dog, Mary, and Richard Erdoes. *Lakota Woman*. New York: Harper Perennial, 1991.
Fortunate Eagle, Adam. *Pipestone: My Life in an Indian Boarding School*. Norman: University of Oklahoma Press, 2010.
Johnson, Broderick H., ed. *Stories of Traditional Navajo Life and Culture by Twenty-Two Navajo Men and Women*. Tsaile: Navajo Community College Press, 1977.
Leupp, Francis E. *The Indian and His Problem*. New York: Charles Schribner's Sons, 1910.
Murillo, Pauline Ormego. *Living in Two Worlds: The Life of Pauline Ormego Murillo*. Highland, CA: Dimples Press, 2002.
Nequatewa, Edmund. *Born a Chief: The Nineteenth Century Hopi Boyhood of Edmund Nequatewa*. Edited by P. David Seaman. Tucson: University of Arizona Press, 1993.
Pratt, Richard Henry. *Battlefield and Classroom: Four Decades with the American Indian, 1867–1904*. Edited by Robert M. Utley. New Haven, CT: Yale University Press, 1964.
Qoyawayma, Polingaysi, and Vada F. Carlson. *No Turning Back: A Hopi Indian Woman's Struggle to Live in Two Worlds*. Albuquerque: University of New Mexico Press, 1977.
Sekaquaptewa, Helen, as told to Louise Udall. *Me and Mine: The Life Story of Helen Sekaquaptewa*. Tucson: University of Arizona Press, 1969.

Sitting Bull. "I came here to give some advice, August 22, 1883." In *Sitting Bull: The Collected Speeches*, edited and compiled by Mark Diedrich. Rochester, MN: Coyote Books, 1998.
Stewart, Irene. *A Voice in Her Tribe: A Navajo Woman's Own Story*. Foreword by Mary Shepardson. Edited by Doris Ostrander Dawdy. Socorro, NM: Ballena Press, 1980. https://archive.org/details/voiceinhertribeno000stew/page/n3/mode/2up.
Talayesva, Don. *Sun Chief: The Autobiography of a Hopi Indian*. New Haven, CT: Yale University Press, 2013.
Zitkala-Ša. *American Indian Stories*. Washington, DC: Hayworth Publishing House, 1921.

Oral History Interviews

CTER Cofounders Conrad Edwards and John Navarro and General Counsel Dan Press, discussion. CTER History Project: The Birth of the TERO Movement video, pt. 1, no date. https://cter-tero.org/videos/#history.
Peter MacDonald, interview by Floyd O'Neil, August 12, 1970. Doris Duke Oral History Collection, #622. American West Center, University of Utah Special Collections.
Dan Press, interview by Sylvia Danovitch, May 26, 1994, Washington, DC, 2, History of the EEOC Oral History Project. Edited transcript in author's possession.

Interviews Conducted by the Author

All recordings and transcripts in the author's possession.
Anonymous Foxwoods worker, August 23, 2012, Ledyard, CT
Anonymous Teamster organizer, August 14, 2012, Oklahoma City, OK
Ron Cobb, August 14, 2012, Oklahoma City, OK
Conrad Edwards and John Navarro, December 6, 2007, Imperial Palace Hotel, Las Vegas
Rodney "Fish" Gervais, December 6, 2007, Imperial Palace Hotel, Las Vegas
Keri Hohne, August 24, 2012, West Hartford, CT
Larry Ketcher, October 4, 2007, Okmulgee, OK
Deron Marquez, June 13, 2012, San Diego State University, San Diego, CA
Daniel Press, June 18, 2007, Washington, DC
Kenneth White, April 4, 2003, Fort Defiance, AZ

SECONDARY SOURCES

Books

Aberle, David. *The Peyote Religion among the Navajo*. Norman: University of Oklahoma Press, 1991.
Adams, David Wallace. *Education for Extinction: American Indians and the Boarding School Experience*, 2nd ed. Lawrence: University Press of Kansas, 2020.
Allison, James. *Sovereignty for Survival: American Energy Development and Indian Self-Determination*. New Haven, CT: Yale University Press, 2015.

Ambler, Marjane. *Breaking the Iron Bonds: Indian Control of Energy Development.* Lawrence: University Press of Kansas, 1990.
Amerman, Steve. *Urban Indians in Phoenix Schools, 1940–2000.* Lincoln: University of Nebraska Press, 2010.
Anderson, Terry L. *Unlocking the Wealth of Indian Nations.* New York: Lexington Books, 2016.
Andrews, Thomas. *Killing for Coal: Colorado's Deadliest Labor War.* Cambridge, MA: Harvard University Press, 2008.
Archuleta, Margaret, Brenda J. Child, and K. Tsianina Lomawaima, eds. *Away from Home: American Indian Boarding School Experiences, 1879–2000.* Phoenix: Heard Museum, 2004. Distributed by the Museum of New Mexico Press, Santa Fe.
Arnesen, Eric. *Brotherhoods of Color: Black Railroad Workers and the Struggle for Equality.* Cambridge, MA: Harvard University Press, 2002.
Ashton, T. H., and C. H. E. Philpin. *The Brenner Debate: Agrarian Class Structure and Economic Development in Pre-Industrial Europe.* Cambridge, UK: Cambridge University Press, 1987.
Bauer, William J., Jr. *We Were All Like Migrant Workers Here: Work Community, and Memory on California's Round Valley Reservation, 1850–1941.* Chapel Hill: University of North Carolina Press, 2009.
Beck, David. *The Struggle for Self-Determination: History of the Menominee Indians since 1854.* Lincoln: University of Nebraska Press, 2005.
Beckert, Sven, and Christine Desan, eds. *American Capitalism: New Histories.* New York: Columbia University Press, 2018.
Bernstein, Alison R. *American Indians in World War II: Toward a New Era in Indian Affairs.* Norman: University of Oklahoma Press, 1991.
Biolsi, Thomas. *Organizing the Lakota: The Political Economy of the New Deal on the Pine Ridge and Rosebud Reservations.* Tucson: University of Arizona Press, 1993.
Blackhawk, Ned. *The Rediscovery of America: Native Peoples and the Unmaking of U.S. History.* New Haven, CT: Yale University Press, 2023.
Boyce, George. *When the Navajos Had Too Many Sheep: The 1940's.* San Francisco: Indian Historian Press, 1974.
Brooks, James. *Captives and Cousins: Slavery, Kinship, and Community in the Southwest Borderlands.* Chapel Hill: University of North Carolina Press, 2002.
Brugge, Doug, Timothy Benally, and Esther Yazzie-Lewis eds. *The Navajo People and Uranium Mining.* Albuquerque: University of New Mexico Press, 2007.
Bsumek, Erika. *Indian-Made: Navajo Culture in the Marketplace, 1868–1940.* Lawrence: University Press of Kansas, 2008.
Byrd, Jodi A. *The Transit of Empire: Indigenous Critiques of Colonialism.* Minneapolis: University of Minnesota Press, 2011.
Cahill, Cathleen D. *Federal Fathers and Mothers: A Social History of the United States Indian Service, 1869–1933.* Chapel Hill: University of North Carolina Press, 2011.
California Nations Indian Gaming Association (CNIGA). *2016 California Tribal Gaming Impact Study: An Economic, Fiscal, and Social Impac Analysis wth Community Attitudes Survey Assessment.* CNIGA, August 2016. https://cniga.com/wp-content/uploads/2021/07/12-2-16-EIS-Full-Report-1-Final.pdf.

Carleton, Sean. *Lessons in Legitimacy: Colonialism, Capitalism, and the Rise of State Schooling in British Columbia*. Vancouver: University of British Columbia Press, 2022.

Carlson, Keith Thor, John Sutton Lutz, David M. Schaepe, and Naxaxalhts'i (Albert "Sonny" McHalsie). *Towards a New Ethnohistory: Community-Engaged Scholarship among the People of the River*. Winnipeg: University of Manitoba Press, 2018.

Carlson-Manathara, Elizabeth, and Gladys Rowe. *Living in Indigenous Sovereignty*. Halifax: Fernwood Publishing, 2021.

Cattelino, Jessica. *High Stakes: Florida Seminole Gaming and Sovereignty*. Durham, NC: Duke University Press, 2008.

Cave, Alfred A. *The Pequot War*. Amherst: University of Massachusetts Press, 1996.

Chamberlain, Kathleen. *Under Sacred Ground: A History of Navajo Oil, 1922–1982*. Albuquerque: University of New Mexico Press, 2000.

Child, Brenda J. *Boarding School Seasons: American Indian Families, 1900–1940*. Lincoln: University of Nebraska Press, 1998.

Child, Brenda J. *Holding Our World Together: Ojibwe Women and the Survival of Community*. New York: Viking, 2012.

Child, Brenda J. *My Grandfather's Knocking Sticks: Ojibwe Family Life and Labor on the Reservation, 1900–1940*. Minneapolis: Minnesota Historical Society Press, 2014.

Cobb, Daniel M. *Native Activism in Cold War America: The Struggle for Sovereignty*. Lawrence: University Press of Kansas, 2008.

Cobble, Dorothy Sue. *The Other Women's Movement: Workplace Justice and Social Rights in Modern America*. Princeton, NJ: Princeton University Press, 2005.

Coleman, Michael C. *American Indian Children at School, 1850–1930*. Oxford: University of Mississippi Press, 1993.

Cooper, Frederick. *Decolonization and African Society: The Labour Question in French and British Africa*. Cambridge, UK: Cambridge University Press, 1996.

Coulthard, Glen Sean. *Red Skin, White Masks: Rejecting the Colonial Politics of Recognition*. Minneapolis: University of Minnesota Press, 2014.

Curley, Andrew. *Carbon Sovereignty: Coal, Development, and Energy Transition in the Navajo Nation*. Tucson: University of Arizona Press, 2023.

Davis, Julie L. *Survival Schools: The American Indian Movement and Community Education in the Twin Cities*. Minneapolis: University of Minnesota Press, 2013.

Deer, Sarah. *The Beginning and End of Rape: Confronting Sexual Violence in Native America*. Minneapolis: University of Minnesota Press, 2015.

DeJong, David H. *The Commissioners of Indian Affairs: The United States Indian Service and the Making of Federal Indian Policy, 1824 to 2017*. Salt Lake City: University of Utah Press, 2020.

Deloria, Philip. *Indians in Unexpected Places*. Lawrence: University Press of Kansas, 2004.

Deloria, Vine, Jr., and David E. Wilkins. *Tribes, Treaties, and Constitutional Tribulations*. Austin: University of Texas Press, 1999.

Denetdale, Jennifer Nez. *Reclaiming Diné History: The Legacies of Navajo Chief Manuelito*. University of Arizona Press, 2007.

Deslippe, Dennis A. *Rights, Not Roses: Unions and the Rise of Working-Class Feminism, 1945–80*. Urbana: University of Illinois Press, 1999.

Effinger-Crichlow, Marta. *Staging Migrations toward an American West: From Ida B. Wells to Rhodessa Jones*. Boulder: University Press of Colorado, 2014.

Eichstaedt, Peter. *If You Poison Us: Uranium and Native Americans*. Santa Fe: Red Crane Books, 1994.

Ellis, Clyde. *A Dancing People: Powwow Culture on the Southern Plains*. Lawrence: University Press of Kansas, 2003.

Ellis, Clyde. *To Change Them Forever: Indian Education at the Rainy Mountain Boarding School, 1893–1920*. Norman: University of Oklahoma Press, 1996.

Etienne, Mona, and Eleanor Leacock. *Women and Colonization: Anthropological Perspectives*. Westport, CT: Praeger, 1980.

Fenn, Elizabeth A. *Encounters at the Heart of the World: A History of the Mandan People*. New York: Hill and Wang, 2015.

Fitzgerald, Deborah. *Every Farm a Factory: The Industrial Ideal in American Agriculture*. New Haven, CT: Yale University Press, 2003.

Fixico, Donald L. *The Invasion of Indian Country in the Twentieth Century: American Capitalism and Tribal Natural Resources*. Boulder: University Press of Colorado, 1998.

Fixico, Donald L. *Termination and Relocation: Federal Indian Policy, 1945–1960*. Albuquerque: University of New Mexico Press, 1986.

Fixico, Donald L. *The Urban Indian Experience in America*. Albuquerque: University of New Mexico Press, 2000.

Frederickson, George. *White Supremacy: A Comparative Study of American and South African History*. New York: Oxford University Press, 1982.

Fromson, Brett Duval. *Hitting the Jackpot: The Inside Story of the Richest Indian Tribe in History*. New York: Grove Press, 2004.

Gabin, Nancy. *Feminism in the Labor Movement: Women and the United Auto Workers, 1935–1975*. Ithaca, NY: Cornell University Press, 1990.

Gilbert, Matthew Sakiestewa. *Education beyond the Mesas: Hopi Students at Sherman Institute, 1902–1929*. Lincoln: University of Nebraska Press, 2010.

Gordon, Theodor P. *Cahuilla Nation Activism and the Tribal Casino Movement*. Reno: University of Nevada Press, 2018.

Gregory, James. *American Exodus: The Dust Bowl Migration and Okie Culture in California*. New York: Oxford University Press, 1989.

Hackel, Steven W. *Children of Coyote, Missionaries of Saint Francis: Indian-Spanish Relations in Colonial California, 1769–1850*. Chapel Hill: University of North Carolina Press, 2005.

Hall, Edward T. *West of the Thirties: Discoveries among the Navajo and Hopi*. New York: Doubleday, 1994.

Hämäläinen, Pekka. *The Comanche Empire*. New Haven, CT: Yale University Press, 2008.

Hämäläinen, Pekka. *Indigenous Continent: The Epic Contest for North America*. New York: Liveright, 2022.

Harmon, Alexandra. *Rich Indians: Native People and the Problem of Wealth in American History*. Chapel Hill: University of North Carolina Press, 2010.

Haskins, Victoria K. *Matrons and Maids: Regulating Indian Domestic Service in Tucson, 1914–1934*. Tucson: University of Arizona Press, 2012.

Hauptman, Laurence M. *The Iroquois and the New Deal*. Syracuse, NY: Syracuse University Press, 1981.

Hauptman, Laurence M., and James D. Wherry, eds. *The Pequots in Southern New England: The Fall and Rise of an American Indian Nation*. Norman: University of Oklahoma Press, 1990.

Hays, Robert. *Editorializing "The Indian Problem": The New York Times on Native Americans, 1860–1900*. Carbondale: Southern Illinois University Press, 2007.

Heaton, John W. *The Shoshone-Bannocks: Culture and Commerce at Fort Hall, 1870–1940*. Lawrence: University Press of Kansas, 2005.

Henson, Eric C. *The State of the Native Nations: Conditions under U.S. Policies of Self-Determination*. New York: Oxford University Press, 2008.

Hoeft, Mike. *The Bingo Queens of Oneida: How Two Moms Started Gaming in Wisconsin*. Madison: Wisconsin Historical Society Press, 2014.

Honey, Michael K. *Going Down Jericho Road: The Memphis Strike, Martin Luther King's Last Campaign*. New York: W. W. Norton, 2008.

Hosmer, Brian. *American Indians in the Marketplace: Persistence and Innovation among the Menominees and Metlakatlans, 1870–1920*. Lawrence: University Press of Kansas, 1999.

Hosmer, Brian C., and Colleen O'Neill, eds. *Native Pathways: American Indian Culture and Economic Development in the Twentieth Century*. Boulder: University Press of Colorado, 2004.

Hoxie, Frederick. *A Final Promise: The Campaign to Assimilate the Indians, 1880–1920*. Lincoln: University of Nebraska Press, 1992.

Hoxie, Frederick. *Parading Through History: The Making of the Crow Nation in America, 1805–1935*. New York: Penguin Press, 2012.

Hoxie, Frederick. *Talking Back to Civilization: Indian Voices from the Progressive Era*. New York: Bedford/St. Martins, 2001.

Hurt, R. Douglas. *American Agriculture: A Brief History*. Ames: Iowa State University Press, 1994.

Hutchinson, Elizabeth. *The Indian Craze: Primitivism, Modernism, and Transculturation in American Art, 1890–1915*. Durham, NC: Duke University Press, 2009.

Hyer, Sally. *One House, One Voice, One Heart: Native American Education at the Santa Fe Indian School*. Santa Fe: Museum of New Mexico Press, 1990.

Iverson, Peter. *Diné: A History of the Navajos*. Albuquerque: University of New Mexico Press, 2002.

Jacobs, Margaret D. *White Mother to a Dark Race: Settler Colonialism, Maternalism, and the Removal of Indigenous Children in the American West and Australia, 1880–1940*. Lincoln: University of Nebraska Press, 2009.

Jagodinsky, Katrina. *Legal Codes and Talking Trees: Indigenous Women's Sovereignty in the Sonoran and Puget Sound Borderlands, 1854–1946*. New Haven, CT: Yale University Press, 2016.

Jensen, Joan M., and Darlis Miller. *New Mexico Women: Intercultural Perspectives*. Albuquerque: University of New Mexico Press, 1986.

Johnson, Susan Lee. *Roaring Camp: The Social World of the California Gold Rush*. New York: W. W. Norton, 2001.

Jorgensen, Joseph G., ed. *Native Americans and Energy Development II*. 2nd ed. Boston: Anthropology Resource Center and Seventh Generation Fund, 1984.

Kamper, David. *The Work of Sovereignty: Tribal Labor Relations and Self-Determination at the Navajo Nation*. Santa Fe: School of Advanced Research Press, 2010.

Keliiaa, Caitlin. *Refusing Settler Domesticity: Native Women's Labor and Resistance in the Bay Area Outing Program*. Seattle: University of Washington Press, 2024.

Kelly, Lawrence. *The Navajo Indians and Federal Indian Policy, 1900–1935*. Tucson: University of Arizona Press, 1968.

Kelm, Mary-Ellen, and Lorna Townsend, eds. *In the Days of Our Grandmothers: A Reader in Aboriginal Women's History in Canada*. Toronto: University of Toronto Press, 2006.

Kersey, Harry A. *The Florida Seminoles and the Indian New Deal, 1933–1942*. Boca Raton: Florida Atlantic University Press, 1989.

Kessler-Harris, Alice. *Gendering Labor History*. Urbana: University of Illinois Press, 2006.

Kessler-Harris, Alice. *A Woman's Wage: Historical Meanings and Social Consequences* Lexington: University Press of Kentucky, 1990.

King, Farina, Michael P. Taylor, and James R. Swensen. *Returning Home: Diné Creative Works from the Intermountain Indian School*. Tucson: University of Arizona Press, 2021.

Klann, Mary. *Wardship and the Welfare State: Native Americans and the Formation of First-Class Citizenship in Mid-Twentieth Century America*. Lincoln: University of Nebraska Press, 2024.

Knight, Rolf. *Indians at Work: An Informal History of Native Labour in British Columbia, 1858–1930*. Vancouver: New Star Books, 1996.

Korstad, Robert Rodgers. *Civil Rights Unionism: Tobacco Workers and the Struggle for Democracy in the Mid-Twentieth Century South*. Chapel Hill: University of North Carolina Press, 2003.

Koshy, Susan, Lisa Marie Cacho, Jodi A. Byrd, and Brian Jordan Jefferson. *Colonial Racial Capitalism*. Durham, NC: Duke University Press, 2022.

Krupat, Arnold. *Changed Forever: American Indian Boarding School Literature*. Albany: State University of New York Press, 2018.

Kvasnicka, Robert M., and Herman J. Viola, eds. *The Commissioners of Indian Affairs, 1824–1977*. Lincoln: University of Nebraska Press, 1979.

LaGrand, James B. *Indian Metropolis: Native Americans in Chicago, 1945–75*. Urbana: University of Illinois Press, 2002.

Lamphere, Louise. *To Run After Them: Cultural and Social Bases of Cooperation in a Navajo Community*. Tucson: University of Arizona Press, 1977.

Latham, Michael E. *Modernization as Ideology: American Social Science and "Nation Building" in the Kennedy Era*. Chapel Hill: University of North Carolina Press, 2000.

Leonard, Thomas C. *Illiberal Reformers: Race, Eugenics, and American Economics in the Progressive Era*. Princeton, NJ: Princeton University Press, 2016.

Leupp, Francis E. *The Indian and His Problem*. New York: Charles Schribner's Sons, 1910.

Leupp, Francis E. *In Red Man's Land: A Study of the American Indian*. New York: Fleming G. Revell, 1914.

Light, Steven Andrew, and Kathryn R. L. Rand. *Indian Gaming and Tribal Sovereignty: The Casino Compromise*. Lawrence: University Press of Kansas, 2005.

Littlefield, Alice, and Martha Knack. *Native Americans and Wage Labor: Ethnohistorical Perspectives*. Norman: University of Oklahoma Press, 1996.

Lomawaima, K. Tsianina. *They Called It Prairie Light: The Story of Chilocco Indian School*. Lincoln: University of Nebraska Press, 1994.

Lutz, John Sutton. *Makuk: A New History of Aboriginal-White Relations*. Vancouver: University of British Columbia Press, 2008.

Madley, Benjamin. *An American Genocide: The United States and the California Indian Catastrophe, 1846–1873*. New Haven, CT: Yale University Press, 2016.

Magnuson, Stew. *The Death of Raymond Yellow Thunder and Other True Stories from the Nebraska–Pine Ridge Border Towns*. Lubbock: Texas Tech University Press, 2008.

Maher, Neil M. *Nature's New Deal: The Civilian Conservation Corps and the Roots of the American Environmental Movement*. New York: Oxford University Press, 2008.

Mankiller, Wilma Pearl, and Michael Wallis. *Mankiller: A Chief and Her People*. New York: St. Martin's Press, 1993.

Maroukis, Thomas Constantine. *We Are Not a Vanishing People: The Society of American Indians, 1911–1923*. Tucson: University of Arizona Press, 2021.

Marx, Karl. *Capital: A Critique of Political Economy, Volume 1*. London: Penguin Classics, 1992.

McCallum, Mary Jane Logan. *Indigenous Women, Work, and History: 1940–1980*. Winnipeg: University of Manitoba Press, 2014.

McCarty, Teresa L. *A Place to Be Navajo: Rough Rock and the Struggle for Self-Determination in Indigenous Schooling*. New York: Taylor and Francis Group, 2002.

M'Closkey, Kathy. *Swept under the Rug: A Hidden History of Navajo Weaving*. Albuquerque: University of New Mexico Press, 2002.

McLerran, Jennifer. *A New Deal for Navajo Weaving: Reform and Revival of Diné Textiles*. Tucson: University of Arizona Press, 2022.

Meeks, Erik V. *Border Citizens: The Making of Indians, Mexicans, and Anglos in Arizona*. Austin: University of Texas Press, 2007.

Metcalf, Warren. *Termination's Legacy: The Discarded Indians of Utah*. Lincoln: University of Nebraska Press, 2002.

Miles, Tiya. *Ties That Bind: The Story of an Afro-Cherokee Family in Slavery and Freedom*. Berkeley: University of California Press, 2015.

Miller, Douglas K. *Indians on the Move: Native American Mobility and Urbanization in the Twentieth Century*. Chapel Hill: University of North Carolina Press, 2019.

Milloy, Jeremy, and Joan Sangster. *The Violence of Work: New Essays in Canadian and US Labour History*. Toronto: University of Toronto Press, 2020.

Moore, John H. *The Political Economy of North American Indians*. Norman: University of Oklahoma Press, 1993.

Muhammad, Khalil Gibran. *The Condemnation of Blackness: Race, Crime, and the Making of Modern Urban America*. Cambridge, MA: Harvard University Press, 2010.

Murphy, Lucy Eldersveld. *A Gathering of Rivers: Indians, Métis, and Mining in the Western Great Lakes, 1737–1832*. Lincoln: University of Nebraska Press, 2000.

Muszynski, Alicja. *Cheap Wage Labour: Race and Gender in the Fisheries of British Columbia*. Montreal: McGill-Queens Press, 1996.

National Indian Gaming Commission (NIGC). *NIGC FY 2023 Gross Gaming Revenue Report*. NIGC, 2023. www.nigc.gov/images/uploads/reports/GGR23_Final.pdf.

Neth, Mary. *Preserving the Family Farm: Women, Community, and the Foundations of Agribusiness in the Midwest, 1900–1940*. Baltimore, MD: Johns Hopkins University Press, 1995.

Newell, Margaret Ellen. *Brethren by Nature: New England Indians, Colonists, and the Origins of American Slavery*. Ithaca, NY: Cornell University Press, 2015.

Norrgard, Chantal. *Seasons of Change: Labor, Treaty Rights, and Ojibwe Nationhood*. Durham, NC: University of North Carolina Press, 2014.

O'Neill, Colleen. *Working the Navajo Way: Labor and Culture in the Twentieth Century*. Lawrence: University Press of Kansas, 2005.

Ostler, Jeffrey. *The Plains Sioux and U.S. Colonialism from Lewis and Clark to Wounded Knee*. New York: Cambridge University Press, 2004.

Parman, Donald L. *The Navajos and the New Deal*. New Haven, CT: Yale University Press, 1976.

Parnaby, Andrew. *Citizen Docker: Making a New Deal on the Vancouver Waterfront, 1919–1939*. Toronto: University of Toronto Press, 2008.

Perdue, Theda. *Cherokee Women: Gender and Culture Change, 1700–1835*. Lincoln: University of Nebraska Press, 1998.

Phillips, George Harwood. *Vineyards and Vaqueros: Indian Labor and the Economic Expansion of Southern California, 1771–1877*. Norman: University of Oklahoma Press, 2010.

Phillips, Katherine M. *Staging Indigeneity: Salvage Tourism and the Performance of Native American History*. Chapel Hill: University of North Carolina Press, 2021.

Philp, Kenneth R. *Indian Self Rule: First-Hand Accounts of Indian-White Relations from Roosevelt to Reagan*. Logan: Utah State University Press, 1995.

Philp, Kenneth R. *Termination Revisited: American Indians on the Trail to Self-Determination, 1933–1953*. Lincoln: University of Nebraska Press, 1999.

Powell, Dana E. *Landscapes of Power: Politics of Energy in the Navajo Nation*. Durham, NC: Duke University Press, 2018.

Press, Daniel. *Indian Employment Rights: A Guide to Tribal Action*. Boulder, CO: ACKCO, 1976.

Price, Douglas T., and Anne Birgitte Gebauer. *Last Hunters, First Farmers: New Perspectives on the Prehistoric Transition to Agriculture*. Santa Fe: School of American Research Press, 1996.

Prucha, Frances Paul, ed. *Documents of United States Indian Policy*. 3rd ed. Lincoln: University of Nebraska Press, 2000.

Prucha, Frances Paul. *The Great Father: The United States Government and the American Indian*. Abridged edition. Lincoln: University of Nebraska Press, 1986.

Quintana, Maria T. *Contracting Freedom: Race, Empire, and U.S. Guestworker Programs*. Philadelphia: University of Pennsylvania Press, 2022.

Rader, Dean. *Engaged Resistance: American Indian Art, Literature, and Film from Alcatraz to the NMAI*. Austin: University of Texas Press, 2011.

Raibmon, Paige. *Authentic Indians: Episodes of Encounter from the Late-Nineteenth Century Northwest Coast*. Durham, NC: Duke University Press, 2005.

Ramirez, Renya K. *Native Hubs: Culture, Community, and Belonging in Silicon Valley and Beyond*. Durham, NC: Duke University Press, 2007.

Reinhardt, Akim. *Ruling Pine Ridge: Oglala Lakota Politics from the IRA to Wounded Knee.* Lubbock: Texas Tech University Press, 2009.

Rivas-Rodríguez, Maggie, and B. V. Olguín, eds. *Latina/os and World War II: Mobility, Agency, and Ideology.* Austin: University Press of Texas, 2014.

Rogge, A. E., D. Lorn McWatters, Melissa Keane, and Richard P. Emanuel. *Raising Arizona's Dams: Daily Life, Danger, and Discrimination in the Dam Construction Camps of Central Arizona, 1890s–1940s.* Tucson: University of Arizona Press, 1995. https://archive.org/details/raisingarizonasd0000unse.

Rose, Nancy. *Put to Work: Relief Programs in the Great Depression.* New York: Monthly Review Press, 1994.

Rosenthal, Nicolas G. *Reimagining Indian Country: Native American Migration and Identity in Twentieth-Century Los Angeles.* Chapel Hill: University of North Carolina Press, 2014.

Rosier Paul. *Rebirth of the Blackfeet Nation, 1912–1954.* Lincoln: University of Nebraska Press, 2004.

Rosier, Paul C. *Serving Their Country: American Indian Politics and Patriotism in the Twentieth Century.* Cambridge, MA: Harvard University Press, 2009.

Ross, Stephanie, and Larry Savage. *Rethinking the Politics of Labour in Canada*, 2nd ed. Winnipeg: Fernwood Publishing 2021.

Rossum, Ralph A. *The Supreme Court and Tribal Gaming: California v. Cabazon Band of Mission Indians.* Lawrence: University Press of Kansas, 2011.

Rubin, Julius H. *Tears of Repentance: Christian Indian Identity and Community in Colonial Southern New England.* Lincoln: University of Nebraska Press, 2013.

Salisbury, Neal. *Manitou and Providence: Indians, Europeans, and the Making of New England, 1500–1643.* New York: Oxford University Press, 1984.

Sangster, Joan. *Transforming Labour: Women and Work in Postwar Canada.* Toronto: University of Toronto Press 2010.

Scott, James C. *Domination and the Arts of Resistance: Hidden Transcripts.* New Haven, CT: Yale University Press, 1990.

Scott, James C. *Seeing Like a State: How Certain Schemes to Improve the Human Condition Have Failed.* New Haven, CT: Yale University Press, 1999.

Scott, James C. *Weapons of the Weak: Everyday Forms of Peasant Resistance.* New Haven, CT: Yale University Press, 1987.

Shoemaker, Nancy. *Negotiators of Change: Historical Perspectives on Native American Women.* New York: Routledge, 1995.

Simonsen, Jane. *Making Home Work: Domesticity and American Indian Assimilation in the American West.* Chapel Hill: University of North Carolina Press, 2006.

Slater, Sandra, and Fay A. Yarbrough. *Gender and Sexuality in Indigenous North America, 1400–1850.* Columbia: University of South Carolina Press, 2022.

Sleeper-Smith, Susan. *Indian Women and French Men: Rethinking Cultural Encounter in the Western Great Lakes.* Amherst: University of Massachusetts Press, 2001.

Sleeper-Smith, Susan. *Rethinking the Fur Trade: Cultures of Exchange in an Atlantic World.* Lincoln: University of Nebraska Press, 2009.

Smith, Paul Chaat. *Like a Hurricane: The Indian Movement from Alcatraz to Wounded Knee.* New York: The New Press, 1996.

Sorkin, Alan L. *American Indians and Federal Aid.* Washington, DC: The Brookings Institution, 1971. https://archive.org/details/americanindiansfoooosork/page/n5/mode/2up.

Sorkin, Alan L. *The Urban American Indian.* Lexington, MA: Lexington Books, 1978.

Stern, Jessica Yirush. *The Lives in Objects: Native Americans, British Colonists, and Cultures of Labor and Exchange in the Southeast.* Chapel Hill: University of North Carolina Press, 2016.

Stoler, Ann Laura. *Along the Archival Grain: Epistemic Anxieties and Colonial Common Sense.* Princeton, NJ: Princeton University Press 2010.

Stratton, Clif. *Education for Empire: American Schools, Race, and the Paths of Good Citizenship.* Berkeley: University of California Press, 2016.

Szasz, Margaret Connell. *Education and the American Indian: The Road to Self-Determination since 1928.* Albuquerque: University of New Mexico Press, 1999.

Theobald, Brianna. *Reproduction on the Reservation: Pregnancy, Childbirth, and Colonialism in the Long Twentieth Century.* Chapel Hill: University of North Carolina Press, 2019.

Thompson, E. P. *The Making of the English Working Class.* New York: Vintage Books, 1963.

Trafzer, Clifford E., Jean A. Keller, and Lorene Sisquoc, eds. *Boarding School Blues: Revisiting American Indian Educational Experiences.* Lincoln: University of Nebraska Press, 2006.

Trennert, Robert A., Jr. *The Phoenix Indian School: Forced Assimilation in Arizona, 1891–1935.* Norman: University of Oklahoma Press, 1988.

Usner, Daniel. *Indian Work: Language and Livelihood in Native American History.* Cambridge, MA: Harvard University Press, 2009.

Valandra, Edward Charles. *Not Without Our Consent: Lakota Resistance to Termination, 1950–59.* Urbana: University of Illinois Press, 2006.

Van Kirk, Sylvia. *Many Tender Ties: Women in Fur-Trade Society, 1670–1870.* Norman: University of Oklahoma Press, 1983.

Vargas, Zaragosa. *Labor Rights Are Civil Rights: Mexican American Workers in Twentieth-Century America.* Princeton, NJ: Princeton University Press, 2007.

Vargas, Zaragosa. *Proletarians of the North: A History of Mexican Industrial Workers in Detroit and the Midwest, 1917–1933.* Berkeley: University of California Press, 1999.

Vučković, Myriam. *Voices from Haskell: Indian Students between Two Worlds, 1884–1928.* Lawrence: University Press of Kansas, 2008.

Wallerstein, Immanuel. *The Modern World-System I: Capitalist Agriculture and the Origins of the European World-Economy in the Sixteenth Century.* New York: Academic Press, 1974.

Weber, Devra. *Dark Sweat, White Gold: California Farm Workers, Cotton, and the New Deal.* Berkeley: University of California Press, 1994.

Weisiger, Marsha. *Dreaming of Sheep in Navajo Country.* Seattle: University of Washington Press, 2009.

Weitzman, David. *Skywalkers: Mohawk Ironworkers Build the City.* New York: Roaring Brook Press, 2010.

Whalen, Kevin. *Native Students at Work: American Indian Labor and the Sherman Institute's Outing Program.* Seattle: University of Washington Press, 2016.

White, Richard. *The Roots of Dependency: Subsistence, Environment, and Social Change among the Choctaws, Pawnees, and Navajos.* Lincoln: University Press of Nebraska, 1983.

Whiteside, Heather. *Proprietary Settler Colonialism and the Making of North America.* New York: Columbia University Press, 2025.

Wilkins, David, and Heidi Kiiwetinepinesiik Stark. *American Indian Politics and the American Political System.* 4th ed. New York: Roman and Littlefield, 2018.

Wilkins, David, and Tsianina Lomawaima. *Uneven Ground: American Indian Sovereignty and Federal Law.* Norman: University of Oklahoma Press, 2002.

Williams, Carol. *Indigenous Women and Work: From Labor to Activism.* Urbana: University of Illinois Press, 2012.

Williams, Eric. *Capitalism and Slavery.* Chapel Hill: University of North Carolina Press, 1944.

Wolf, Eric. *Europe and the People Without History.* Berkeley: University of California Press, 1982.

Articles, Papers, and Book Chapters

Akee, Randall K. Q., Katherine A. Spilde, and Jonathan B. Taylor. "The Indian Gaming Regulatory Act and Its Effects on American Indian Economic Development." *Journal of Economic Perspectives* 29, no. 3 (2015): 185–208.

Albers, Patricia. "From Legend to Land to Labor." In *Native Americans and Wage Labor: Ethnohistorical Perspectives,* edited by Alice Littlefield and Martha C. Knack, 245–73. Norman: University of Oklahoma Press, 1996.

Alder, Stephen. "Further Reasons for the NLRB's Inability to Guarantee American Workers' Freedom to Organize and Bargain Collectively: Comment on Autonomous and Politicized: the NLRB's Uncertain Future." *Comparative Labor Law and Policy Journal* 26, no. 2 (2005): 261–68.

Ambler, Marjane. "The Three Affiliated Tribes at Fort Berthold—Mandan, Hidatsa, Arikara—Seek to Control Their Energy Resources." In *Native Americans and Energy Development, II,* edited by Joseph Q. Jorgenson, 194–99. Boston: Anthropology Resource Center and Seventh Generation Fund, 1984.

Anderson, Hugh Allen. "Richard Henry Pratt: Pioneer of Indian Education and Founder of Carlisle Indian School." *Handbook of Texas Online,* May 1, 1995. Last updated January 14, 2021. www.tshaonline.org/handbook/entries/pratt-richard-henry.

Axtell, James. "The Rise and Fall of the Stockbridge Indian Schools." *Massachusetts Review* 27, no. 2 (Summer 1986): 367–78.

Baca, Lawrence R. "American Indians, the Racial Surprise in the 1964 Civil Rights Act: They May, More Correctly, Perhaps, Be Denominated a Political Group." *Howard Law Journal* 48 (Spring 2005): 971–97.

Bess, Jennifer. "The New Egypt, Pima Cotton, and the Role of Native Wage Labor on the Cooperative Testing and Demonstration Farm, Sacaton, Arizona, 1907–1917." *Agricultural History* 88, no. 4 (Fall 2014): 491–516.

Blackhawk, Ned. "I Can Carry On from Here: The Relocation of American Indians to Los Angeles." *Wicazo Sa Review* 11, no. 2 (October 1995): 16–30.

Blanchard, David. "High Steel! The Kahnawake Mohawks and the High Construction Trade." *Journal of Ethnic Studies* 11 (Summer 1983): 43–44.

Breinig, Helmbrecht. "Native Survivance in the Americas: Resistance and Remembrance in Narratives by Asturias, Tapahonso, and Vizenor." In *Survivance: Narratives of Native Presence*, edited by Gerald Vizenor, 39–60. Lincoln: University of Nebraska Press, 2008.

Brodie, Keith. "NLRB Jurisdiction over Indian Tribes—Uncertainty Abounds." *National Law Review* 15, no. 94 (June 2015). www.btlaborrelations.com/nlrb-jurisdiction-over-indian-tribes-uncertainty-abounds/.

Brownlie, Robin Jarvis. "'Living the Same as the White People': Mohawk and Anishinaabe Women's Labour in Southern Ontario, 1920–1940." *Labour/Le Travail* 61 (Spring 2008): 41–68.

Bunten, Alexis Celeste. "More Like Ourselves: Indigenous Capitalism through Tourism." *American Indian Quarterly* 34, no. 3 (Summer 2010): 285–311. https://doi.org/10.5250/amerindiquar.34.3.285.

Burow, Paul Berne, Samara Brock, and Michael R. Dove. "Unsettling the Land: Indigeneity, Ontology, and Hybridity in Settler Colonialism." *Environment and Society: Advances in Research* 9 (2018): 57–74.

Burrill, Fred. "The Settler Order Framework: Rethinking Canadian Working-Class History." *Labour/Le Travail* 83 (Spring 2019): 173–98.

Byrd, Jodi A., and Michael Rothberg. "Between Subalternity and Indigeneity: Critical Categories for Postcolonial Studies." *Interventions* 13, no. 1 (March 2011): 1–12.

Calcaterra, Angela. "A 'Second Look' at Charles Alexander Eastman." *Studies in American Indian Literatures* 27, no. 4 (Winter 2015): 1–36.

Campbell, Brooke. "Cobell Settlement Finalized after Years of Litigation: Victory at Last?" *American Indian Law Review* 37 (2013): 629–47. https://digitalcommons.law.ou.edu/ailr/vol37/iss2/7.

Campisi, Jack. "The Emergence of Mashantucket Pequot Tribe, 1637–1975." In *The Pequots in Southern New England: The Fall and Rise of an American Indian Nation*, edited by Laurence M. Hauptman, and James D. Wherry, 117–40. Norman: University of Oklahoma Press, 1990.

Campisi, Jack. "The New England Tribes and Their Quest for Justice." In *The Pequots in Southern New England: The Fall and Rise of an American Indian Nation*, edited by Laurence M. Hauptman, and James D. Wherry, 179–93. Norman: University of Oklahoma Press, 1990.

Carstensen, Fred, William Lott, Stan McMillen, Bobur Alimov, Na Li Dawson, and Tapas Ray. *The Economic Impact of the Mashantucket Pequot Tribal Nation Operations on Connecticut*. Storrs, CT: Connecticut Center for Economic Analysis, University of Connecticut, November 28, 2000. www.indian.senate.gov/wp-content/uploads/johnson_1.pdf.

Cattelino, Jessica. "Casino Roots: Cultural Production of Twentieth Century Seminole Economic Development." In *Native Pathways: American Indian Culture and Economic Development in the Twentieth Century*, edited by Brian Hosmer and Colleen O'Neill, 66–90. Boulder: University Press of Colorado, 2004.

Cattelino, Jessica. "The Double Bind of American Need-Based Sovereignty." *Cultural Anthropology* 25, no. 2 (2010): 235–62. https://doi.org/10.1111/j.1548-1360.2010.01058.x.

Cattalino, Jessica. "Tribal Gaming and Indigenous Sovereignty, with Notes from Seminole Country." *American Studies* 46, nos. 3–4 (Winter–Fall 2005): 187–204.

Champagne, Duane. "Tribal Capitalism and Native Capitalists: Multiple Pathways of Native Economy." In *Native Pathways: American Indian Culture and Economic Development in the Twentieth Century*, edited by Brian Hosmer and Colleen O'Neill, 308–29. Boulder: University Press of Colorado, 2004.

Clow, Richmond L. "The Indian Reorganization Act and the Loss of Tribal Sovereignty: Constitutions on the Rosebud and Pine Ridge Reservations." *Great Plains Quarterly* 7, no. 2 (Spring 1987). https://digitalcommons.unl.edu/greatplainsquarterly/317/.

Connell, Raewyn. "Masculinities in Global Perspective: Hegemony, Contestation, and Changing Structures of Power." *Theory and Society* 45 (August 2016): 303–18.

Cooke William N., and Frederick H. Gautschi III. "Political Bias in NLRB Unfair Labor Practice Decisions." *Industrial and Labor Relations Review* 35, no. 4 (July 1982): 539–49.

Cothran, Boyd. "Working the Indian Field Days: The Economy of Authenticity and the Question of Agency in Yosemite Valley." *American Indian Quarterly* 34, no. 2 (Spring 2010): 194–223.

Cramer, Renee Ann. "The Common Sense of Anti-Indian Racism: Reactions to Mashantucket Pequot Success in Gaming and Acknowledgment." *Law and Social Inquiry* 31, no. 2 (Spring 2006): 313–41.

Croghan, Lore. "Scott Butera, the 37-Year-Old EVP of Trump Hotels and Casino Resorts, Has Tall Order—Building Trust Between Bondholders and Donald Trump." *Hotel Online: News for the Hospitality Industry*, April 12, 2004 (no longer available).

Curley, Andrew. "T'ááa hwó ají t'éego and the Moral Economy of Navajo Coal Workers." *Annals of the American Association of Geographers* 109, no. 1 (2019): 71–86.

Dawson, Susan E. "Navajo Uranium Workers and the Effects of Occupational Illnesses." *Human Organization: Journal of the Society for Applied Anthropology* 51, no. 4 (Winter 1992): 389–97.

Doran, Kwinn H. "Ganienkeh: Haudenosaunee Labor-Culture and Conflict Resolution." *American Indian Quarterly* 26, no. 1 (Winter 2002): 1–23.

Dorsey, Peter A. "Going to School with Savages: Authorship and Authority among the Jesuits of New France." *William and Mary Quarterly* 55, no. 3 (July 1998): 399–420.

Durand, Jorge, Douglas S. Massey, and Emilio A Parrado. "The New Era of Mexican Migration to the United States." *Journal of American History* 86, no. 2 (September 1999): 518–36.

Eastman, Charles. "The Indian in School." *Journal of Education* 80, no. 24 (1914): 653–64. www.jstor.org/stable/42768165.

Ellis, Clyde. "Five Dollars a Week to be 'Regular Indians:' Shows, Exhibitions, and the Economics of Indian Dancing, 1880–1930." In *Native Pathways: American Indian Culture and Economic Development in the Twentieth Century*, edited by Brian Hosmer and Colleen O'Neill, 184–208. Boulder: University Press of Colorado, 2004.

Firkus, Angela. "Agricultural Extension and the Campaign to Assimilate the Native Americans of Wisconsin, 1914–1932." *Journal of the Gilded Age and Progressive Era* 9, no. 4 (October 2010): 473–502. www.jstor.org/stable/i20799402.

Fixico, Donald L. "Understanding the Earth and the Demand on Energy Tribes." In *Indians and Energy: Exploitation and Opportunity in the American Southwest*, edited by Sherry Smith and Brian Frehner, 21–34. Santa Fe, NM: School of Advanced Research Press, 2010.

Fletcher, Matthew L. M. "Little River Band Enters into Collective Bargaining Agreement with United Steelworkers." *Turtle Talk* (blog), December 21, 2010. https://turtletalk.blog/2010/12/21/little-river-band-enters-into-collective-bargaining-agreement-with-united-steelworkers/.

GBB. "Pequots' Financial Problems Mount." *Global Gaming Business Magazine*, August 2, 2010. https://ggbmagazine.com/article/pequots-financial-problems-mount/.

Ghan, Derek. "Federal Labor Law and the Mashantucket Pequot: Union Organizing at Foxwoods Casino." *American Indian Law Review* 37, no. 2 (2013): 515–48. https://digitalcommons.law.ou.edu/ailr/vol37/iss2/4.

Glaser, Leah S. "'An Absolute Paragon of Paradoxes': Native American Power and the Electrification of Arizona's Indian Reservations." In *Indians and Energy: Exploitation and Opportunity in the American Southwest*, edited by Sherry Smith and Brian Frehner, 161–202. Santa Fe: School of Advanced Research Press, 2010.

Glenn, Evelyn Nakano. "Settler Colonialism as Structure: A Framework for Comparative Studies of U.S. Race and Gender Formation." *Sociology of Race and Ethnicity* 1, no. 1 (January 2015): 54–74.

Goldberg, Carole, and Duane Champagne. "Ramona Redeemed? The Rise of Tribal Political Power in California." *Wicazo Sa Review* 17, no. 1 (Spring 2002): 43–63.

Gordon, Theodor. "Nation, Corporation or Family? Tribal Casino Employment and the Transformation of Tribes." Center for Gaming Research Occasional Paper Series: Paper 5, July 2010. https://oasis.library.unlv.edu/occ_papers/17/.

Gouveia, Grace Mary. "'We Also Serve': American Indian Women's Role in World War II." *Michigan Historical Review* 20, no. 2 (Fall 1994): 153–82.

Grandjean, Katherine A. "New World Tempests: Environment, Scarcity, and the Coming of the Pequot War." *William and Mary Quarterly* 68, no. 1 (January 2011): 75–100.

Grant, Kenneth W., II, Katherine A. Spilde, and Jonathan B. Taylor. "Social and Economic Consequences, of Indian Gaming in Oklahoma." Joint Occasional Papers on Native Affairs, No. 2003-04. Harvard Project on American Indian Economic Development, 2003. https://nnigovernance.arizona.edu/sites/nnigovernance.arizona.edu/files/2022-09/2003_GRANT_etal_JOPNA_socialeconomicconsequences.pdf.

Green, Elna C. "Relief from Relief: The Tampa Sewing-Room Strike of 1937 and the Right to Welfare." *Journal of American History* 95, no. 4 (March 2009): 1012–37.

Grossman, James. "A Chance to Make Good: 1900–1929." In *To Make Our World Anew: A History of African Americans*, edited by Robin D. G. Kelley and Earl Lewis, 378–79. Oxford, UK: Oxford University Press, 2000.

Guss, Jonathan. "Gaming Sovereignty? A Plea for Protecting Worker's Rights While Preserving Tribal Sovereignty." *California Law Review* 102, no. 6 (December 2014): 1623–69.

Harmon, Alexandra. "Tribal Enrollment Councils: Lessons on Law and Indian Identity." *Western Historical Quarterly* 32, no. 2 (Summer 2001): 175–200.

Harmon, Alexandra, Colleen O'Neill, and Paul Rosier. "Interwoven Economic Histories: American Indians in a Capitalist America." *Journal of American History* 98, no. 3 (December 2011): 698–722.

High, Steven. "Native American Wage Labour and Independent Production during the 'Era of Irrelevance.'" *Labour/Le Travail* 37 (Spring 1996): 243–64.

Hollermann, Ephrem. "Where There Was Need: Evangelization and North American Benedictines." *American Benedictine Review* 63 (September 2012): 303–20.

Hosmer, Brian. "'A Dollar a Day and Glad to Have It': Work Relief on the Wind River Reservation as Memory." In *Native Pathways: American Indian Culture and Economic Development in the Twentieth Century*, edited by Brian Hosmer and Colleen O'Neill, 283–307. Boulder: University Press of Colorado, 2004.

Hurtado, Albert L. "'Hardly a Farmhouse—A Kitchen without Them': Indian and White Households on the California Borderland Frontier in 1860." *Western Historical Quarterly* 13, no. 3 (July 1982): 245–70. www.jstor.org/stable/969413.

Ishiyama, Noriko. "Environmental Justice and American Indian Tribal Sovereignty: Case Study of a Land-Use Conflict in Skull Valley, Utah." *Antipode* 35, no. 1 (2003): 119–39.

Jacobs, Margaret D. "Diverted Mothering among American Indian Domestic Servants, 1920–1940." In *Indigenous Women and Work: From Labor to Activism*, edited by Carol Williams, 179–92. Urbana: University of Illinois Press, 2012.

Jacobs, Margaret D. "Shaping a New Way: White Women and the Movement to Promote Pueblo Indian Arts and Crafts, 1900–1935." *Journal of the Southwest* 40, no. 2 (Summer 1998): 187–215. www.jstor.org/stable/40170017.

Jacobs, Margaret D. "Working on the Domestic Frontier: American Indian Domestic Servants in White Women's Households in the San Francisco Bay Area, 1920–1940." *Frontiers: A Journal of Women Studies* 28, nos. 1–2 (2007): 165–99. https://digitalcommons.unl.edu/historyfacpub/49/.

Jensen, Joan M. "Canning Comes to New Mexico: Women and the Agricultural Extension Service, 1914–1919." In *New Mexico Women: Intercultural Perspectives*, edited by Joan Jensen and Darlis Miller, 201–26. Albuquerque: University of New Mexico Press, 1986.

Johansen, Bruce E. "The BIA as Banker: Trust Is Hard When Billions Disappear." *Native Americas* 14, no. 1 (Spring 1997): 14–23.

Johnston, Barbara Rose, Susan Dawson, and Gary Madsen. "Uranium Mining and Milling: Navajo Experiences in the American Southwest." In *Indians and Energy: Exploitation and Opportunity in the American Southwest*, edited by Sherry Smith and Brian Frehner, 111–34. Santa Fe: School of Advanced Research Press, 2010.

Kamper, David, and Katherine A. Spilde. "The Legal Regimenting of Tribal Wealth: How Federal Courts and Agencies Seek to Normalize Tribal Governmental Revenue and Capital." *American Indian Culture and Research Journal* 40, no. 2 (2016): 1–29. https://doi.org/10.17953/aicrj.40.2.kamper.spilde.

Kantor, Harvey. "Choosing a Vocation: The Origins and Transformation of Vocational Guidance in California, 1910–1930." *History of Education Quarterly* 26, no. 3 (Autumn 1986): 351–75.

Kauanui, Kēhaulani. "A Structure, Not an Event." *Lateral* 5 (Spring 2016). www.jstor.org/stable/48671433.

Kelly, Lawrence C. "The Indian Reorganization Act: The Dream and the Reality." *Pacific Historical Review* 44, no. 3 (August 1975): 291–312.

La Farge, Oliver. "Termination of Federal Supervision: Disintegration and the American Indians." *Annals of the American Academy of Political and Social Science* 311 (May 1957): 41–46.

LaPier, Rosalyn, and David R. M. Beck. "A 'One-Man Relocation Team': Scott Henry Peters and American Indian Urban Migration in the 1930s." *Western Historical Quarterly* 45 (Spring 2014): 17–36.

Laudenschlager, David D. "The Utes in South Dakota, 1906–1908." *South Dakota History* 9 (Summer 1979): 233–46.

Laukaitis, John J. "Indians at Work and John Collier's Campaign for Progressive Educational Reform, 1933–1945." *American Education History Journal* 33, no. 2 (2006): 97–105.

Lewis, David Rich. "Skull Valley Goshutes and the Politics of Nuclear Waste: Environment, Economic Development, and Tribal Sovereignty." In *Native Americans and the Environment: Perspectives on the Ecological Indian*, edited by Michael E. Harkin and David Rich Lewis, 304–42. Lincoln: University of Nebraska Press, 2007.

Littlefield, Alice. "Indian Education and the World of Work in Michigan, 1893–1933." In *Native Americans and Wage Labor: Ethnohistorical Perspectives*, edited by Alice Littlefield and Martha C. Knack, 111–14. Norman: University of Oklahoma Press, 1996.

Littlefield, Alice. "Learning to Labor: Native American Education in the United States, 1880–1930. In *The Political Economy of North American Indians*, edited by John H. Moore, 43–59. Norman: University of Oklahoma Press, 1993.

Lofthouse, Jordan K. "Institutions and Economic Development on Native American Lands." *Independent Review* 24, no. 2 (Fall 2019): 227–48. www.independent.org/pdf/tir/tir_24_2_04_lofthouse.pdf.

Lomawaima, K. Tsianina. "Estelle Reel, Superintendent of Indian Schools, 1898–1910: Politics, Curriculum, and Land." *Journal of American Indian Education* 35, no. 3 (Spring 1996): 5–31.

Magliari, Michael F. "Free State Slavery: Bound Indian Labor and Slave Trafficking in California's Sacramento Valley, 1850–1864." *Pacific Historical Review* 81, no. 2 (May 2012): 155–92.

Maher, Neil M. "A New Deal Body Politic: Landscape, Labor, and the Civilian Conservation Corps." *Environmental History* 7, no. 3 (July 2002): 435–62.

Maher, Neil M. "'Work for Others but None for Us': the Economic and Environmental Inequalities of New Deal Relief." *Social History* 40, no. 3 (August 2015): 312–34.

Marr, Carolyn J. "Assimilation through Education: Indian Boarding Schools in the Pacific Northwest." Topical Essays, American Indians of the Pacific Northwest Collection, Digital Collections, University of Washington Libraries. Accessed June 30, 2025. https://content.lib.washington.edu/aipnw/marr.html.

McKellips, Karen K. "Educational Practices in Two Nineteenth Century American Indian Mission Schools." *Journal of American Indian Education* 32, no. 1 (October 1992): 12–20.

McLaughlin, Castle. "Nation, Tribe, and Class: The Dynamics of Agrarian Transformation on the Fort Berthold Reservation." *American Indian Culture and Research Journal* 22, no. 3 (1998): 101–38. https://doi.org/10.17953.

Meadows, William. "The Return of the Numu Pukutsi: Reclaiming a Comanche Warrior Tradition." *American Indian Quarterly*, 46, no. 3 (Summer 2022): 189–224.

Meeks, Eric V. "The Tohono O'odham, Wage Labor, and Resistant Adaptation, 1900–1930." *Western Historical Quarterly* 34, no. 4 (Winter 2003): 469–90.

Merjian, Armen H. "An Unbroken Chain of Injustice: The Dawes Act, Native American Trusts, and *Cobell v. Salazar*." *Gonzaga Law Review* 46, no. 3 (2010–11): 609–58. https://blogs.gonzaga.edu/gulawreview/files/2011/09/Merjian.pdf.

Miller, Douglas K. "Willing Workers: Urban Relocation and American Indian Initiative, 1940s–1960s." *Ethnohistory* 60, no. 1 (January 2013): 51–76.

Mills, Suzanne E., and Tyler McCreary. "Which Side Are You On?: Indigenous Peoples and Canada's Labour Movement." In *Rethinking the Politics of Labour in Canada*, 2nd ed., edited by Stephanie Ross and Larry Savage, 133–15. Halifax: Fernwood Publishing, 2021.

Mitchell, Joseph. "The Mohawks in High Steel." In *Apologies to the Iroquois*, edited by Edmund Wilson, 1–36. New York: Farrar, Straus and Giroux, 1959.

Moore, John H. "Cheyenne Work in the History of US Capitalism." In *Native Americans and Wage Labor: Ethnohistorical Perspectives*, edited by Alice Littlefield and Martha C. Knack, 122–43. Norman: University of Oklahoma Press, 1996.

Morales, Eduardo. "Tejano Migrants and the Creation of an Ethnic Mexican National Community in Indiana and the Great Lakes Region before World War II." *Journal of the West* 53 (Summer 2014): 12–24.

National Congress of Native Americans. "Securing Our Futures." Policy paper, 2013. https://archive.ncai.org/attachments/PolicyPaper_CUFUHjKqlcEhGLtpcwrDyiUgrDgqOFUWmxMiRzAFFaxJWsCZDSK_Securing%20Our%20Futures%20Final.pdf.

Needham, Andrew. "'A Piece of the Action': Navajo Nationalism, Energy Development and Metropolitan Inequality." In *Indians and Energy: Exploitation and Opportunity in the American Southwest*, edited by Sherry Smith and Brian Frehner, 203–30. Santa Fe: School of Advanced Research Press, 2010.

Norrgard, Chantal. "Indigenous Unions: What the Native Brotherhoods Can Teach Us about Labor." Unpublished paper in the author's possession; used with permission.

Novak, Steven J. "The Real Takeover of the BIA: The Preferential Hiring of Indians." *Journal of Economic History* 50, no. 3 (1990): 640–46.

Nykiel, Ronald. "An Assessment of the Many Contributions of Native American Gaming." *UNLV Gaming Research and Review Journal* 8, no. 2 (2004): 51–56. https://doi.org/10.9741/2327-8455.1173.

Oakes, Leslie S., and Joni J. Young. "Reconciling Conflict: The Role of Accounting in the American Indian Trust Fund Debacle." *Critical Perspectives on Accounting* 21, no. 1 (January 2010): 63–75.

O'Neil, Floyd. "An Anguished Odyssey: The Flight of the Utes 1906–1908." *Utah Historical Quarterly* 36, no. 4 (1968): 315–27. https://issuu.com/utah10/docs/uhq_volume36_1968_number4/s/104768.

O'Neill, Colleen. "Testing the Limits of Colonial Parenting: Navajo Domestic Workers, The Intermountain Indian School, and the Urban Relocation Program, 1950–1962." *Ethnohistory* 66, no. 3 (July 2019): 565–92.

Osmond, Colin Murray. "'I Was Born a Logger': Stó:lō Identities Forged in the Forest." In *Towards a New Ethnohistory: Community-Engaged Scholarship among the People of the River*, edited by Keith Thor Carlson, John Sutton Lutz, David M. Schaepe and Naxaxalhts'i (Albert "Sonny" McHalsie), 215–35. Winnipeg: University of Manitoba Press, 2018.

Ostler, Jeffrey. "Locating Settler Colonialism in Early American History." *William and Mary Quarterly* 76, no. 3 (July 2019): 443–50.

Parham, Vera. "'These Indians Are Apparently Well to Do': The Myth of Capitalism and Native American Labor." *International Review of Social History* 57, no. 3 (2012): 447–70. https://doi.org/10.1017/S002085901200051X.

Parman, Donald L. "The Indian and the Civilian Conservation Corps." *Pacific Historical Review* 40 (February 1971): 39–56.

Philp, Kenneth R. "Termination: A Legacy of the Indian New Deal." *Western Historical Quarterly* 14, no. 2 (April 1983): 165–80.

Plumer, Riley. "Overriding Tribal Sovereignty by Applying the National Labor Relations Act to Indian Tribes in *Soaring Eagle Casino and Resort v. National Labor Relations Board*." *Law and Equality: A Journal of Theory and Practice* 35, no. 1 (2017): 131–32. https://scholarship.law.umn.edu/lawineq/vol35/iss1/6.

Potter, Lori. "The Domino-Effect of Really Bad Decisions." *Lori Potter: Memoirs and Musings of a Mashantucket Pequot* (blog), May 7, 2012. https://loripotter.wordpress.com/2012/05/07/the-stinking-domino-effect-of-really-bad-decisions.

Powell, Dana, and Dailan J. Long. "Landscapes of Power: Renewable Energy Activism in Diné Bikéyah." In *Indians and Energy: Exploitation and Opportunity in the American Southwest*, edited by Sherry Smith and Brian Frehner, 231–62. Santa Fe: School for Advanced Research, 2010.

Pratt, Richard Henry. "The Advantages of Mingling Indians with Whites." *Proceedings of the National Conference of Charities and Correction at the Nineteenth Annual Session Held in Denver, Col., June 23–29, 1892*. Edited by Isabel C. Barrows. Boston: Press of Geo. H. Ellis, 1892. https://hdl.handle.net/2027/wu.89030648919.

Quinnell, Kenneth. "National Native American Heritage Month Profiles." *AFL-CIO* (blog), November 29, 2024. https://aflcio.org/2024/11/29/national-native-american-heritage-month-profiles.

Raibmon, Paige. "The Practice of Everyday Colonialism: Indigenous Women at Work in the Hop Fields and Tourist Industry of Puget Sound." *Labor: Studies in Working-Class History of the Americas* 3, no. 3 (2006): 23–56. https://doi.org/10.1215/15476715-2006-004.

Rawls, James J. "Gold Diggers: Indian Miners in the California Gold Rush." *California Historical Quarterly* 55, no. 1 (April 1976): 28–45.

Reinhardt, Bob H. "Drowned Towns in the Cold War West: Small Communities and Federal Water Projects." *Western Historical Quarterly* 42, no. 2 (Summer 2011): 149–72.

Robbins, Lynn. *Navajo Participation in Labor Unions*. Lake Powell Research Project Bulletin, No. 15. Institute of Geophysics and Planetary Physics, University of California, Los Angeles, December 1975. https://files.eric.ed.gov/fulltext/ED127091.pdf.

Roosevelt, Eleanor. "My Day: November 12, 1936." The Eleanor Roosevelt Papers Project, George Washington University. Accessed April 4, 2025. https://www2.gwu.edu/~erpapers/myday/displaydoc.cfm?_y=1936&_f=md054486.

Rosenthal, Nicolas G. "Representing Indians: Native American Actors on Hollywood's Frontier." *Western Historical Quarterly* 36, no. 3 (October 2005): 328–52. https://doi.org/10.2307/25443194.

Rosier, Paul C. "Crossing International and Historiographical Boundaries: American Indians and Twentieth Century American Foreign Policy." *Diplomatic History* 39, no. 5 (November 2015): 955–66.

Rosier, Paul C. "'The Old System Is No Success:' The Blackfeet Nation's Decision to Adopt the Indian Reorganization Act of 1934." *American Indian Culture and Research Journal* 23, no. 1 (1999): 1–37. https://escholarship.org/uc/item/42w6s9gj.

Rothberg, Emma. "Elouise Cobell (Yellow Bird Woman): 1945–2011." National Women's History Museum. Accessed June 26, 2023. www.womenshistory.org/education-resources/biographies/elouise-cobell-yellow-bird-woman.

Sangster, Joan. "Colonialism at Work: Labour Placement Programs for Aboriginal Women in Post-War Canada." In *Aboriginal History: A Reader*, edited by Kristen Burnett and Geoff Read, 293–302. New York: Oxford University Press, 2012.

Sium, Aman, Chandni Desai, and Eric Ritskes. "Towards the 'Tangible Unknown': Decolonization and the Indigenous Future." *Decolonization: Indigeneity, Education and Society* 1 (2012): i–xiii. www.ufv.ca/media/assets/race-antiracism-network-ran/Decolonization-and-the-Indigenous-Future.pdf.

Smith, Kaighn, Jr. "The NLRB and Indian Gaming Three Ways." Drummond Woodsum, Attorneys at Law. Accessed December 5, 2017. www.dwmlaw.com/the-nlrb-and-indian-gaming-three-ways (no longer available).

Smith, Kaighn, Jr., and Joel West Williams. "Native Americans, Tribal Sovereignty, and Unions." *International Union Rights* 25, no. 4 (2018): 22–28.

Spilde, Katherine, and Jonathan B. Taylor. "Economic Evidence on the Effects of the Indian Gaming Regulatory Act on Indians and Non-Indians." *UNLV Gaming Research and Review Journal* 17, no. 1 (May 2013): 13–30.

Stevens, Ernie, Jr. "IGA Report: Indian Gaming Continues to Anchor American and Oklahoman Economies." *Indian Gaming Magazine*, August 6, 2024. www.indiangaming.com/iga-report-indian-gaming-continues-to-anchor-american-and-oklahoman-economies.

Sturm, Circe. "Blood Politics, Racial Classification, and Cherokee National Identity: The Trials and Tribulations of the Cherokee Freedmen." *American Indian Quarterly* 22, nos. 1–2 (Winter–Spring, 1998): 230–58. https://nativeappropriations.com/wp-content/uploads/2020/06/Sturm-Blood-Politics.pdf.

Swain, Martha. "'The Forgotten Woman': Ellen S. Woodward and Women's Relief in the New Deal." *Prologue* 15, no. (1983): 201–13.

Szaz, Margaret Connell. "The Path to Self Determination: American Indian Education, 1940–1990." In *One House, One Voice, One Heart: Native American Education at the Santa Fe Indian School*, edited by Sally Hyer, 95–98. Santa Fe: Museum of New Mexico Press, 1990.

Taylor, Quintard. "Facing the Urban Frontier: African American History in the Reshaping of the Twentieth-Century American West." *Western Historical Quarterly* 43, no. 1 (Spring 2012): 6–27.

Tetzloff, Lisa. "Elizabeth Bender Cloud: 'Working for and with Our Indian People.'" *Frontiers: A Journal of Women Studies* 30, no. 3 (2009): 77–115.

Tidd, James Francis, Jr. "Stitching and Striking: WPA Sewing Rooms and the 1937 Relief Strike in Hillsborough County." *Tampa Bay History* 11, no. 1 (Spring/Summer 1989): 1–17. https://digitalcommons.usf.edu/tampabayhistory/vol11/iss1/3/.

Trennert, Robert A. "The Federal Government and Indian Health in the Southwest: Tuberculosis and the Phoenix East Farm Sanatorium, 1909–1955." *Pacific Historical Review* 65, no. 1 (February 1996): 61–84.

Tuck, Eve K., and Wayne Yang. "Decolonization Is Not a Metaphor." *Decolonization: Indigeneity, Education and Society* 1, no. 1 (2012): 1–40.

Watkins, Arthur V. "Termination of Federal Supervision: The Removal of Restrictions over Indian Property and Person." *Annals of the American Academy of Political and Social Science* 311(May 1957): 47–55.

Way, Evan. "Raising Capital in Indian Country." *American Indian Law Review* 41, no. 1 (2016): 167–200. https://digitalcommons.law.ou.edu/ailr/vol41/iss1/5.

Wayne, Frank Anthony. "The Federal Role in American Indian Education." *Harvard Educational Review* 52, no. 4 (1982): 423–30.

Whalen, Kevin. "Labored Learning: The Outing System at Sherman Institute, 1902–1930." *American Indian Culture and Research Journal* 36, no. 1 (2012): 151–75.

Wolfe, Patrick. "Settler Colonialism and the Elimination of the Native." *Journal of Genocide Research* 8, no. 4 (December 2006): 387–409. www.tandfonline.com/doi/pdf/10.1080/14623520601056240.

Dissertations and Theses

Fish, Lewis J. "A Study of the Reasons for Failure on the Job of Some Graduates of Intermountain School." Master's thesis, Utah State University, 1960.

Fluharty, Sterling. "'For a Greater Indian America': The Origins of the National Indian Youth Council." Master's thesis, University of Oklahoma, 2003.

Garrett, Matthew R. "Mormons, Indians and Lamanites: The Indian Student Placement Program, 1947–2000." PhD diss., Arizona State University, 2010.

Kamper, David. "The Politics and Poetics of Organizing Navajo Laborers." PhD diss., University of California–Los Angeles, 2003.

Lamb, Joe. "Coughing Cows and Utter Disaster: Bovine Tuberculosis at the Genoa Indian Industrial School." Master's thesis, Utah State University, 2014.

Rzeczkowski, Frank. "Reimagining Community: Intertribal Relations on the Northern Plains, 1885–1925." PhD diss, Northwestern University, 2003.

Shreve, Bradley Glenn. "Red Power Rising: The National Indian Youth Council and the Origins of Intertribal Activism." PhD diss, University of New Mexico–Albuquerque, 2007.

Tonnies, Carol. "Away for the Homeland: Why Students Fought to Keep Intermountain Indian School Open." Master's thesis, Utah State University, 2016.

Websites

American Gaming Association. www.americangaming.org.

San Manuel of Mission Indians website. Accessed December 31, 2024. https://sanmanuel-nsn.gov/.

INDEX

Page numbers in italics indicate illustrations.

Abramoff, Jack, 137
ACKCO American Indian Professional Services, 99
Acord, Enola, 32–33
activism, Native, 145. *See also* Red Power movement
Adams, David Wallace, 27
Administration for Native Americans, 105
Africa: postwar development strategies, 170n54; and western development model, 82
African Americans, 6, 30
agriculture. *See* farming
Akimel O'odham people, 10, 65
Alaskan Brotherhood, 147
Alvarez, David, 119
Ambler, Marjane, 106
American Indian Movement, 146
American Indians. *See* Native Americans
Andrews, Thomas, 9
Apache people, 65
artisans, Native, 44
assimilationism: in boarding schools, 143–44; challenges to, 90; in Civilian Conservation Corps, 48; criticism of relocation, 78; Native resistance, 12; "total assimilation," policy of, 2; into working class, 98
Astor, Betty, 88

author's methodology: chapter outlines, 13–15; research, 15–17
auto industry, 135

Bad River Ojibwe people, 10
Bagley, Jeff, 86–87
Battlefield and Classroom (Pratt), 1
Bauer, William, 4, 11
beet farming, 22, 36
Begay, Myrtle, 39
Begay, Peter, 73
Bernstein, Alison, 66
Berrien, Jacqueline, 141–43
BIA. *See* Bureau of Indian Affairs
Biden, Joe, 138
bingo operations, 113–14. *See also* gaming industry
Black Americans, 6, 30
Blackfeet Community Action Project, 100
Blackfeet Indian Welfare, 55–56, 62
Blackfeet National Bank, 25
Blackfeet Tribal Business Council, 104
Blackfeet Tribal Council, 101
Blackfoot Nation, 25
boarding schools, 2, 4–5, 19–40; abuse in, 37–40; "civilizing mission," 33–34; contemporary transformations of, 146–47; curricula and schedules, 27–28; dependency, reinforcement of, 23–29; domestic training, 32; gendered roles and female subservience, 32–33;

boarding schools (*continued*)
    Indian employment bureau (OIA), 35–37; as labor contractors, 34–35; and labor exploitation, 22, 27–28; low-wage labor, preparation for, 21; opposition and criticism, 37–40; outing system, 21–23, 39; pressure to assimilate, 143–44; race and gender, frameworks of, 29–34; rationale and history, 19–20; and settler-colonial labor demands, 20–21, 155n8; student wages, withholding of, 23–25; vocational training, 32. *See also names of individual boarding schools*
Brodie, Keith, 136
Brown, Janice, 121–22
Brown, Larry, 103
buffalo soldiers, 29
Bureau of Indian Affairs (BIA): positive programming emphasis, 76–78; recordkeeping, 162n33; relocation services, 71; TOB Study, 84–90; Voluntary Relocation Program, 68. *See also* Relocation Program (BIA)
Burlington Railroad, 36, 37
Burton, E. R., 49–50
Butera, Scott, 112, 125, 126

Cabazon band, Mission Indians, 114, 122
Cahuilla Indians, 78
California: gaming industry, 116–22; Proposition 5, 116–18
Canada: Aboriginal Labour Placement Program, 168n30; Canadian history, 151n12
Canadian Pacific Railroad, 10
capitalism: origins of, 151–52n20; wage work, 7
Carlisle Indian School (US Indian Industrial School), 2
casinos. *See* gaming industry
Castillo, Francisco, 65
Cattelino, Jessica, 12
CCC-ID. *See* Civilian Conservation Corps–Indian Division

Chee, Byron, 80
Chemehuevi people, 65
Cherokee Nation, 103
Cherokee people, 44
Chickasaw Nation, 123, 131–36; removal treaties, 135
Child, Brenda J., 12, 38, 146
Chilocco, Oklahoma, 27
Christianity as "civilizing" force, 8
Civilian Conservation Corps, 160n5, 161n22
Civilian Conservation Corps–Indian Division (CCC-ID), 42, 43, 45–52, 46, 162n32; academic coursework, 50–51; National Defense Training Center, 65
civil rights: laws, 141–42; narratives, 5–8
Civil Rights Act (1964), 99, 173–74n26
Civil Works Administration (CWA), 56
Cobell, Elouise P. (Yellow Bird Woman), 25
Cobell v. Salazar, 25
Cody, Kenneth, 96
Cold War, development during, 81
Collier, John, 42–44, 47–48, 50, 52–53, 55–56, 63–64, 66, 144
colonial frameworks, 3–4; anti-colonial struggle, 7–8; in Canada, 151n12; colonizers' perspectives, 154n43; legacy of exploitation, 5–7. *See also* decolonization; settler colonialism
Colville Reservation, 101
Colville Tribe, 100
Communications Workers of America (CWA), 120
Comprehensive Employment and Training Act (CETA), 100, 174n31
Cronemeyer, Hoska, 79, 79–80
Connecticut, 124–25. *See also* Mashantucket Pequot Tribal Nation
conservation work, 45–47
Constitution, and Indian sovereignty, 113
Cooper, Frederick, 82–83, 145
Council for Tribal Employment Rights (CTER), 91–92, 98, 105, 129, 141–42,

174n31; creation of, 109; Workforce Protection Ordinance, 142
Council of Energy Resource Tribes (CERT), 105; criticism of, 105–6
Covington, Laura, 60
Crockett, Henrietta, 59
Crow Indian Women's Club, 60
Crow Indian Women's Federated Club, 61
Crow Indian Women's Federation, 59
Crow people, 37, 59, 60, 84
Crow Reservation, 59
CTER. *See* Council for Tribal Employment RightsCurley, Nat, 79
Cut Bank Boarding School, 58

Dagenett, Charles E., 36
Damon, Sam, 96
Davis, Gray, 121, 137
Davis, M. H., 41
Dawes Act (1887), 2, 16, 19, 122
decolonization, 7, 81–82, 90, 151n18. *See also* colonial frameworks
Deernose, Kitty, 60
Desai, Chandni, 7
Diné be'iiná Náhiiłna be Agha'diit'ahii (DNA), 94
Diné College, 146
Diné people, 44, 65, 83; federal relief projects, 42; workers, 104
disenrollment, 84
DNA. *See* Diné be'iiná Náhiiłna be Agha'diit'ahii
domestic work: "home improvement" programs, 57; for Native girls, 31, 32, 164–65n67
Donner, William, 58
Doyle, Morgan J., 21–22
Durazo, Maria Elena, 118
Duro, Henry, 122

Eastman, Charles, 37
education: education reform, 20; Native attendance in public schools, 159n99; schools, contemporary, and sovereignty, 146; survival schools, 146

education for Native Americans: boarding schools and assimilation, 2; as "civilizing" project, 23; Navajo Special Program curriculum, 83
Edwards, Conrad, 91, 100, 101–3, *102*, 107
EEOC. *See* Equal Economic Opportunity Commission
Emergency Conservation Work (ECW), 52–53
Emmons, Glen, 76–77
energy industry, 92–93, 99–100, 107
Equal Economic Opportunity Commission (EEOC), 97, 141; and CTER, 109
Europe, postwar development, 81–82
extension agents, 52, 56–57, 58, 59, 61, 62

family relocation, 72–73, 168n28. *See also* relocation programs
Fanon, Frantz, 7
farming: beet farming, 22, 36; as "civilizing" force, 8; commercial agriculture, 153n38; family farm, ideal of, 23; independent small farms, ideal of, 21
Federal Emergency Relief Administration (FERA), 54
federal policies, 2–3; Indian policies post–World War II, 67–70
film industry, 44–45
Flake, Jeff, 138
Forman, George, 119
Fort Apache Agency, 58
Fort Apache Boarding School, 39
Fort Berthold Indian School, 32
Fort Hall Reservation, 103
Fortunate Eagle, Adam, 29, 38–40
Fox people, 10
Foxwoods Resort Casino, 123, *124*, 124–25, 126–31; financial struggle, 128–29; union election, 129–31

Gage, Maynard L., 63
Gallup Supply Center Warehouse, 94–95, 96, 173n12
Gamble, Mary Nan, 71, 72

gaming industry: California, 116–22; compacts and regulation, 114–15; court cases, 114; debt restructuring, 126; Foxwoods Casino, 126–31; gambling, legalization of, 113; Mashantucket Pequot Tribal Nation (MPTN), 123–25; overview, 109–16; seniority systems, 129, 130; stereotypes of "rich Indians," 117–18; and wealth creation, 111–12, 124–25; WinStar World Casino, Oklahoma, 131–36, 132

Garcia, Joe, 136

gendered roles: in capitalism, 153n34; under economic development, 12–13, 161n17; masculine ideals in Civilian Conservation Corps, 46–47; and monitoring of relocated workers, 73–74; subservience of women, 32–33; women in relief work, 56–57

General Allotment Act (Dawes Act, 1887), 16, 19, 113–14

General Federation of Women's Clubs, 60

Genoa, Nebraska, 27, 31, 157n37

George, Elizabeth, 123

Gervais, Rodney "Fish," 100–101, 103–4

Gila River Pima-Maricopa Reservation, 70

Gingrich, Newt, 137

"global motherhood," 33

grazing permits, 83–84

Grijalva, Raúl, 138

Hampton Normal Institute, 29–30, 157n43

Hanley, Max, 23

Harris, William Torrey, 31–32

Hartigan, Michael, 120

Harvard Project on American Indian Economic Development, 116

Haskell Indian Boarding School, 38, 146

Haskell Indian Nations University, 146

Haskins, Victoria, 4–5, 32

Hauptman, Laurence M., 45

Hayward, Richard "Skip," 123

Hayworth, J. D., 136–37

Heart of the Earth Survival School, 146

Hena, James, 95

HERE. *See* Hotel Employees and Restaurant Employees Union

"high steel" work, 10

hiring preference agreements, 94–97, 98–99, 103–4

Hohne, Keri, 127–28

Hollywood, Florida, 114

Hoopa Valley Agency, 48

Hoopa Valley reservation, 50, 51

Hopkins, Harry, 54, 55, 58

Hosmer, Brian, 50

Hotel Employees and Restaurant Employees Union (HERE), 116–17, 118, 120, 177n27

Housing and Urban Development (HUD) projects, 100

Hoxie, Frederick, 2

Hualapai people, 65

Huerta, Dolores, 118–19

Hunkpapa Lakota people, 2

IGRA. *See* Indian Gaming and Regulatory Act

indentured labor, 11

Indian Arts and Crafts Act (1935), 44, 161n12

Indian Citizenship Act (1924), 150n6

Indian Craftsman (magazine), 36

Indian Emergency Conservation Work (IECW), 49

Indian Freedom Program, 68

Indian Gaming and Regulatory Act (IGRA), 112, 114, 115, 121

Indian Industrial School, 2

"Indian New Deal," 43–44, 122, 161n12

Indian Reorganization Act, 43–45, 61

Indians. *See* Native Americans

Indians at Work (OIA publication), 50

Indian Women's Federation, 62

Indigenous lifeways, disruption of, 7. *See also* Native Americans

Individual Indian Money accounts, 25, 49

individual rights vs. tribal identities, 77–78

industry: industrial time clocks, 26; and labor supply, 20

Institute of American Indian Arts, 146–47
Intermountain Indian School, 70, 72, 73, 74–75, 83

Jacobs, Margaret, 32
Japanese internment camps, 81
Johnson, Lyndon B., 146
Jones, Paul, 78, 83–84
Jones, Rena, 75
Jones, William, 23

Kahnawà:ke people, 10
Kamper, David, 120
Kantor, Harvey, 20
Killing for Coal (Andrews), 9
kin networks, 9, 12, 77, 146
Klamath people, 68, 69
Kumeyaay Indians, 119, 120

Laborers International Union of North America, 123, 147
labor systems: racialized, 3; white employers' expectations, 31
labor unions. *See* unions
La Farge, Oliver, 73, 77
La Flesche, Francis, 37
Lakeside Mine Management, 91–92
Lakota people, 37
land policies: allotment, 10; land ownership, 2; settler colonial practices, 12; and work programs, linked with, 16
Latham, Michael, 81
Latinx people, 151n11
Lay, Brice, 70, 72
Lester, David, 105
Leupp, Francis E., 26–27, 35–36
Light, Steven, 115
Lincoln, Tom, 96
Little River Band, Ottawa, 123, 133, 134
Little River Casino, Michigan, 123, 133, 135
"Loafers and Laborers" (*Puck* cartoon), 3–4, 4
Lomawaima, K. Tsianina, 19, 26
Lower Brule Reservation, 44
Lyon, Marcus, 87

MacDonald, Peter, 97, 146
Maher, Neil, 45–46
Marquez, Deron, 109, 111, 119–20, 154n46
Marshall, Edward E., 52
Marshall, Gilbert, 52
Marshall Plan, 81
Mashantucket Pequot Labor Relations Law (MPLRL), 126–27
Mashantucket Pequot Tribal Nation (MPTN), 112, 123; Foxwoods Casino, 124–25; Foxwoods Casino unionization, 126–31; tribal lands, 123–24
McCain, H., 54–55
McCarty, Teresa, 146
McKay, Douglas, 77–78
McNickle, D'Arcy, 83
Menominee people, 68, 69
Meriam, Lewis, 22
Meriam Report, 22, 28–29, 33–34
Merjian, Armen H., 25–26
Mexican American workers, 6
Meyer, Linda, 128
migration. *See* relocation programs
Miller, Bob, 87
Miller, Doug, 59, 78
Miller, Robert A., 51–52
mining, 92–93, 172n1
Mission Indian Agency, California, 65
Mission Indians, 114
Miwok people, 10
"modernization" projects, 81–82, 83, 90. *See also* settler colonialism
Montana Indian Civil Rights Commission, 104
Moolenaar, John, 138
Moran, Jerry, 137, 138
Morley, Bill, 86
Moye, Laura, 127
MPTN. *See* Mashantucket Pequot Tribal Nation
Murillo, Pauline Ormego, 111–12
Murphy, Daniel (D. E.), 47–48, 51
Murray, James E., 60–61
Myer, Dillon, 81

Index

Nash, Jay B., 48, 49
National Archives and Records Administration (NARA), 15
National Congress of American Indians (NCAI), 37, 136
National Indian Gaming Commission, 114
National Indian Youth Council (NIYC), 95
National Labor Relations Act (NLRA) (1935), 122, 127, 134, 135
National Labor Relations Board (NLRB), 120–21, 130; court cases, 134; employers' interests, 180n76; jurisdiction of, 136; union establishment, 178n38
Native Americans: civil rights, concern for, 119; economic dependency, 110–11; genocidal conditions, 9–10; kin networks, 9, 12, 77, 146; languages, 42–43; Native-centered development, 13; Native voices, 15–16; precolonial workscapes, 9–13; seasonal cycles vs. subsistence farming, 20; terminology to identify, 149–50n1; US policies and international development, overlap of, 81–82. *See also names of individual tribes*
natural resources, control of, 92–93
Navajo Community College, 146
Navajo Construction Workers Association, 97, 99
Navajo Generating Plant case, 94–97, 95
Navajo Nation, 144–45; electricity, access to, 93; labor policies, 99; Rough Rock Demonstration School, 146; ties with relocated urban members, 78–79; tribal leadership and relocation program, 83
Navajo people, 12, 39; construction workers' lawsuit, 94–97; Navajo preference clauses, 105
Navajo Relocation Committee, 78–80
Navajo Reservation, 76
Navajo Special Program, 83
Navarro, John, 91–92, 100, 101, 103
Nequatewa, Edmund, 23–25
New Deal relief programs, 144; criticism of, 61–62

Nichols, John, 81
NLRB. *See* National Labor Relations Board
NLRB v. Pueblo of San Juan, 136
Norrgard, Chantal, 4, 9
Northrup Corporation, Los Angeles, 79
Novak, Steve, 98

Obama, Barack, 134, 137–38
Office of Indian Affairs (OIA), 10, 25, 98; Indian Employment Service, 35–37
Office of Navajo Labor Relations (ONLR), 97, 99
Ohkay Owingeh (San Juan Pueblo), 136, 138
OIA. *See* Office of Indian Affairs
oil and gas leases, 64
Ojibwe people, 9–11; wage work, adaptation to, 11; wage work and control, 4; wild rice harvest, 11
Oklahoma: WinStar World Casino, 131–36, 132
One Goose, Mary, 60
Oneida people, 45
Osage people, 11
Ottawa Indians, 123, 133, 134
Ouray Boarding School, 38
outing system, 21–23, 39, 75–76, 157n44

Parker, Arthur C., 37
Parker, Joseph, 61
Parman, Donald, 44
Parsons, Steve, 134
paternalistic attitudes, 30; at the CCC-ID, 48–49
Paul, William, 88–89
Pawnee Agency, 66
Peters, Scott Henry, 67
Phoenix Indian School, 23
Pico, Anthony, 119
Pipestone Indian Training School, 29, 38
Plenty Coups (Crow headman), 98–99
Point Four Program, 81, 83
positive programming, 76–78
Potter, Lori, 125
Pound, Thad C., 27

poverty: public assistance, 45; reservation poverty vs. urban poverty, 85; War on Poverty, 146
Pratt, Richard Henry, 1; on education for Native Americans, 2; "kill the Indian in him" policy, 19; military service, 29–30; OIA blocked from boarding school labor, 36; outing system, 21–23; schools as labor contractors, 34–35; vision for Indian schools, 30
Press, Dan, 94–97, 99, 100–102, *102*, 143
Problem of Indian Administration, The (Meriam), 22
Progressive Era: racial uplift, 60; relief projects (1930s), 45–46
Proposition 5, California, 116–21
public assistance, 45
Public Law 280, 68
Public Works Administration (PWA), 52

Quechan people, 65

racial structures: anti-Indian rhetoric in union elections, 130–31; racialized labor systems, 3; in settler society, 31
racial uplift, 37, 60
Radtke, Leonard, 48, 51
Raibmon, Paige, 11
railroad work, 10, 36, 37
Ramirez, Ken, 118
Rand, Kathryn, 115
Red Cliff Ojibwe people, 10
Red Lake Bank of Chippewa, 104
Red Lake Nation, 29
Red Power movement, 38, 69, 90, 145
Red School House (survival school), 146
Reel, Estelle, 23, 24, 26, 30
relief programs, gendered roles in, 61–62
relief projects (1930s), 41–43; Civilian Conservation Corps–Indian Division (CCC-ID), 45–52, *46*; Indian Reorganization Act, 43–45; Works Progress Administration (WPA), 52–62
Relocation Program (BIA), 76. *See also* relocation programs

relocation programs, 63; economic influences, 80–83; family relocation, 72–73, 168n28; migrant ties to reservation communities, 83–84; Native workers' lived experiences, 83–90; political economy of relocation, 80–83; positive programming, 76–78; postwar Indian policy, 67–70; relocation, Native American experience of, 70–76; relocation, Native American views on, 83–90; relocation to urban areas, 64; relocation for work, 10; return to reservations, 86, 87, 89; training programs, quality of, 87–89; tribal government involvement, 78–80, 81–82; World War II labor programs, 64–67, *65*, *66*, 166n1
reservations: attempts to eliminate, 64; economic development on, 105; as employment agencies, 103; successful economies, 68
"right-to-work" laws, 127, 143
Ritskes, Eric, 7
Rocky Ford, Colorado, 36
Rokita, Todd, 137
Roosevelt, Eleanor, 53, 54
Rosebud Sioux, 84
Rosenthal, Nick, 69
Rosier, Paul, 81–82
Rough Rock Demonstration School, 146
Round Valley Reservation, California, 4, 11
Russell, Don, 89
Rzeczkowski, Frank, 98

Saginaw Chippewa, 123
Salois, Mary B., 55–56, 57, 59, 62
Sanders, William, 86
San Ildefonso Pueblo, 78
San Manuel Band: gaming, impact on community, 111–12; HERE complaint filed against, 120–21; HERE decision, ruling in appeal, 121–22, 137–38; Proposition 5 campaign, 117–18
San Manuel Business Committee, 111
San Manuel Indian Bingo and Casino v. NLRB, 134–35

Santa Fe Indian School, 146–47
Santa Fe Railway, 37
Schildt, Carl, 100
Schultz, Jessie Donaldson, 58
Schwab, Robert W., 55
Scott, James C., 38
Seasons of Change (Norrgard), 4
Seminole people, 11–12, 44
Seminole Tribe, 114
settler colonialism: anti-colonial struggle, 7–8; land use policies, 12; and wage work, 8–9. *See also* colonial frameworks
Sherman Institute, California, 23, 25, 27, 31, 66, 74, 83, 98, 147
Sho-Ban News, 104
Sho-Ban (Shoshone-Bannock) office, Fort Hall, 103
Sitting Bull, 1, 2, 21, 150n3
Sium, Aman, 7
Smith, Kaighn, 135
Soaring Eagle Resort and Casino, 123, 135
Society of American Indians, 156n19
Sokolove, Michael, 125
sovereignty: and control of employment, 92–93; and control over gaming industry, 115–16; expanding concepts of, 100; and labor unions, 128–29; natural resources on reservation land, 92–93; sovereignty rights, 77. *See also* tribal sovereignty
Spanish colonization, 3
Spokane Tribe, 103
Standing Rock Sioux, 78
stereotypes: in film and tourist industries, 45; "rich Indians," 117–18
subsistence practices, 10–12, 44
survival schools, 146
survivance, 20, 62, 154n5
Swain, Martha, 54

Tauchin, Able, 79
Teamsters, 123, 133–34
termination policy, 68–69, 76, 170n57
TERO. *See* Tribal Employment Rights Ordinance
Thomas, Stanley, 70
Thorpe, Grace, *66*
Tlingit people, 44
Tobar, Hector, 117
Tohono O'odham people, 65
Tohono O'odham Reservation, Arizona, 100
Tohono O'odham Tribal Council, 101
tourism industry, 44–45
trade unions. *See* unions
Treaty of Dancing Rabbit Creek (1830), 135
Treaty of Washington (1866), 135
Tribal Council of the Three Affiliated Tribes, 84
Tribal Employment Rights offices, 107
Tribal Employment Rights Ordinance (TERO), 91–92, 99–101, 129; activists' stories, 102–3; expansion after Warm Springs conference (1977), 103; overview, 93–94; positive impact of, 104–5; worker leadership, 106
tribal governments, 43; collective bargaining agreements, 120; enrollment and disenrollment, 84; federal oversight, termination of, 68–69; fiscal institutions, 176n5; labor and sovereignty, 121–22; labor regulation, 103; relocation, involvement in, 78–80, 81–82; tribal preference laws, 129–30
Tribal Labor Sovereignty Act, 136–39
tribal sovereignty: clash with states over gaming industry, 114; in conflict with civil rights laws, 141–42; in conflict with unions, 138–39; and contemporary schools, 146; San Manuel case, 120–22; tribal identities vs. individual rights, 77–78; wage work as destructive force, 19–20; weakening of, 3. *See also* sovereignty
Tribal Sovereignty Protection Act, 137
Trump, Donald, 131, 138
Trump Enterprises, 126

UAW. *See* United Auto Workers
unemployment among Native Americans, 45

unions: gaming industry, 115–16; Indian involvement, 106–7; opposition to hiring preference programs, 104–5; and Proposition 5, 118–21; "right-to-work" provisions, 127, 143
United Auto Workers (UAW), 123; at Foxwoods Casino, 126
United Farm Workers, 118
United Food and Commercial Workers, 123, 127, 128–29
United Mine Workers, 147
United States government policies. *See* federal policies
United Steelworkers, 147
Ute people, 65

Valentine, Robert, 36
Vallasis, George, 96
Vennoch, Joan, 126
Viejas Band, Kumeyaay Indians, 119, 120
Vizenor, Gerald, 62
vocational training, 32
Voluntary Relocation Program, 68

Waddell, Oscar M., 38
wage work, 92; as component of capitalism, 7; and settler colonialism, 8–9; and tribal sovereignty, 19–20
War on Poverty, 146
Warren, Jenifer, 117
Watkins, Arthur, 68, 76
Wayne, Clinton, 87
wealth creation, 124–25; gaming industry, 111–12
Weisiger, Marsha, 12–13
We Were All Like Migrant Workers Here (Bauer), 4
Whalen, Kevin, 4–5, 21, 25, 31
Wheeler-Howard Act, 43
White, Kenneth, 94, 96, *96*, 97–98, 99–100, 104, 107

Whitefeather, Bobby, 104
White Mountain Apache, 138
White River Ute people, 37
Wild West shows, 44
Williams, Aubry, 54
Williams, David, 70–71, 72
Williams, Elizabeth, 70–71, 72
Williams, Minnie, 60
Wilson, Pete, 116–17, 119
Wind River Reservation, 50
WinStar World Casino, Oklahoma, 123, 131–36, *132*; Chickasaw lawsuit, 133–34
Women Accepted for Volunteer Emergency Service (WAVES), 66–67
Women's Army Auxiliary Corps (WAAC), 66
Woodward, Ellen S., 54
work: "moral value" of, 19; wage work, 7, 8–9, 19–20, 92; workers' rights, 6; working conditions, 98
Workforce Protection Ordinance (CTER), 142
"workscape," concept of, 9
Works Progress Administration (WPA), 42, 52–62, 160n3; mattress project, 42, 54–55, 164n59, 164n62; sewing projects, 52–54, *53*
World War II labor programs, 64–67, *65*, *66*
WPA. *See* Works Progress Administration

Yaamava' Resort and Casino, 178n31. *See also* San Manuel Band
Yaqui Indian Center, 119
Yazzie, Elizabeth, 72
Yellow Bird Woman (Elouise P. Cobell), 25
Yellowtail, Robert, 59, 60, 61, 165–66n76
Yuhaaviatam of San Manuel Nation, 175n2. *See also* San Manuel Band
Yuma Reservation, 21–22

Zitkala-Ša, 19, 26

www.ingramcontent.com/pod-product-compliance
Lightning Source LLC
Chambersburg PA
CBHW021854230426
43671CB00006B/392